The Marine Aquarium Problem Solver

Practical & Expert Advice
on Keeping Fish & Invertebrates

Nick Dakin

Tetra✿Press

No 16839

Contents

AN ANDROMEDA BOOK

Copyright © 1996
Andromeda Oxford Limited

Reprinted 1998, 1999, 2000, 2001

Planned and produced by
Andromeda Oxford Limited,
11–13 The Vineyard, Abingdon,
Oxfordshire,
England, OX14 3PX

Published in North America by
Tetra Press,
3001 Commerce Street.
Blacksburg, VA 24060

ISBN 1-56465-187-8

Advisory Editor   DR. KEITH BANISTER

Project Editor	Fiona Gold
Art Editor and Designer	Chris Munday
Proofreader	Lin Thomas
Editorial Assistant	Marian Dreier
Picture Research Managers	Martin Anderson, Claire Turner
Indexer	Barbara James
Production	Nicolette Colborne
Publishing Director	Graham Bateman

Colour origination by AD.VER, Italy
Printed in Slovakia by Polygraf Print, Prešov.

Introduction

In recent years, interest in marine fishkeeping as a hobby has blossomed and a whole industry has grown up around providing the latest equipment and a variety of livestock. The constant improvements in husbandry techniques and advances in technology have often outstripped reliable sources of information available to the aquarist; sometimes it seems that there are many more questions to ask than answers available! Until now, that is. The purpose of this book has been to draw on a lifetime's experience in fishkeeping, and over twelve years of acting as an "agony uncle" to marine aquarists through the pages of specialist magazines, to identify and respond to the concerns of hobbyists everywhere.

This book is aimed both at the beginner and at the experienced marinist who is thirsty for more useful knowledge and practical help. It will advise the newcomer on how to enjoy the hobby to the full and avoid some of the pitfalls of inexperience, while also providing the established hobbyist with a wealth of information.

The responsibilities of marine aquarists are generally far greater than those of freshwater fishkeepers. Much marine livestock comes directly from the sea and cannot be readily supplied from captive breeding programmes, although most species are easily sustainable with conscientious harvesting. Breeding most of the popular marine fish and invertebrates in captivity could be a reality if the will and the finance were available, but such programmes would inevitably make the hobby so expensive that it would put it well out of reach of the majority of aquarists. Therefore, each and every marinist must regard their livestock as precious, to be loved, nurtured and cared for as part of our planet's heritage.

Marine aquaria provide some of the most stunning displays of natural life to be witnessed on Mother Earth. We can protect that gift (for it is a gift, not a right) by planning before we purchase, and making informed decisions about care and conditions. Having said that, we are only human, and humans make mistakes. I hope that this book will help you avoid those mistakes, or at least overcome them to reach a happy conclusion.

I wish you every fishkeeping success,

Nick Dakin

NICK DAKIN

Tank Set-up and Care

For many hobbyists, the preparation of a suitable tank environment can be just as exciting and interesting as the introduction of the live-stock. Such enthusiasm is to be encouraged, as it will certainly be reflected in the success of the end result. Advance planning is the chief secret of success; it costs nothing but time and a note pad to ensure that the aquarium is suitable to house the delicate creatures that will finally know it as home.

Although marine husbandry can be neatly divided into separate areas, it is important to remember that each one overlaps with the others at some stage, particularly with regard to water quality, tank maintenance and the compatibility of the livestock.

Foremost on the hobbyist's list of priorities should be where the basic tankwater comes from. It has become clear over recent years that using ordinary mains water as the basis of a salt-water mix is no longer good practice. Many other factors can be improved upon as time progresses, but high water quality must be maintained from the very beginning. Pure, clean water is essential for the modern aquarist, not optional.

▶ *Pyjama Cardinals* (Sphaeramia nematoptera) *see page 83.*

Aquarium Design

THE AQUARIUM IS PROBABLY THE SINGLE MOST important and expensive purchase that the hobbyist will make, so it is vital to choose a high-quality tank that meets all the most essential needs. Unusual shapes may attract the eye, but practicality is the key issue. Nearly all designs are capable of supporting a marine community, but knowing the limitations of a particular pattern and staying within them can prove very restrictive. There are several main criteria to keep in mind.

Volume/Surface Area Ratio

The aquarium must have enough surface area to exchange carbon dioxide for life-giving oxygen. Trickle filters can aid in this process, but deep tanks with a limited surface area are still at a major disadvantage. In nature, coral reefs are saturated or super-saturated with dissolved oxygen and replicating this concentration can be difficult to achieve even in the best designs. Small tanks are convenient, but they present enormous difficulties for the marine hobbyist. Creatures of the coral reef are reliant on the stability of their environment and have adapted to predictable conditions over many thousands of years. Larger tanks offer far more stability in terms of pH and temperature than small tanks, where stability can rarely if ever be achieved.

Unnatural Territories

The vast majority of marine fish are territorial and nearly always protect a horizontal, rather than vertical, area. Choosing a tall, thin tank is likely to bring its inhabitants into unnaturally close contact and may lead to serious territorial disputes as the more dominant species try to establish their boundaries. Even when moderately stocked, such an aquarium can take on an abnormally crowded appearance, a condition that may not appeal to everyone.

● *What is the smallest volume of water recommended for the marine aquarium?*

If the tank is to house fish only, then 20 gallons (91 l; 24 US gallons) nett (excluding rockwork, substrate, etc.,) is an absolute minimum. An invertebrate aquarium would need to accommodate more water for greater stability and 30 gallons (136 l; 36 US gallons) nett is a good starting point.

● *How thick should the tank walls be for safety?*

The dimensions of the aquarium will dictate the optimum thickness for safety, but in general the deeper the aquarium, the thicker the material. It is a false economy to invest in very cheap aquaria, established professional aquarium builders can usually be relied upon to supply safe products.

● *How will I know if the shape of the aquarium will make the contents look distorted?*

This entirely depends on the design of the aquarium, and it is wise to check for distortion before purchasing. Hold a book or piece of printed paper inside the aquarium close to any vertical joints or corners; the degree of distortion will easily be gauged. The same process should be carried out before buying bow-fronted or circular tanks.

● *Should the tank be purchased first and the filtration adapted to it?*

No! The tank, stand, filtration and other equipment need to be considered as a complete system, allowing for ease of maintenance, efficiency of filtration, lighting and other sundries. Always suit the aquarium to the equipment, never the reverse.

● *Should I choose glass or acrylic?*

Glass and acrylic technology have both advanced so far that each type is practical and affordable, and there is no real advantage of one over the other. Acrylic is hard, very scratch-resistant and can be moulded into a jointless unit. All-glass tanks now use bonding cements and advanced construction techniques and are no longer prone to leakage.

Choosing a shape

An aquarium of irregular shape is generally subject to viewing distortion. Livestock can appear to become "split" between two or more pieces of glass or acrylic, and having to adjust position to view livestock can leave the aquarist frustrated long after the novelty of the complicated design has worn off. It is no coincidence that the vast majority of aquarists choose the traditional rectangular design as most of the potential problems are more easily overcome. Since this design has been popular for so many years, equipment has been designed to be accommodated easily.

Lighting and Other Equipment

Illumination is a perennial problem for unusually shaped tanks, as the options are so limited. Octagonal, hexagonal and irregular designs can make fluorescent lighting complicated, and largely ineffectual. The only realistic option may be a mercury vapour or metal halide pendant spotlight, leaving little space for support lighting.

The space available to house filtration and other equipment must also be considered

▲ A rectangular aquarium like this one is ideal for viewing livestock since it combines maximum viewing area with minimum distortion. The housing conceals all the lighting and additional equipment.

carefully. Tank restrictions often mean that a vital piece of equipment is omitted due to sheer lack of space, putting livestock at risk. Adding pieces of equipment around the tank can prove extremely unsightly and detract from the beauty of the livestock within.

Stands and Safety

Every gallon of sea water weighs roughly 10lbs (a litre weighs approximately one kilogram) and the total contents of a fully stocked aquarium will be extremely heavy. Whichever design you choose, safety is of paramount importance. A faulty, uneven or incompatible stand will cause the tank to rupture, leading to possible human injury, the loss of livestock and a great deal of mess! The ideal stand would be professionally purpose-built for the aquarium in question and should accommodate all the necessary equipment while also looking attractive.

Heating and Chilling

POIKILOTHERMS ARE "COLD BLOODED" animals whose metabolism and body temperature is completely controlled by their environment. If the water is too cold, metabolic activity slows down; too warm and metabolic rates increase. In either case, the result could be severe stress, leading to disease or death. Many sessile invertebrates, for example, respond to high water temperatures by expelling their symbiotic algae (zooxanthellae) which, if not recolonized swiftly, can lead to the death of the host animal.

Coral reefs are very stable as far as temperatures are concerned. Indeed, local vacillation notwithstanding, recorded values only vary by a few degrees throughout the year. As a consequence, fish and invertebrates are seldom subjected to temperature variation except during freak weather or unusual ocean current patterns. Replicating temperature stability in the aquarium is of the utmost importance and choosing reliable equipment cannot be over-emphasized.

Heating Equipment

Several suitable heating methods are available to the hobbyist: the combined heater/thermostat; the glass tube immersion heater controlled by an external thermostat; and the under-tank heater mat, also controlled by an external thermostat. Of these, the combined heater/thermostat remains by far the most popular choice, but it should be a model that is clearly calibrated and accurate to ±1°.

Glass tube immersion heaters have declined in popularity over recent years, but even so they remain a good choice. Large tanks, in particular, benefit from having several heater units in different locations, all controlled by one accurate thermostat. Not only is this a reasonably economic method, it also generates efficient heat dispersal and maintains stable water temperatures.

This reef off the coast of Indonesia is an extremely stable environment for marine life. Water quality, pH, temperature and other variables are constant and ideal.

A recent arrangement, gaining in popularity, is the under-tank heater mat, controlled by an external thermostat. This extremely reliable method is capable of maintaining temperatures to within ± 0.25°C (0.5°F). In addition, the fear of livestock burning themselves against heating elements is removed and there is no fragile equipment in the aquarium to risk breakage nor look unsightly. As heat is dispersed over almost the entire area of the base, cool spots are almost entirely eliminated. Forward planning is imperative here as heating mats cannot be fitted retrospectively!

● Is there an optimum temperature for the tropical marine aquarium?

... Yes, 25°C (77°F) suits most, but specific set-ups vary. Livestock starts to suffer below 22°C (72°F) and above 27°C (80°F).

● Is there a scale of heater wattages for a given volume of water?

In most household living areas, where the ambient temperature is already warm, the following scale would be applicable:

watts	tank size (nett)
100–150	up to 30 gallons (136 l; 37 US gallons)
150–200	up to 80 gallons (364 l; 96 US gallons)
300	up to 150 gallons (682 l; 180 US gallons)
500	up to 300 gallons (1364 l; 360 US gallons)

If the room housing the aquarium is particularly cool, then wattage values may have to be increased by as much as 50–100%.

● Is good water circulation important to stable water temperatures?

Yes, it is vital that heated water is circulated efficiently, avoiding cool spots behind and below rockwork.

● Is there any concern for heaters that fail "on".

Most modern heaters are very reliable and often designed to fail in the "off" mode, but one large unit may heat the water dangerously quickly and two smaller units of half the wattage are safer. Not only is it highly unlikely that both would fail "on" at the same time, but one smaller unit would take longer to increase the temperature, giving the aquarist a better chance to detect the fault before any losses occur.

Here are some of the different kinds of equipment available: 1-3 are heaters with built-in thermostats; 4 is a heater only and should be used with a temperature controller (5a) and sensor probe (5b). A digital temperature controller can also be used along with any heater-thermostat to increase its accuracy.

Under-tank heating mats are a good option for aquarium heating.

● Do any other pieces of equipment heat the water?

Lighting, ultraviolet sterilizers, canister filters, water pumps and fluorescent starter units stored beneath the tank all help to warm the water to a greater or lesser degree. If temperatures rise too much, chilling may be necessary to achieve stability.

● What steps should be taken to preserve livestock if a heater fails in the "off" position?

If the heater has failed "off", and the tank has cooled to dangerously low levels (20°C/68°F or below), take the following actions:

1 Reconnect a spare heater
2 Using an enamelled pan (not aluminium), warm some aquarium water and slowly reintroduce it back into the tank.
3 Float sealed bottles of hot water in the tank, making sure that the displacement does not cause an overflow.
4 Avoid feeding for at least 24 hours after the temperature has normalized.
5 In the event of a more general power failure, insulate the tank with blankets and polystyrene sheets.

Temperature Measurement

Accurate measurement of the aquarium temperature is as important as efficient heating. If the thermostatic control does not possess a built-in digital temperature display, then it would be advisable to invest in a high-quality thermometer capable of recording incremental readings of a fraction of a degree. It would also be wise to avoid fragile mercury-filled thermometers since any breakage within the aquarium will poison all the livestock.

Chilling

Chilling a tropical aquarium may seem like a contradiction in terms; however, there are many occasions where the temperature may rise dangerously out of control. Any aquarium with high-intensity lighting may overheat, especially if the room temperature is also high. Tropical, and even temperate, climates may experience prolonged daytime temperatures well in excess of those recommended for the marine aquarium. Simply turning down the heater-thermostat will not reduce the temperature of the tank below the ambient temperature of the room.

During hot weather there are several steps that you can take to keep the room temperature down, aside from chilling the tank. Keeping blinds or curtains closed will reduce the effects of the sun. Tanks containing light-loving invertebrates can have their photoperiod reduced to eight hours, spilt into two four-hour periods (7am – 11am and 6pm – 10pm). This will avoid exposure during the hottest part of the day from noon to late afternoon. Even so, some invertebrates may suffer if the tank has no facility for chilling.

Before the invention of purpose-built aquarium chillers, many inventive hobbyists were purchasing old, but serviceable, refrigerators or freezers. Holes were cut in the external walls and coils of canister-filter tubing carrying aquarium water were passed into the cooling cavity. The more coils, the greater the cooling effect on the water, but the degree of cooling could not be controlled accurately. This option is only for the committed enthusiast with plenty of time to experiment.

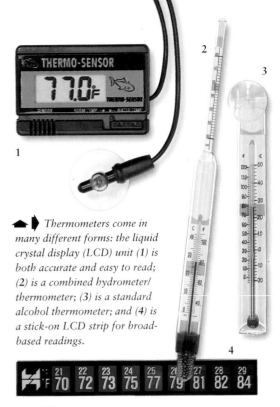

Thermometers come in many different forms: the liquid crystal display (LCD) unit (1) is both accurate and easy to read; (2) is a combined hydrometer/thermometer; (3) is a standard alcohol thermometer; and (4) is a stick-on LCD strip for broad-based readings.

Q&A

● *Will a chiller affect the quality of the aquarium water in any way?*

... No. Apart from lowering the temperature by the required amount, a chiller cannot alter the water passing through it.

● *Temperatures have increased and fish are gasping at the surface, what has happened?*

The warmer water becomes, the less dissolved oxygen it can hold, although carbon dioxide can still rise dangerously higher than normal. An increase in water circulation is vital as oxygen-depleted water will be more frequently presented to the surface to absorb oxygen and disperse unwanted carbon dioxide.

● *Will an increase in normal temperature affect biological filtration?*

Yes. As with fish and invertebrates, most bacteria require a certain amount of dissolved oxygen to perform effectively; rapidly increasing the temperature reduces the oxygen content and bacteria die or fail to function. The remaining bacteria will further endanger livestock as they compete for available oxygen. Therefore, stable temperatures are essential if an efficient biological filter is to be maintained.

➤ *Chiller units work to their greatest advantage when positioned outside the house, where they will not be affected by ambient room temperatures. It is important, however, to arrange for some degree of protection against the weather and inquisitive animals.*

● *What steps should be taken if a heater fails "on"?*

If the aquarium has seriously overheated (reaching temperatures of 30°C/86°F or above), take the following actions:

1) Disconnect the power to all heating units.

2) Switch the lighting off.

3) Install a large fan to blow across the surface of the water. Evaporation is increased and latent heat removed along with it. (Keep replacing the water).

4) Aerate the water using several airstones

5) If fitted, immerse a canister filter into a container filled with ice and water – take care not to cover the motor section.

6) Float sealed bags full of ice cubes, or cooler packs in the aquarium water – taking care to lower the water level, thus avoiding an overflow.

7) Relocate the airpump to the refrigerator (not the freezer); the cooled air is not only oxygen-laden but will help to cool the water it contacts.

8) Install a chiller, if available, for long-term, guaranteed results.

9) After the temperature has returned to normal, avoid feeding for 24 hours.

Some of the above methods may prove very variable in their effectiveness, reducing temperature by no more than one or two degrees and are only designed as short-term remedies.

Proprietary Chilling Equipment

Chillers range in capacity and it is important to choose the correct model for the size of tank. As a general rule, chillers should be capable of reducing the aquarium water temperature by at least 5°C (9°F) from ambient room temperature without being in continuous operation. For the sake of convenience, some models also incorporate a heater facility which helps to keep the amount of equipment in the tank down to a minimum. Owing to the highly corrosive nature of saltwater, most purpose-built aquarium chillers have either a thin layer of platinum sealing the waterways, or use inert substances to make water/metal contact impossible. Such specialized safety treatments usually cause the final product to be very expensive. Even stainless steel piping will eventually corrode under the influence of saltwater, releasing toxins into the water and putting the safety of the whole system at risk should severe corrosion occur.

A pump of the correct flow will be needed to transport the aquarium water through the chiller and a suitable canister filter is usually very effective for this purpose. Chillers need to be positioned outside, or at least not in the same room as the aquarium, for maximum efficiency. In the cooling process, copious quantities of warm air is given off (exchanged heat from the tank), if this is re-introduced back into the same room, the ambient temperature will rise, leading to an increase in tank temperature, and so on. Therefore, the chiller will work very hard and produce little temperature reduction to show for it! If positioned outside, make sure that it is protected from inclement weather and that all the grilles are made of metal and not plastic; this will deter rodents finding their way into the inner workings of the unit as they seek out a warm, dry home and possibly cause damage to themselves and the chiller in the process.

A chiller that is installed as an emergency measure on an aquarium that is already too warm should be adjusted to reduce the temperature slowly over a period of 48 hours. A gradual return to normal will avoid undue stress to the livestock.

Lighting

CORRECT ILLUMINATION PLAYS A CRUCIAL role in the whole presentation of any marine display and lack of consideration in this area can turn a potentially stunning aquarium into a dismal mediocre-looking feature.

The Science of Light

Light falls within a broad spectrum of wavelengths with each wavelength representing a particular colour. For our purposes the spectrum ranges from ultraviolet through blue, green, yellow, orange, red and infrared.

Natural sunlight contains all of these wavelengths but they do not penetrate water at equal rates. Reds and oranges have little penetration, yellow and green penetrate further, with only blue light capable of exceeding depths greater than 15–20 feet (4.5–6m). Most tanks are, of course, very shallow compared with the sea and none of the wavelengths are filtered out to any noticeable degree. The predominance of any one wavelength is controlled by the type of lighting. In this way, aquaria can take on a yellow, pink, blue or very white hue. Carefully employed, and at the correct intensity, these colours can be used merely to enhance the appearance of fish, or they may be absolutely essential to the well-being of light-loving corals.

Illuminating the Fish-Only Tank

Lighting the fish-only tank is a matter of personal taste as it is rarely vital to the health of any particular species. However, extremes of red or very blue light are best avoided as much of the beauty of coral fish can be lost (blue lights can be used if a particular deep water effect is wanted, but bright colours will disappear in the process). If possible, choose lighting that is slightly yellow or red, with a hint of blue. That way, the beauty of the colours will be retained and enhanced for the human eye to enjoy.

● *How do I choose the best lighting for the fish-only tank?*

... Visit as many retailers as possible. Witness a wide variety of display lighting and choose a system that appeals to you personally; it should complement the colours of the fish without being too garish.

● *How many pendant spotlamps will be needed for a 5ft (150cm) tank?*

Either two mercury vapour with a value of 80 or 125 watts each for fish-only applications, or two 150 watt metal halides where light-loving corals are housed. As a general guide, one spotlamp will cover approximately 2 sq ft (0.18 sq m) of water surface area.

● *Can domestic spotlamps or tungsten halogen security lamps be used?*

The domestic spotlamp is very wasteful of electricity, runs too hot to be close to water safely and provides the wrong colour spectrum for invertebrates. Tungsten halogen lamps may resemble metal halide spotlamps, and be much cheaper, but their lighting quality is totally unsuited to the marine aquarium hobby.

● *How often will bulbs need replacing if they are on for 10–12 hours daily?*

Many highly specified fluorescent tubes are now designed to maintain much of their efficiency for at least 18 months of usage, although some models will still require to be changed every 6 months. Read the manufacturer's instructions to discover into which category they fall. Mercury vapour bulbs lose much of their intensity within the first 3–6 months and after one year become very dim when compared with new bulbs. Metal halide bulbs must be replaced every 12–15 months if the blue end of the spectrum is to be preserved. While this may prove expensive, it is essential to the health of light-loving invertebrates.

● *How many fluorescent tubes should illuminate a reef tank?*

As many as will fit over the aquarium! There is no danger of over-illuminating the tank but there is a real risk of under-lighting where corals are concerned.

Lighting the Invertebrate Tank

Not all invertebrates are light-loving; lobsters, crabs, some shrimps, sponges and many sea whips absolutely thrive in conditions of subdued lighting and proper provision should be made for these species. Having said that, most tropical invertebrates require high-intensity lighting of the correct wavelength to prosper. Living within their surface tissues is a species of algae called zooxanthellae. This is a truly symbiotic relationship whereby the algae provides the coral with oxygen and certain nutrients, and in return, the host furnishes the algae with a secure and convenient home as well as a supply of carbon dioxide. Like all plants, zooxanthellae require light to photosynthesize, otherwise both the algae and their host coral will suffer, or even die.

It is almost impossible to over-illuminate this sort of aquarium, even with the most

▲ This superb reef tank has been beautifully enhanced by the use of correct lighting. Not only are the light-loving invertebrates fully satisfied, but the recessed metal halides are also pleasing to the human eye.

powerful of lamps. When compared with natural sunlight, artificial lighting is still relatively weak (anyone who has witnessed sunlight shining on a brightly lit tank will have seen just how dim artificial light is in comparison). Good invertebrate lighting should peak strongly at the violet/blue, as well as the red end of the colour spectrum as this is where most plants absorb their light. Unfortunately, human eyes do not register blue and red light as strongly as say, yellow, which is of little use to algae. As a result many artificial lights are designed to peak heavily in the blue, red and yellow areas of the spectrum, to meet the needs of algae and humans alike.

Types of Lighting

Mercury Vapour (HQL) pendant lamps are to be found in two wattages, 80 and 125. They look similar to metal halide lamps but are nowhere near as effective in intensity and spectrum. These lamps peak in the green/yellow/orange wavelengths with some smaller peaks in the violet end of the spectrum. This makes for excellent viewing with the added advantage of a natural "rippling" effect that only pendant spotlamps provide.

If these lamps are used for light-loving invertebrates, then it would be wise to add extra actinic blue fluorescent tubes to support that end of the spectrum. Mercury vapour bulbs lose their efficiency quickly and will need replacing every 3–6 months if you are keeping light-loving corals.

▲ *Mercury vapour pendant spotlamps need to be suspended from the ceiling and carefully positioned over the tank. Bringing the bulb just below the lip of the aquarium will prevent any glare affecting the viewer.*

Fluorescent Tubes have improved immensely. Convenience, and their relatively cool operation, make them the most popular aquarium lighting. New high-specification models give greater output in vital parts of the lighting spectrum, as well as providing a longer usable life-span with very little loss in efficiency. The choice is so great now that tubes are available to provide light specifically for the fish-only tank, intense illumination for corals, or blue light for a dusk/dawn effect. To increase the intensity of fluorescent tubes even further, external reflectors can be fitted to benefit corals. Some tubes have internal reflectors to achieve the same effect.

Whichever tubes are used they produce an even, some would say bland, effect. Fluorescents cannot create the dappled sunlight display, so beloved by marinists.

Metal Halide (HQI) pendant spotlamps are ideal for invertebrates as well as the fish-only aquarium. They provide high-intensity lighting with an excellent colour spectrum, not only for corals but for viewing as well.

Metal halides are also useful for deep tanks where light needs to be punched right down to the substrate. They give a pleasant blue-tinged viewing light that closely resembles natural sunlight. If the surface of the water is

▲ *The efficiency of a fluorescent tube can be maximized by using a suitable reflector. The complete unit can then be concealed beneath an aquarium hood.*

● *Can I mix different types of fluorescent tubes?*

... Yes, they can be mixed to cover the colour spectrum or to achieve a desired effect. This is probably the best approach for lighting an invertebrate aquarium with tubes.

● *When choosing metal halide lighting are there any special points to note?*

For light-loving invertebrates, choose bulbs with a colour temperature of 6500°Kelvin (K), this encourages healthy growth of corals. Metal halide lights emit a high level of ultraviolet rays which can be harmful to human eyesight. Screen them with glass designed to reduce ultraviolet rays to safe levels. Bulbs are also available with internal protective coatings that perform much the same task. Make sure that protection is in place before switching on the bulbs.

● *What is the minimum safe distance between the spotlamp and the water surface?*

Approximately 8in (20cm). If there is a high degree of water splash from the surface, then the lamps should be raised to a greater distance. Always remember that the farther away a light is from the water surface, the less effective it will be.

disturbed the underwater rippling effect can be stunning and very realistic.

Although this is the type of lighting most marinists aspire to, there are two major disadvantages. The first is its high price. Even though the cost of metal halides has halved in the last few years, the cheapest models are still out of reach to all but the most committed aquarists. Second, metal halides produce a great deal of heat; enough to raise tank temperatures to dangerously high levels during the summer months. If this heat cannot be adequately dispersed, a water coolant unit may have to be fitted and that could also prove to be very expensive. (See Chilling pages 10–11). In view of the extra heat generated, planning ahead before you install metal halides is essential. Extra room ventilation may well be necessary, as well as a fan to disperse heat away from the aquarium.

▼ *Using some ingenuity, several metal halide pendants can be linked as one unit. Sheets of glass are used to fill in the gaps, reducing evaporation from the tank and glare for the viewer.*

Testing and Water Conditions

MARINE FISH AND INVERTEBRATES ARE VERY sensitive animals, requiring the utmost care and attention to water quality, lighting and filtration. If the aquarist hopes to keep a good selection of these special animals for any length of time, then all water parameters need to be monitored constantly. A good grounding in these areas will help the newcomer and intermediate hobbyist alike to progress to more challenging species.

Most fish are far easier to keep than invertebrates and will tolerate a degree of variance where water quality is concerned, this is, of course, not a trend to be encouraged and the marinist will find that by improving water parameters to invertebrate levels in the fish-only tank, fish remain healthier, display better coloration and are longer lived.

Testing and Test Kits

The only satisfactory way of confirming the presence of various dilute toxic substances such as ammonia and nitrite is to use an accurate test kit. It is surprising how many hobbyists possess few or no test kits; perhaps they make the hobby seem too technical. However, it is vitally important for the marine fishkeeper to understand the major

● *Can tests be taken at any time of the day?*

... It is best that tests are performed at the same time every day to give a reliable base from which to compare unusual readings.

● *Are test kits always accurate?*

No. Kits wrongly stored, used incorrectly or beyond their recommended expiry date cannot be expected to give reliable information. Faulty kits also exist and if this is suspected should be compared with another identical kit for confirmation.

● *Are test kit reagents toxic?*

Yes, they can be very dangerous and it is strongly recommended that they are stored in a safe location out of the reach of children and animals.

● *Are all nitrate test kits the same?*

No. Some kits read nitrate-nitrogen (NO_3-N), whilst others read total nitrate (NO_3). The readings are not the same and a simple calculation must be performed to convert one to another. To convert nitrate-nitrogen to total nitrate multiply the NO_3-N reading by 4.4. To convert NO_3 to NO_3-N divide by 4.4. Nitrate levels are generally quoted as total nitrate (NO_3) unless otherwise stated. It would be wise to inspect the kit prior to purchase to discover which method has been adopted.

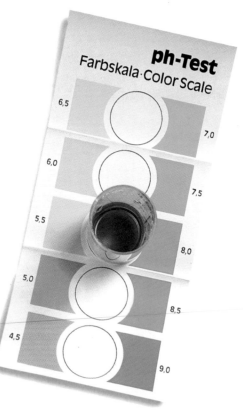

◀ *A broad range pH test kit may be suitable for the newcomer but the advanced hobbyist will soon want more accurate results.*

processes going on in their aquarium, to give themselves the best chance of success.

There are six basic test kits which every marine hobbyist should own and know how to use: ammonia, nitrite, nitrate, pH, specific gravity and copper. Ammonia and nitrite will enable the initial maturation of the aquarium filters to be monitored and confirm when it is complete. They will, subsequent to stocking, also warn of a mortality, overfeeding, overstocking and a breakdown in biological filtration. Specific gravity (S.G.) and pH are very useful in enabling the stability of the water to be managed, as these parameters are easily adjustable. The nitrate test kit will have no initial use, as far as the maturing aquarium is concerned, but it will prove a vital aid in assessing the quality of mains water. After all, if the mains water has a value of 45ppm, it may well be thought necessary to consider the purchase of a mains water filter to assist in the continuing fight to keep nitrates as low as possible. Once the aquarium has received its first inhabitants, nitrates will start to build up and must be constantly monitored. If invertebrates are to be kept at any stage, testing the mains water for copper is important. If the aquarium is for fish only, then this kit will prove very useful should disease need to be treated with a copper-based medication.

There are many other test kits available to mark the progress of an aquarium and confirm that there are no impending disasters: dissolved oxygen, carbon dioxide, alkalinity, phosphate, silicate, calcium, redox potential, conductivity, KH (carbonate hardness), iron, ozone, iodine, and strontium. Tests carried out by electronic meters are highly accurate, but their price might deter hobbyists.

When To Test
Monitoring a brand new set up will certainly mean an ammonia and nitrite test every day. pH can be measured every few days at the beginning, and more often as livestock is introduced. Once the tank has matured, ammonia and nitrite tests can be reduced to weekly for the first few months but every day for a week subsequent to every new livestock

addition. Nitrates can rise very quickly once an aquarium has become established and a test every fortnight, before and after water changes, is advisable.

Keeping an Aquarium Log
It is strongly recommended that every aquarium should have its history recorded from the beginning. Test results, registered with the date and time of testing, will help detect trends in water quality in the long term, particularly when compared with livestock additions. As a bonus, the age, growth and health of livestock can also be monitored.

Be warned that practically every test kit with liquid reagents, once opened, will have a limited shelf life, usually about six months. After that, they cannot be guaranteed accurate and may give misleading information. A good idea is to write the date that it was opened on the side of the package and the approximate expiry date. Store these kits in a cool, dark place, for full potential shelf life and refrain from purchasing any test kit that has been previously opened.

Kits with tablet or powdered reagents only, have an almost indefinite shelf life but still should be stored in a cool, dry location to retain accuracy. Store all colour charts out of strong light as the colours will fade.

Electronic Metering
A large number of water parameters can be measured electronically and the levels revealed on a digital display. These readings may be produced by single-test dip-in models, or permanently fitted probes enabling constant displays. Whichever model is chosen, the probe will require calibrating at regular intervals with special solutions. In this way, full accuracy can be maintained. More sophisticated equipment will also combine metering with the control of other facilities such as heaters, chillers or ozone. The most widely available electronic meters include: pH, temperature, redox potential, conductivity, dissolved oxygen, and salinity. Advanced fishkeeping usually relies on more sophisticated monitoring and this is to be encouraged.

TESTING WATER QUALITY

Ammonia (NH₃/NH₄⁺)
Optimum level: zero at all times

Ammonia is the primary enemy of invertebrates and fish, capable of causing death in very low concentrations. Causes of ammonia include: an immature filter, overfeeding, overstocking and dead or dying stock. By vigilance and regular testing, the presence of ammonia can be avoided.

Nitrite (NO₂)
Optimum level: zero at all times

Even trace levels of nitrite can destroy a well presented invertebrate aquarium and cause fish much distress. All comments regarding ammonia apply equally as well here.

Nitrate (NO₃)
Optimum levels: below 10 parts per million (ppm)
total NO₃ preferably zero

Some fish may tolerate well in excess of 25ppm. A reasonably harmless substance where many fish are concerned but a good overall indicator of general water quality and one that should be kept extremely low if invertebrates are to thrive. Constantly high nitrate levels usually reflect high fish stocking ratios. This must be monitored and the aquaria de-stocked if necessary.

Phosphates (PO₄)
Optimum level: zero

Invertebrates do not prosper when levels of phosphate get too high. Phosphates arrive in the aquarium through unfiltered mains water (used in the mixing of fresh or saltwater changes), poor quality carbon and marine salts, but mostly through the waste products of fish. Nuisance algae thrive where phosphate levels are high and destocking, high-quality water changes in the correct proportion or phosphate-removing resins can all help alleviate the problem.

Temperature
Optimum level: 25°C (77°F)

A stable temperature is essential to the well-being of invertebrates and fish. Hot weather may force the temperature up and a cooler may have to be installed if valuable livestock is not to be lost. Always use an accurate thermometer.

pH
Optimum level: 8.1–8.3

pH is a measure of the alkalinity or acidity of aquarium water. Invertebrates are sensitive to wide variations, although some natural changes are to be expected during the day. Dissolved oxygen assists in the increase of pH and as this builds up due to activity of photosynthesis by micro and macro algae; test meters or kits will detect it. Aquarium water could drop to as low as 7.9 at the end of the night, and peak at around 8.4 just before lights out. These natural pH cycles are gradual and tend not to stress livestock to any great degree. Owing to their ingredients, pH buffers can also increase KH values to dangerously high levels. Regular water changes are essential.

Alkalinity
Optimum level: approx 600 microequivalents

Sodium carbonate is an important constituent of sea water as it helps prevent the dangerous lowering of pH by buffering it to optimum levels. As it is depleted, the buffering capacity of the water is reduced and the pH becomes unstable. Alkalinity test kits can now warn of low buffering levels and potential problems.

(K)arbonate Hardness (KH)
Optimum level: Natural
Sea water (NSW) is 7dKH

KH is a measurement of various carbonates and bicarbonates of calcium and magnesium, and borates within fresh and sea water. A stable KH will prevent rapid declines in alkalinity and subsequent drops in pH. Boosting the KH of aquarium seawater to between 12–18dKH using a proprietary generator has been recommended. However, left to their own devices, most aquaria settle naturally to around 7dKH and there appears to be no advantage in constantly increasing dKH to unnatural levels. Indeed, it could prove harmful as pH levels might be adversely affected.

Salinity
Optimum level:
between 1.021–1.024 (S.G.)

Salinity measures the total amount of dissolved solids in sea water. It is usually recorded as specific gravity (S.G.) but can also be referred to as parts per

Reverse Osmosis

NOT SO VERY LONG AGO IT WAS ACCEPTABLE to use mains water when making up fresh salt mixes. But over recent years domestic water supplies seem to have deteriorated with an increase in the number of impurities such as nitrates, phosphates, other mineral salts, bacteria, dissolved organics and heavy metals, to name but a few. These are, arguably, of little consequence to the health of humans but have become a real obstacle to fishkeepers, especially those keeping marines. Poor water quality can encourage nuisance algae, put extra stress on fish and invertebrates leading to disease and death, cause unexplained losses and a general failure in the hobby. Consequently, more and more people are filtering their mains water. The high filtering efficiency of reverse osmosis (RO) units has attracted a large number of hobbyists to use one to help preserve valuable livestock.

What is Reverse Osmosis?
Osmosis is the natural process by which selective molecules in an aqueous solution can pass through a semi-permeable membrane, while the movement of other molecules due to size, shape or other reasons is restricted (see pages 78–79).

In order to preserve a balance, nature deems that water molecules will pass from a less dense solution into a denser solution in order to dilute it and create an equilibrium; for our purposes this is *not* what we want. Therefore, mains water pressure is used to force water molecules the "wrong way" through the membrane, leaving the unwanted pollutants behind and flushed to waste.

The Mechanics
TFC (Thin Film Composite) membranes have proved to be the most suitable for the fishkeeper owing to their high efficiency rating with over 90% of pollutants capable of being removed, including nitrates, phosphates, pesticides, heavy metals and a whole host of other substances. However, TFC membranes are sensitive to chlorine in mains water and need an activated carbon pre-filter to remove it and prevent premature deterioration.

In areas where there is a high concentration of total dissolved solids (TDS) in the mains supply, a particulate (sediment) filter will also be necessary. This will help to protect the membrane and prolong its life. A TFC membrane will last 1–5 years depending on the original quality of the water it has to filter,

THE REVERSE OSMOSIS PROCESS

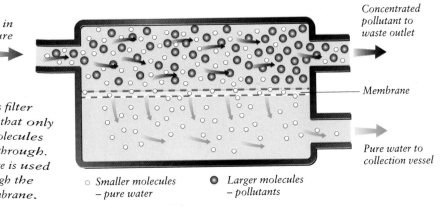

Mains water in under pressure

A reverse osmosis filter membrane is so fine that only the smaller water molecules are allowed to pass through. Mains-water pressure is used to force water through the highly resistant membrane.

Concentrated pollutant to waste outlet

Membrane

Pure water to collection vessel

○ *Smaller molecules – pure water*   ● *Larger molecules – pollutants*

thousand (ppt) or 0/00 (eg 35 0/00 is 1.026). Constant evaporation of freshwater from the aquarium causes the salts to become more concentrated and the salinity to rise. To maintain stability, automatic dosing systems called osmo-regulators or osmolators are often used. These systems use conductivity meters to a very accurate level. They take their readings in micro Siemens (µS) and may be set to replenish freshwater as it evaporates

Calcium
Optimum level: 350–400 ppm

Calcium is a vital element in any marine aquarium. A host of invertebrates draw it from the surrounding water in copious amounts and calcium reserves need to be replenished on a regular basis. Regular water changes may achieve this but a well-stocked invertebrate tank may require the addition of biologically available calcium to keep levels optimum.

Dissolved Oxygen (O_2)
Optimum level: 6–7 ppm

Both fish and invertebrates benefit greatly from high levels of dissolved oxygen. Good water circulation is the key, as oxygen is drawn mainly from the interface between air and water. Dissolved oxygen also affects pH (see pH).

Copper
Optimum levels: zero in the invertebrate aquarium; variable in the fish-only tank

Copper-based medications have proved very reliable in the treatment of various fish diseases such as whitespot and *Oodinium*. It is, however, highly toxic to invertebrates and should never be used in aquaria housing these animals. Accurate measurement of copper is essential as it can even prove lethal to fish at certain levels. (see Fish Health pages 70-73). Copper can even be introduced to the marine aquarium by way of the domestic water supply and this should be tested from time to time.

Redox Potential (ORP)
Optimum level:
approx 350 millivolts

Oxygen Reduction Potential is, broadly speaking, a measurement of the water's ability to cleanse itself. Highly efficient filtration and the use of ozone will help to boost values. OR can only be measured using electronic meter with a high quality probe. As with ma "advanced" tests, ORP is absolutely essential and t ings may be difficult to i without a full understa the multiple parameter

✓ WATER TESTING CHECKLIST

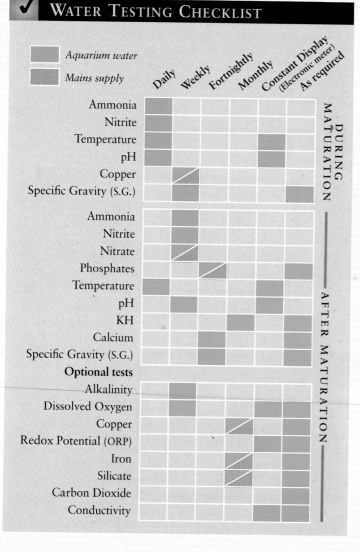

Legend: Aquarium water / Mains supply

	Daily	Weekly	Fortnightly	Monthly	Constant Display (Electronic meter)	As required
DURING MATURATION						
Ammonia	■					
Nitrite	■					
Temperature	■				■	
pH	■				■	
Copper		◨				
Specific Gravity (S.G.)		■				
AFTER MATURATION						
Ammonia		■				
Nitrite		■				
Nitrate		◨				
Phosphates			◨			
Temperature	■				■	
pH		■			■	
KH				■		
Calcium		■				
Specific Gravity (S.G.)		■				
Optional tests						
Alkalinity		■				
Dissolved Oxygen		■				
Copper				◨		
Redox Potential (ORP)					■	
Iron				◨		
Silicate				◨		
Carbon Dioxide		■				
Conductivity					■	

● *Can an RO unit be used if the mains water pressure is low?*

... A specialized pump may be required should the water pressure be less than 40 psi (2.8 kg/cm2).

● *Can RO water be used immediately?*

Being so efficient, the RO process strips the water of oxygen and must be aerated for 24 hours before use.

● *Will the unit still work if the flow of water through it is restricted?*

Yes, as long as the pressure remains high.

● *Are there any other parameters that affect the flow through an RO filter?*

Yes, the temperature. The lower the temperature, the slower the flow.

➤ *Reverse osmosis units may take on different designs but the process remains the same. Here, the particulate filter is in the cylinder on the left; the carbon filter is in the center and the TFC membrane is in the right-hand cylinder.*

while carbon and particulate pre-filters should be changed every 4–6 months. The membrane can filter to 1/10,000 micron (the naked eye can just see 40 microns!) so the process is slow and only one part pure water is saved out of every five rejected. There are no electrical connections and a standard RO unit will operate on mains water pressure of 40–100 psi (2.8–7.0 kg/cm2).

Reverse osmosis units can be bought to produce varying quantities of pure water in each 24-hour period and, as it is not wise to switch the unit off for long periods, the correctly rated unit must be purchased to suit the needs of the individual. Hence, it is useless buying a unit that will yield 10 gallons a day (140 gallons every two weeks) if the requirement is for 25 gallons a fortnight! (Although the excess could be shared with friends.) If you are confused as to your needs, be guided by a specialist supplier to the aquarist, and not the drinking-water trade.

Positioning

Most RO units will fit neatly under the sink but can be positioned just about anywhere there is a mains water supply with plenty of pressure. It can be plumbed in easily using a butterfly connection device (usually supplied) that requires no plumbing or other skills. A waste outlet will have to be found, and many people will be able to put this water to good use irrigating the garden or topping up a pond, etc. Store pure RO water in food quality containers like those used in wine making; the use of any other vessels may prove unsuitable as RO water will easily "soak up" toxins in the plastic.

A Sound Investment

Although the initial investment may seem high, an RO unit can save the marine aquarist much heartache by limiting the possibilities of losing valuable livestock to impurities. Nuisance algae will also be brought under control far more easily. Miracle cures in a bottle are few and far between in marine fishkeeping and there is no real substitute for pure, clean, water.

Undergravel Filtration

UNDERGRAVEL FILTRATION HAS BEEN USED for many years as the principal means of biological filtration in the marine aquarium, and despite the development of newer rival systems (see pages 24–25 and 26–27) it remains the most popular option today. Two basic methods are available.

The Downflow Method

Downflow is the traditional and most widely adopted method because it is easy to understand and set up. Start by covering the base of the tank as completely as possible with undergravel filter plates. These can be either of the small, lock-together variety, or the larger all-in-one type with fine slits. Some aquarists prefer to glue these to the base using silicone sealant. Next, for a four foot tank, an uplift should be fitted to the plate(s) at either end in the back corner. The tubes may have to be cut with a hacksaw to accommodate a powerhead on each one.

Once the plates are in position, cover them with a suitably coarse medium such as coral

● *Is it essential to glue the filter plates to the base glass?*

... No, the weight of the filter bed tends to seal the plates from any leakage.

● *Can air be used to operate the uplifts?*

Yes, but powerheads perform the task much more efficiently and just as cheaply.

● *Can I put a layer of floss over the filter plates as a gravel tidy substitute?*

The floss will become clogged and impenetrable to water within a few months. Replacement means major disturbance of the whole aquarium on a regular basis.

● *How can the media be checked for contaminants?*

A strong magnet placed inside a polythene bag can be passed over the media to remove any metal fragments.

● *What will happen if two different powerheads are used for the same filter bed?*

The stronger pump will reduce the flow of the weaker one as it pulls against it. In extreme cases, water will be drawn down the weaker pump, rendering the whole filter bed useless.

Strengths of Undergravel Filtration

1) Universally understood and very widely available
2) Easy to operate, a bonus for beginners
3) Relatively cheap for smaller tanks
4) A natural environment for substrate dwellers
5) Quiet in operation
6) Calcium levels are higher and more stable due to calcium-rich substrate
7) pH is buffered by alkalinity of the substrate
8) There is a large natural surface upon which bacterial colonies can thrive
9) Since undergravel filtration has been in use for many years, the correct stocking levels can be calculated very accurately using the formulas on pages 57 and 59.

Weaknesses of Undergravel Filtration

1) Displaces large amounts of water
2) Filter bed looks unnatural
3) Tends to clog with detritus
4) Bacteria consumes oxygen from the tank (but extra turbulence from the pumps may compensate)
5) Coral sand requires gradual renewal after two years
6) Calcium carbonates in substrate may interfere with effectiveness of medication
7) Collecting coral sand and gravel for the aquarium trade is less environmentally acceptable
8) Contamination of the tank by fragments of rusting metal collected from the sea bed with coral sand and gravel.

Downflow Method

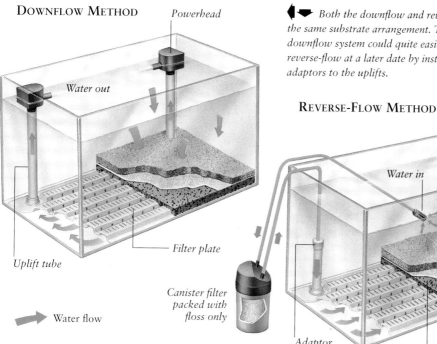

Powerhead

Water out

Uplift tube

Filter plate

Water flow

Canister filter
packed with
floss only

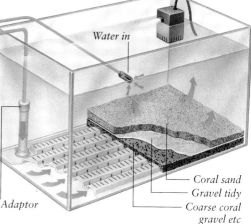

☜☛ *Both the downflow and reverse-flow filters use the same substrate arrangement. This means that a downflow system could quite easily be upgraded to reverse-flow at a later date by installing the appropriate adaptors to the uplifts.*

Reverse-Flow Method

Water in

Adaptor

Coral sand
Gravel tidy
Coarse coral
gravel etc

gravel, crushed shells or dolomite chips at a rate of 10lb (4kg) for every square foot of base area; in this case, 40lb (16kg) in total. A gravel tidy, which is no more than a fine plastic mesh, must then be placed over the coarse media and neatly trimmed to fit tightly into all the corners and around the uplifts. Cover the gravel tidy with a layer of coral sand, again at a rate of 10lb (4kg) per sq ft. The mesh will prevent the two media from mixing together to form a compacted, ineffectual filter bed. It is wise to wash all media thoroughly prior to positioning and to give it a thorough visual examination for foreign objects and contaminants.

The powerheads should draw the total water volume of the tank through the filter bed at least three times every hour. If several powerheads are used, they must all be of the same make and power rating to provide maximum efficiency. The coral sand will require raking through on a regular basis to prevent compaction, which reduces the through-flow. Any mulm and detritus can be siphoned off at the same time.

The Reverse-Flow Method

The filter bed arrangement for reverse-flow is exactly the same as the downflow method but the direction of the water is reversed and pumped down the uplifts and up through the various media. Power is best supplied by one or more canister filters capable of circulating the total volume of tank water at least three times every hour. For even distribution of water throughout the filter bed, a filter plate with fine slits is usually more effective.

An extra water pump will be necessary for good water circulation. The advantage of reverse-flow is that the water can be constantly filtered for detritus and debris that would otherwise be drawn into the coral sand, packing it down and clogging it. Therefore, place only mechanical media (filter floss) in the canister and change it every two weeks, depending on stocking levels. Biological media is totally unnecessary as all the bacterial activity should be limited to the filter bed. Activated carbon must also be avoided as this will rob some of the nutrients from the filter bed, reducing the biological activity.

Trickle Filters

HUMAN WASTE HAS BEEN PROCESSED THROUGH trickle filters since the turn of the century, but it is only recently that the techniques have been adapted for use in domestic aquaria. Water containing various nitrogenous compounds (ie ammonia and nitrites) is trickled or sprayed over a medium very suitable for bacterial colonization. As the water soaks through the medium, aerobic (oxygen-using) bacteria utilize the dissolved compounds as food and convert them into less toxic substances. *Nitrosomonas* species convert ammonia into nitrites and *Nitrobacter* species convert the nitrites into nitrates; yet another bacterium can be called upon to convert nitrates into free nitrogen gas but this is only achieved under anaerobic (oxygen-free) conditions and is not usually encompassed by trickle filtration systems.

Trickle filters are far more efficient than traditional undergravels. Again, the reasoning is surprisingly simple. The *Nitrosomonas* and *Nitrobacter* bacteria require access to copious amounts of oxygen to perform their tasks efficiently; with normal undergravels the friendly bacteria can only call upon the available oxygen dissolved in the water, if this is low then the bacteria count will be equally low, making the filter increasingly inefficient. Trickle filters, on the other hand, have access to unlimited supplies of free oxygen and the bacteria can not only perform their functions at peak efficiency but have a favourable environment in which to multiply quickly.

Undergravel filtration can still contribute to a successful tank set-up. Some aquarists use a combination of undergravel and trickle filters on the same tank with exceptional results.

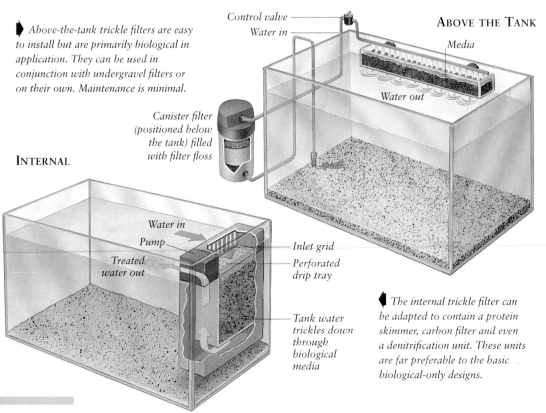

▶ *Above-the-tank trickle filters are easy to install but are primarily biological in application. They can be used in conjunction with undergravel filters or on their own. Maintenance is minimal.*

Control valve
Water in

ABOVE THE TANK

Media

Water out

Canister filter
(positioned below
the tank) filled
with filter floss

INTERNAL

Water in
Pump
Treated
water out

Inlet grid
Perforated
drip tray

Tank water
trickles down
through
biological
media

◀ *The internal trickle filter can be adapted to contain a protein skimmer, carbon filter and even a denitrification unit. These units are far preferable to the basic biological-only designs.*

Strengths of Trickle Filters

1) Most equipment can be concealed
2) Increased surface area promotes bacteria
3) Ease of maintenance
4) Detritus is pre-filtered out
5) No water or space is lost to filter media within the tank
6) High levels of dissolved oxygen are produced as water is filtered
7) Medications are more effective since they are not interfered with by a calcareous media
8) Convenient for automatic or semi-automatic water change systems
9) A vast range of associated equipment can be installed with the filter or at later intervals

Weaknesses of Trickle Filters

1) Expense
2) Limited range of models
3) Some are difficult to assemble and install
4) Back-up service can be poor
5) Can be noisy in operation
6) Some tanks require drilling or a proper failsafe overflow mechanism
7) Risk of leaking joints
8) Pre-filters generally need daily attention
9) Livestock can be drawn into the overflow
10) KH, pH and calcium buffers will probably be required
11) Stocking levels cannot be determined as accurately as with undergravel filters

● *Are trickle filters just for large tanks?*

... No, any size of tank would benefit where high quality water is essential.

● *Can more fish be stocked if a trickle filter is fitted?*

No. Trickle filters should be seen as a means to improve water quality and not as an excuse to increase livestock beyond a reasonable level.

● *Do trickle filters reduce the need for water changes?*

No. A 15–25% water change every two weeks should be standard practice for every tank whatever the filtration.

● *Will trickle filters reduce nitrates?*

No, a separate denitrifying filter will be required, although this may be housed within the trickle filter.

● *Is extra turbulence required in the showtank?*

Experience has shown that extra circulatory pumps are usually needed in the main tank to supplement the return flow from the trickle filter.

● *Is it better to use plastic, ceramic or coral gravel in the filter?*

Each model will come with a recommendation from the manufacturer as to which medium suits their own product and this should be followed for best results. All of the media mentioned are perfectly acceptable.

➤ *Many marine aquarists find that a trickle filter sited below the tank provides many advantages. After the initial expense has been absorbed, the overall flexibility makes for a more natural and successful display.*

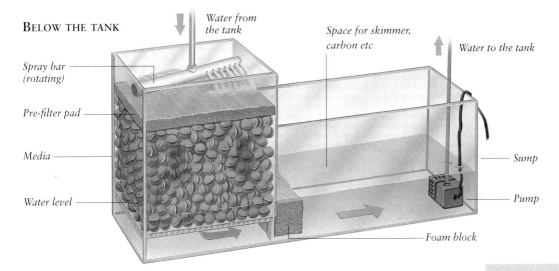

BELOW THE TANK

Water from the tank

Space for skimmer, carbon etc

Water to the tank

Spray bar (rotating)

Pre-filter pad

Media

Water level

Sump

Pump

Foam block

Canister Filters

EXTERNAL CANISTER FILTERS ARE ONE OF THE most versatile but misunderstood pieces of aquarium equipment. Canister filters can be used in three main ways.

For Mechanical Filtration

In this case the filter will be packed with filter floss to extract particles of suspended solids and act as a pre-filter for reverse-flow systems and trickle filters. To achieve a good through-flow of water and extended media life, it is important to pack all materials fairly lightly. Depending on how heavily stocked the tank is, the filter media will need replacing every one to two weeks.

For Chemical Filtration

The canister filter should be packed with an adsorbative medium such as activated carbon or specific removal resin. This may act entirely independently or as a pre-filter to an ultra-violet sterilizer, in which case the packing should include some filter floss just before the water return. The chemical medium should be contained in a nylon mesh bag specially made for the purpose, but if this is not available then it may be placed between two pieces of filter floss. If this latter method is used, then the filter floss will have to be changed once a week to prevent clogging and a restriction in water flow; some filters allow for packing in self-contained modules. Replace the filter medium every two months in the case of carbon but follow manufacturer's instructions with respect to resins and other filtration substances.

For Biological Filtration

The filter should be packed with a porous material that is also fairly coarse and allows a good water flow. If flow is restricted in any way, the bacteria will begin to die. Encase the biological media in a nylon bag to prevent it being drawn into the pump motor impeller.

As this type of filter must be disturbed as little as possible, it is not advisable to mix it with other media that require regular attention, such as filter floss. If the filter is large

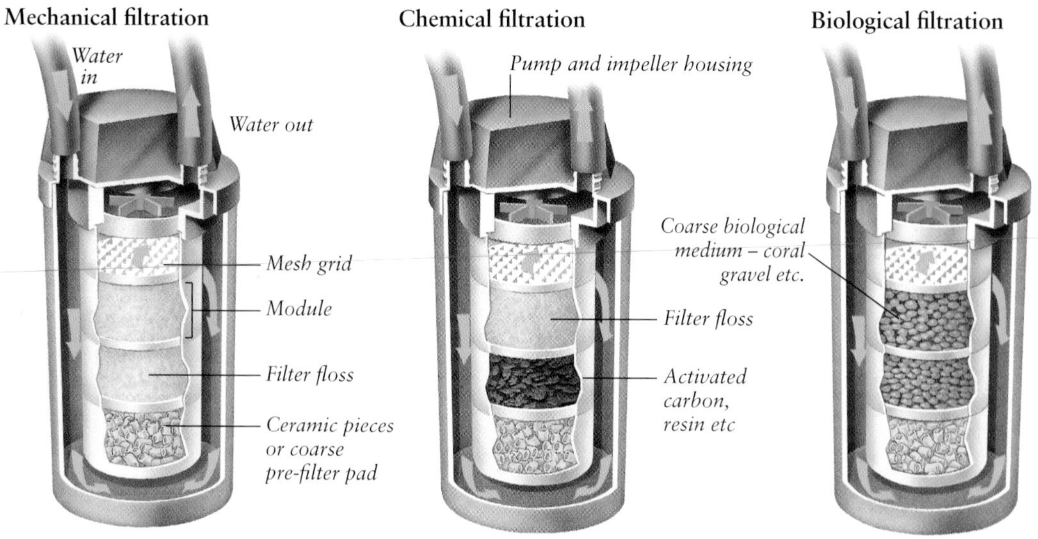

▼ *The three main ways to utilize a canister filter are illustrated here. These models use internal clip-together modules, each holding a different medium.*

Mechanical filtration	Chemical filtration	Biological filtration

Mechanical filtration: Water in — Water out — Mesh grid — Module — Filter floss — Ceramic pieces or coarse pre-filter pad

Chemical filtration: Pump and impeller housing — Filter floss — Activated carbon, resin etc

Biological filtration: Coarse biological medium – coral gravel etc.

● *Can coral sand be used as a biological medium?*

... No, it will quickly compact down hard, preventing proper water flow.

● *What is the correct canister packing to operate an undergravel filter?*

If a reverse-flow undergravel filter (pages 22–23) is in use, extra biological filtration is unnecessary within the canister and only mechanical media should be used.

● *How can canister maintenance be made less of a chore?*

Maintenance is considerably easier if twin valves are fitted to both the inlet and outlet hoses. The syphon need not be broken when the canister is removed and the risk of water leakage is much reduced.

● *How can algae be discouraged from forming inside the hosing?*

A useful tip is to exclude all light completely from the hosing by wrapping it in strips of thin black plastic, thereby depriving any algae of all light. In theory, the algae should not form at all.

● *Why has the impeller become noisy in its housing?*

The impeller can become noisy for several reasons:
1) there is insufficient water flowing past it to lubricate its action
2) there is air trapped in the impeller housing
3) the impeller, or impeller housing is worn.
Avoid very cheap canister filter models as construction materials tend to be inferior and they can become noisy in a short time. High quality, but more expensive filters are always a good investment.

▶ *There are many varying designs of canister filter available to the hobbyist. Take care to choose a good quality product of the correct capacity and pumping power. Too large is better than too small.*

enough and stocking levels are kept reasonably low, it is possible to use a canister filter as the sole means of biological filtration, and to dispense with the undergravel media, gaining the tank valuable extra water volume. This is not, however, to be recommended to the inexperienced unless under expert advice.

It is vitally important that canister filters are packed fairly loosely and maintained properly to ensure that the correct amount of water reaches the pump impeller. If the impeller runs dry, irreparable damage can occur, or at the very least you will have clattering, noisy units.

Always make sure canister filters are sited below the aquarium and not on the same level or above. This enables the syphon to work correctly. In an ideal world, the top of the canister should be just below the bottom of the tank; the greater the distance below, the less water will be pumped due to back-pressure. Equally, never use more hose than is absolutely necessary as increased back-pressure will reduce water flow and put an unnecessary strain on the pump. Friction will also cause much the same effect.

Clean inlet strainers and outlets once a week, or more often if required. All tubing should be cleared of obstructive algae and detritus with a proprietary hose brush every three months. Lastly, do not underestimate the usefulness of the coarse pre-filter pad or ceramic pieces. These not only extract larger pieces of debris but also enable the pump to draw the water through the various media much more effectively. Never be tempted to dispense with the pre-filter stage to make space for other media.

Protein Skimming

PROTEIN SKIMMING, ALSO CALLED FOAM fractionation or air stripping, is a mechanical process for removing waste substances from saltwater at a primary stage, long before they can be treated biologically or chemically.

The theory behind protein skimming is relatively simple. Molecules of many organic and inorganic substances are strongly attracted to the interface between water and gas. This is because each molecule has a "water loving" (hydrophilic) end and a "water hating" (hydrophobic) end. Substances that react in this way are called surface active agents, commonly shortened to surfactants. These include: proteins, amino acids, dyes, fatty acids, albumin compounds, fats, carbohydrates, enzymes, detergents, copper ions and many inorganic compounds.

How Does It Work?

A protein skimmer creates a huge water/air interface area by producing millions of tiny bubbles in a confined space to which the surfactants become attracted. As the bubbles rise naturally, an oily scum is produced at the surface which is continuously pushed up by the pressure of the foaming column below until it overflows into the waste collection cup. Here the bubbles burst and the liquid residue is captured, ready for disposal. Its colour may vary from dark brown to yellow.

It follows that the more bubbles there are, and the longer they are kept in suspension, the more efficient the skimming process will be. Indeed, studies on the most advanced models indicate that up to 80 percent of all organic waste can be removed from the marine aquarium by an efficient skimmer of the correct size. One drawback is that protein skimmers may reduce the efficacy of medications as some inorganic ions (such as copper) are surfactants and are readily removed. In this case, switch the skimmer off for 12 hours immediately after each treatment dosage. It is questionable whether the skimmer should be switched off for the duration of medication as the resultant build-up of waste products could very likely offset the advantages of treatment owing to increased stress levels.

Three Basic Types of Protein Skimmer

The basic types of protein skimmer available are the direct-current, the counter-current and the powered venturi skimmer.

The direct-current skimmer, positioned inside the aquarium, is the simplest and least efficient of the designs. In its basic form, a wooden air diffuser is positioned below a hollow acrylic tube above which a collection cup is placed. Bubble generation and contact time are minimal, limiting this design to the very smallest and lightly stocked aquaria. Ozone *cannot* be used with this model.

An improvement on the direct-current model is the counter-current skimmer. This is probably the most popular method in common use and, though some designs are outdated, the unit is generally easy to install and fairly efficient. Physically it can resemble the direct-current model with the addition of an extra counter-flow feature. This keeps the bubbles inside the acrylic tube in suspension for a much longer period, so that a greater number of surfactants can be attracted and collected. Counter-current models come in several lengths and the greatest length that will fit in a particular depth of water should always be chosen for maximum efficiency. It is important for both the direct-current and counter-current model to be set at the correct height in the water. The grid just below the collection cup should be at the same level as the water surface.

An improvement on the counter-current skimmer, known as the advanced counter-current skimmer, is also available. These are positioned outside the aquarium. Tank water is pumped into the top of a cylinder and mixed with the stream of fine bubbles produced from a limewood air diffuser. A counter-current effect is set up as the water exits from the bottom of the unit and the bubbles try to rise against the flow. Contact times can be very prolonged and consequently make this type of skimmer extremely efficient. It can be highly recommended to the vast majority of marine hobbyists. The collection cup will fill with a liquid that may resemble dark coffee or weak orange juice. The colour and amount collected each day will depend very much on the amount of live-stock kept. In any case, the collection cup should be emptied and cleaned regularly to prevent bacterial build-ups and consequent nasty smells. In the normal course of events, the liquid waste is practically odourless.

The third type of protein skimmer is the powered venturi model, the most efficient skimming device to date (and usually the most expensive of the three types). Such is the versatility of the powered skimmer that several designs exist, enabling positioning above, beside or inside the tank or external trickle filter sump. The larger powered venturi skimmer is highly recommended for the heavily stocked, fish-only aquarium in particular.

THE ADVANCED COUNTER-CURRENT PROTEIN SKIMMER

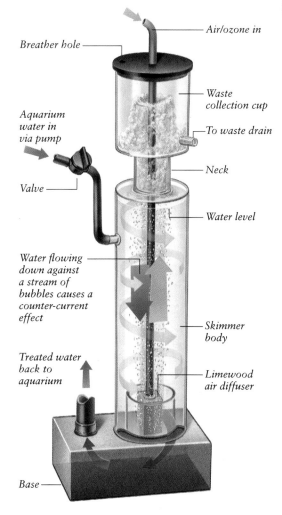

- Air/ozone in
- Breather hole
- Waste collection cup
- Aquarium water in via pump
- To waste drain
- Neck
- Valve
- Water level
- Water flowing down against a stream of bubbles causes a counter-current effect
- Skimmer body
- Treated water back to aquarium
- Limewood air diffuser
- Base

● *Must all marine aquaria be fitted with a protein skimmer.*

... Yes, it is an essential piece of equipment, removing pollutants that other filtration methods fail to eliminate.

● *What should be done if the waste liquid is colourless and copious in quantity?*

The skimmer requires further careful adjustment to air and water flow. This situation is not uncommon with new set-ups.

● *How often should the wooden air diffusers be replaced?*

To maintain maximum efficiency renew air diffusers every two months. The internal body of the unit can be cleaned at the same time.

● *Does the collection cup have to be emptied of waste liquid every day?*

No, most modern skimmers have a bleed-off tube redirecting the liquid into a drain or larger container to be emptied once or twice a week.

● *Is it essential to use ozone with a protein skimmer?*

No, many skimmers work very well without the use of ozone, although their efficiency can be markedly improved with its use (see Ozone pages 30–32).

◀ *Advanced counter-current protein skimmers are invariably made from clear acrylic, enabling the hobbyist to monitor the density of bubbles and the correct water level. A wide, firm base is essential to keep the whole structure stable.*

Ozone

Since its inception, the use of ozone within the marine aquarium has caused much confusion among hobbyists. Put simply, the ozonizer increases the efficiency of the protein skimmer and the destruction of dissolved solids, increasing the overall quality of the aquarium water.

The Ozonizer

Ozone (O_3) is an unstable gas produced by passing dehumidified air through a very high voltage field, usually within a unit called an ozonizer. Ordinary oxygen (O_2) is a stable molecule but the effect of the ozonizer causes an extra atom to be added to this structure to form unstable ozone (O_3) molecules. The extra atom is eager to break this temporary partnership and interact with other organic and inorganic molecules. When this happens, ozone oxidizes the chemicals with which it comes into contact.

Used in conjunction with a protein skimmer, as it must nearly always be, ozone oxidizes dissolved solids that have accumulated in the water (almost "burning" them out of existence). This results in an increase of redox potential. Redox potential, or ORP (Oxygen Reduction Potential) measures the water's ability to clean itself — the cleaner the water, the higher the ORP (see page 19).

In addition, ozone will clarify the water by oxidizing discolouring dyes that cause the "yellowing" of marine water. It will slightly increase oxygen saturation levels and kill the cells of free-swimming bacteria, viruses and algae, resulting in a mild sterilization of infected water. Unfortunately, the beneficial organisms and substances are also destroyed as ozone makes no distinction between the harmful and the harmless. However ozone cannot compete with the effectiveness of ultraviolet sterilizers in their ability to rid the aquarium of free-swimming parasites.

● *How does the aquarist calculate the correct amount of ozone for a given tank?*

Apart from observing the physical effects on livestock, the only way to make sure that ozone is improving water quality is to use a redox potential meter. All other means are unreliable.

● *What redox level should the aquarist aim for?*

Many fish-only tanks will be fine at readings of 250–350 mv. Sensitive invertebrates are best between 350–450 mv, but no livestock should be kept at levels approaching or exceeding 500 mv.

● *How can the hobbyist tell if ozone is in the main tank water?*

By testing with a residual ozone kit available from a well-stocked aquarium retailer.

● *What are the effects of residual ozone on livestock?*

It damages the gills of fish causing them to flick, scratch and breathe heavily. Death occurs in severe cases. Coral invertebrates will fail to display properly for long periods and, like crustaceans, can die for no apparent reason.

▲ *Modern ozonizers are compact units. The inside of this model illustrates the chamber (bottom) that exposes ordinary air to a high voltage field to create ozone.*

Using Ozone Safely

You must ensure that ozone is never allowed direct access to the aquarium water as it is extremely harmful to the delicate tissues of fish, invertebrates and algae, not to mention friendly nitrifying bacteria, even in quite low residual amounts. Used correctly with a counter-current skimmer, for example, ozone must only be fed down the central column and through the wooden air diffuser. It must not be injected into the counter-current feature, otherwise ozone will flood into the show tank with potentially disastrous results. Venturi skimmers, designed to take ozone, present a problem as the throughput of water is so great, much of the ozone fails to escape and is pumped straight into the main tank. Only careful attention to the level of ozone and the rate at which the venturi skimmer operates can alleviate the potential risks.

An alternative to the protein skimmer is a safe vessel in which ozone can treat aquarium water. This device, called an ozone reactor, can normally be found associated with under-tank trickle filters, but surplus ozone must still be disposed of safely. Any excess ozone should be ducted out of the room or filtered through activated carbon that will neutralize its effects on humans. Failure to take suitable

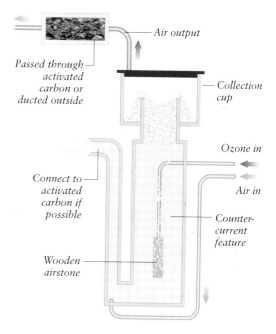

Air output

Passed through activated carbon or ducted outside

Collection cup

Ozone in

Connect to activated carbon if possible

Air in

Counter-current feature

Wooden airstone

▲ *Introducing ozone gas into a counter-current skimmer can only be done through the wooden air diffuser in the central column. Maximum contact time with the water is achieved through this method while, in theory, none leaks into the aquarium.*

▼ *Given the potential hazards involved in using ozone, the schematic diagram below must be followed as closely as possible.*

THE SAFE WAY TO INSTALL OZONE

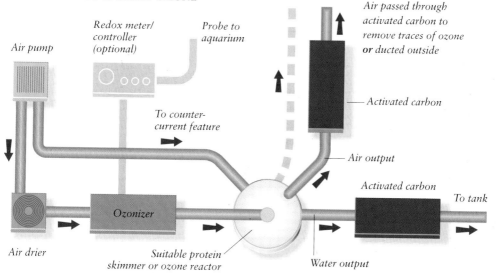

Air pump

Redox meter/ controller (optional)

Probe to aquarium

Air passed through activated carbon to remove traces of ozone **or** ducted outside

Activated carbon

To counter-current feature

Air output

Activated carbon

To tank

Ozonizer

Air drier

Suitable protein skimmer or ozone reactor

Water output

precautions could cause nausea, headaches, depression and irritation of the eyes.

Although ozone has a distinctive smell, it is somewhat difficult to define in words; to some, it reminds them of the seaside and to others, electricity. A slight smell of ozone beneath the tank hood is quite normal, but if it can be detected in the room as a pungent odour, then it must be dealt with in one of the ways previously described.

Exposure to ozone will destroy a great many items including plastic airline and even the protein skimmer itself, given time! As plastic airline will become brittle in a relatively short period of time, it is safer to use silicone airline instead and keep the levels of ozone as low as possible to prolong the life of the skimmer. Rubber is also affected by ozone and those skimmers using rubber sealant rings cannot be used with this gas, even for short periods.

Measuring Ozone

Ozone supply is measured in milligrams per hour (mg/h) and can be controlled automatically by means of a redox potential measuring/control unit. In this way, a desired redox level is set (in millivolts) and the ozonizer is switched on and off automatically. However, redox controllers are expensive and most marine aquarists will set their ozonizer manually at a constant rate. For example, the ozone level for an average aquarium is usually accepted to be in the region of 3–5 mg/h per 10 gallons (45 l; 12 US gallons) of water, although this can be increased by a factor of three depending on stocking levels, etc. Equally, this dose can be vastly reduced if amounts detected in the room become intolerable or if the livestock are showing signs of stress. Remember that more is not always better and a small background level of ozone may be all that is needed to improve the health of livestock.

Ozone and Invertebrates

Ozone is lethal to the larvae of marine invertebrates and if it is hoped that tubeworms, sponges and other organisms will reproduce in the aquarium by such means, the use of ozone must either be foregone, or limited to extremely low levels.

There is also some evidence to suggest that calcium reacts with ozone, which depletes the water of this important mineral, thus starving such animals as hard corals of an extremely important supplement. Those marinists who hope to specialize in keeping hard corals and other invertebrates that utilize calcium would do well to consider a system that is devoid of an ozonizer.

Ozone is also inappropriate when treating the same aquarium with medications since it renders such treatments ineffective.

● *Can ozone have an effect on nuisance algae?*

... Yes. Owing to the cleaner water, slime algae can be kept under control or sometimes eradicated altogether.

● *Can I make fewer water changes if ozone is in use?*

No. Ozone cannot replace the vital elements lost as seawater mix becomes aged and stale. Only regular water changes can do this.

● *Should any safety precautions be taken when an ozonizer is in use?*

Yes, water must never be allowed to back-syphon into the unit. Either position it above the tank or use an anti-syphon valve. Avoid a humid or damp location.

● *Is the efficiency of an ozonizer greatly reduced if humid air is drawn into it?*

Yes. Ozonizers should be used with a purpose-built air drier containing small beads that absorb moisture from the atmosphere and feed the ozonizer with dry air.

● *Some ozonizers are set to a specific output such as 25 mg/h or 50 mg/h, are these safe?*

Only when operated in conjunction with a redox controller, otherwise there is no way to keep an accurate control over the amount of ozone dosing the tank. Always remember that ozone is a potentially dangerous gas and must be treated with respect. Any strong pungent smell (such as reminiscent of the seaside or electricity) in a room housing an aquarium, indicates an excess of ozone.

Ultraviolet Sterilizers

As with the ozonizer, it is important that the hobbyist tries to understand how the ultraviolet sterilizer operates in order to make the correct informed decision.

How It Works

Light within a certain wavelength has long been known to have a germicidal effect in both air and water. Broadly speaking, these wavelengths fall between the blue/violet range of the visible spectrum and the shorter invisible wavelengths of X-rays. Measurements of these wavelengths are made in nanometers (nm) and the most efficient wavelength for germicidal purposes is 254 nm, although the actual lamp producing ultraviolet light may cover a wider range from 100–280 nm. This range is usually referred to as UVC radiation. If aquarium water is passed close to a lamp producing UVC radiation, most micro-organisms will be destroyed or severely disrupted. These organisms may include various bacteria, fungal spores, free-swimming algae, viruses and dinoflagellates such as *Oodinium* and *Cryptocaryon* species.

To be fully effective several conditions must be met: the water passing around the lamp must be clean and free from suspended particles and discolouration; the flow rate over the lamp should be correctly adjusted; the lamp must be of the right wattage for the volume of water it is to treat (see table page 34), and the housing must be kept clean and the tube renewed regularly.

Noting these conditions it will become increasingly obvious that the ultraviolet sterilizer would best be connected to the return hose of a suitable canister filter or other such pre-cleaning device. This filter should be packed with filter floss to trap any particulate matter and a good quality activated carbon to adsorb any discoloration that may interfere with the treatment of the water. Opti-

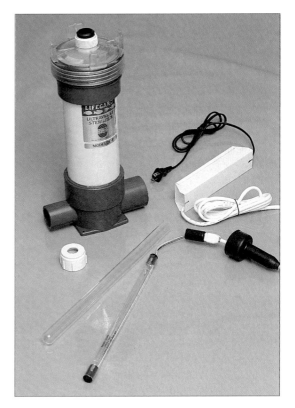

Marine aquarium sterilizers are easily dismantled into their component parts for cleaning and repair purposes. Aquarists would do well to familiarize themselves with the internal design before installation.

mum flow rates through the sterilizer are essential. Too fast and the organisms will not be destroyed; too slow and unwanted organisms may multiply faster than they can be treated. The correct flow rates for marine tanks are to found on table overleaf.

UV Sterilizer Maintenance

It is vitally important that the quartz sleeve surrounding, and protecting, the ultraviolet tube be kept clean from any sludge build-up. Failure to do so will result in a severe lowering of efficiency, leaving the aquarium, in some cases, totally unprotected.

UV Specifications for Marine Tanks

Lamp	Aquarium Size	Flow Rate per hour
8 watt	up to 40 gal (180 l; 48 US gal)	about 160 gal (725 l; 190 US gal)
15 watt	up to 80 gal (365 l; 96 US gal)	about 300 gal (1360 l; 360 US gal)
25 watt	up to 100 gal (455 l; 120 US gal)	about 400 gal (1820 l; 480 US gal)
30 watt	up to 150 gal (680 l; 180 US gal)	about 450 gal (2045 l; 540 US gal)
50 watt	up to 200 gal (910 l; 240 US gal)	about 500 gal (2275 l; 600 US gal)

◀ *It is virtually impossible to "over-sterilize" marine aquarium water and is, therefore, quite acceptable to install a higher wattage model than indicated if so desired. It is also in order to connect two or more sterilizers in series to give a more pronounced effect; flow rates can be multiplied accordingly.*

Clean the sleeve by gently scouring with a soft brush and rinsing with clean, fresh water. Stubborn deposits may require the assistance of a household non-abrasive cleaning solution, but care must be taken not to scratch the sleeve and all traces of the solution must be removed before re-use. Carry out this cleaning procedure once every three months. It may be of interest to know that a quartz sleeve is used because ultraviolet rays have difficulty passing through glass whereas quartz allows unimpeded passage. The useful life of an ultraviolet lamp is about 5,000 hours or about 6 months of continuous use. There is no way of detecting whether a lamp has reduced in efficiency and it is best to change it every 6 months.

Are All Sterilizers the Same?

UVC radiation has an extremely limited effective range and the distance across the cavity holding the water is crucial. For marine aquaria and fresh/brackish water aquaria, this distance should be no more than 6mm (0.25in); any greater and many harmful organisms will escape treatment. Those sterilizers designed for pond use usually have a much larger cavity of 12mm (0.5in), or greater, to facilitate the extra turnover required for a much greater volume of water. As the main aim here is to destroy less resistant single-celled algae ("green water") a larger cavity is quite acceptable. The marine aquarist cannot have it both ways, so take care to choose the right model. Always investigate the manufacturer's technical specification of each model to confirm its suitability.

Standard Equipment

The usefulness of an ultraviolet sterilizer in helping to control the most common water-borne diseases and algal blooms is not in question, but there are many other ailments that do not have a free-swimming stage and cannot be treated. Therefore, the sterilizer cannot be regarded as a general "cure-all", nor as an excuse for slack aquarium maintenance. In its favour, the UV is easy to install, cannot damage livestock in the way that a misused ozonizer can and it requires very little maintenance. For the hobbyist who keeps a mixed fish/invertebrate tank, a sterilizer can help fend off fish diseases that might otherwise have to be treated with medications proving fatal to invertebrates. In this respect, all of those possessing such a set up would be wise to invest in a sterilizer to protect their investment.

SAFETY WARNING: UV radiation is highly dangerous to the eyes and should *never* be looked at directly!

ULTRAVIOLET STERILIZATION

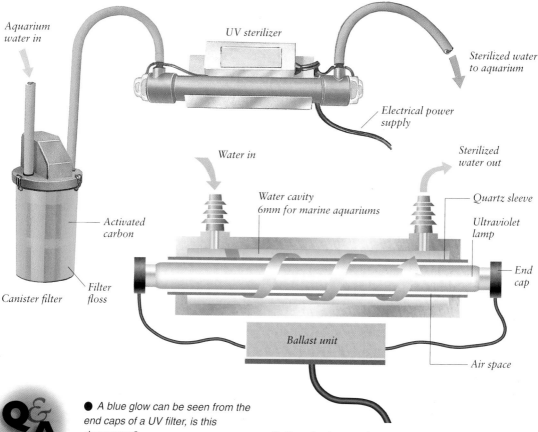

Aquarium water in

UV sterilizer

Sterilized water to aquarium

Electrical power supply

Water in

Sterilized water out

Water cavity 6mm for marine aquariums

Quartz sleeve

Ultraviolet lamp

Activated carbon

End cap

Canister filter

Filter floss

Ballast unit

Air space

Q&A...

● *A blue glow can be seen from the end caps of a UV filter, is this dangerous?*

No. It is designed in this way to assure the owner that the unit is on. The plastic cups filter out any harmful rays.

● *Where should the unit be placed?*

In a dry position with good air circulation – beneath the tank if possible. Never position it under the tank hood!

● *When the tank is dark, a blue glow can be seen emanating from the tank return pipe from the UV filter; is this normal?*

Yes, perfectly normal. It will do no harm whatsoever to fish or invertebrates as the harmful rays will be filtered out long before the visible blue rays can be observed.

● *Can the length of tube life be extended by switching the unit on for only 12 hours each day?*

This practice is not to be recommended as, although the tube life will be extended, the aquarium will be left unprotected for unacceptable periods. The whole point is to provide continuous protection.

● *Can cloudy water be controlled with a UV sterilizer?*

Yes. If it is caused by free-swimming algae or bacteria a sterilizer is usually very effective.

● *Some models claim to be suitable for both marine aquaria and ponds, can this be right?*

Possibly. Tests have shown that the optimum cavity space for marine applications must be no more than 6mm and this could be used on a pond as well. But if the cavity space is 12mm, or even greater, it is suitable for pond use only. If the model you are considering does not specify cavity space, look for one that does.

● *Is there a simple way to know when to change the ultraviolet lamp?*

Yes. Write the date for renewal on the unit and in an aquarium log or diary.

● *Will a UV sterilizer kill the hair and slime algae already in a tank?*

No. It can only kill the spores that pass close to the tube in the unit.

Activated Carbon

SEVERAL SUBSTANCES CAN BE USED TO MAKE activated carbon, including animal bone, wood, coconut and other nut shells, and, of course, coal. After processing the carbon is highly porous and can perform two important functions in the aquarium: it adsorbs hydrophobic (water-hating) organic molecules by bonding these to the actual structure of the material; and it absorbs organic molecules into the maze of microscopic channels where they are effectively "trapped".

Along with unwanted organic matter, other substances including copper, trace elements and heavy metals are also removed from the tank water. If activated carbon is not used these substances may build up to unacceptably toxic levels. Copper is the only one that would register in a test, but the aquarist will be able to judge the effectiveness of carbon filtration by the clarity of the water. Look along the length of the aquarium; if the water is anything less than crystal clear (tinged with yellow in the worst cases), then either the carbon needs replacing or possibly not enough carbon of the right quality is being used.

Many aquarists will be surprised to learn that the best quality activated carbon granules are generally only 1–2mm in diameter and are light, quite hard but not solid. Placed in water, the granules will float and give off a hissing sound as the water is taken in and air expelled. The benefits of using good quality activated carbon, renewed on average every two months, cannot be stressed too greatly. While it is possible to operate a tank without it, the potential risks are not worth taking.

● Where is the carbon best positioned?

... Some purpose-built filtration systems possess a special compartment for carbon. If not, then it is best loaded into an external canister filter with mechanical or other chemical media, but not biological media.

● Why is ordinary carbon not used?

Activated carbon is much more efficient and will remove many toxins that are tolerated by the majority of freshwater fish but not by marine animals.

Activated carbon made from coconut shells

● Does using activated carbon reduce or eliminate the need for water changes?

No, water changes still remain an essential part of maintenance.

● Are all carbons designed for aquarium use?

No, usually quite the opposite. Most carbons are destined to be used in the chemical industry and air purifiers. Many are treated with phosphoric acid, which will leach phosphates into the aquarium. Test activated carbons for phosphates by introducing a few fresh granules into 10ml (0.3 US fl oz) of distilled water. After 10 minutes, test the water with a phosphate test kit. Those carbons revealing no phosphates are to be recommended.

● Can a good quality activated carbon help restore flagging sessile invertebrates?

Yes, in many cases, especially with a 33% high quality water change.

● Does the use of carbon eliminate the need for a protein skimmer?

No. Skimmers and carbon remove different pollutants and one can only complement the other.

Phosphates

PHOSPHATES HAVE BEEN KNOWN TO FARMERS and growers for a long time as useful fertilizers; much in the same way as nitrates. Like nitrates, excess phosphates are washed from the land, into the streams and rivers, and eventually into our mains water. Certainly, the levels of phosphate pollution are far less measurable than nitrates and we are often talking in terms of less than 1–2ppm (mg/l) in the main, but the effects can be much the same even at these low levels – increased amounts of nuisance algae (slime and filamentous) and a general deterioration in water quality. Mains water is not the only way phosphates can find their way into the aquarium. Some marine salts contain high levels of phosphates, as do a few makes of activated carbon. It has also been suggested that harmful levels of phosphates can leach from coral sand and even tufa rock into the aquarium, although this may be rather more connected with a die-back of organic life on, or within, it. Finally, the most obvious phosphate-generators are fish. Their waste products, in common with most other animals, contain significant amounts of phosphate.

Test kits are now available and the aquarist should measure phosphate levels in the local mains water to assess contamination. Levels in marine salts and carbon can be checked by testing a solution made up with distilled (confirmed phosphate-free) water. (Tests can be carried out after 10 minutes.) Phosphate contamination can be reduced by a change of media, or installation of a mains water filter such as a deionizer, reverse osmosis unit or a proprietary resin.

Safe Levels

Fish-only aquaria will be safe at around 1–2 ppm (or sometimes much higher depending on the species), unless there is an outbreak of nuisance algae, in which case levels should be

● *Excluding external factors, what else causes phosphate pollution?*

... High levels of phosphate are caused by overstocking and/or overfeeding, insufficient water changes (15–25% fortnightly is recommended), insufficient filtration (lack of protein skimmers, carbon, etc.) or a combination of all these.

● *Are phosphates essential for decorative algae growth?*

Only in very small quantities; too much and nuisance algae will flourish instead.

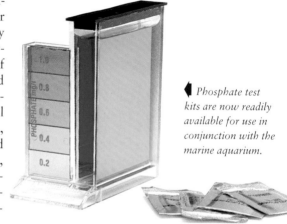

◀ *Phosphate test kits are now readily available for use in conjunction with the marine aquarium.*

reduced to 0.5ppm or below. Invertebrate aquaria need to be maintained at very low levels on a continuous basis. An absolute maximum for healthy invertebrates and the prevention of nuisance algae is 0.05ppm.

Phosphate-removing media are effective, but they all have one big drawback – both macro- and micro-algae are largely destroyed within 24 hours of installation. *Caulerpa* and other species must be removed before treatment to avoid massive pollution. The sudden deprivation of phosphate is often given as the reason for this die-back of algae. This seems extremely unlikely and may also be due to toxins leached from the media or sudden changes in water parameters, such as a large drop in KH.

Nitrates

WITH GOOD CAUSE, MANY MARINE AQUARISTS are worried about the unduly high levels of nitrates in their mains water, and subsequently in their tanks. While nitrate is nowhere near as toxic as ammonia or nitrite, it can still considerably weaken fish, leaving them vulnerable to nitrate poisoning and a variety of potentially lethal diseases. Invertebrate species fare very badly, except at the very lowest concentrations.

Nitrates in mains water are now relatively easy for the hobbyist to eliminate. In addition, other potentially harmful compounds such as phosphates and sulphates are often extracted at the same time. Resins, deionizers and reverse osmosis units will all do the job. A reverse osmosis unit (see pages 20–21) will give impeccable water quality, but it is also the most expensive option (well worth the expense, in the opinion of many). Most hobbyists, however, invest in a rechargeable resin that is effective and easy to use.

The build-up of nitrates in the aquarium can occur through contaminated water changes, but is also self-generated as part of the biological filtration cycle. Heavily stocked or overfed tanks suffer the most where nitrate levels can easily rise out of control.

Reducing Nitrates in the Aquarium

There are three main ways of reducing nitrates in the aquarium. The first, and simplest, is the regular water change with nitrate-free water. Depending on how heavily stocked it is, most tanks require a 15–25% change every fortnight. This method of control is called **dilution**.

The second, less predictable method, is to grow plenty of macro algae such as *Caulerpa* spp. Algae use nitrate as a food source. If harvested modestly on a regular basis, the toxins are removed from the aquarium and new growth is encouraged to continue the process. This method is called **assimilation**.

NITRATE FILTER

Mains water in

Nitrate-free water out

Filter pad *Resin beads* *Filter pad*

◀➥ *Nitrate filters will require re-charging from time to time to maintain peak efficiency. This is done by trickling through a saturated solution of saltwater. Most models can be re-charged as many as 1,000 times.*

● *How do high nitrates affect fish?*

Poor appetite, insipid coloration, ... tumours, fin-rot and a generally lowered resistance to disease.

● *Can nitrates be introduced in any other way apart from in the main water supply?*

Yes, some low-grade salt mixes have been found to contain nitrates, as have some algal fertilizers. It would be wise to test your chosen brand of salt mix after making it up with distilled, or other nitrate-free water. Algal fertilizers are nearly always based on sodium nitrate and they should also be tested. Low-grade carbon can also be a source of nitrates, although most marine carbons are usually nitrate-free.

● *Can high nitrate levels indicate a wider problem?*

Yes. High levels of nitrate are usually associated with deteriorating water conditions, and water changes should be increased to compensate.

● *Will changing half the water in the aquarium decrease nitrate levels by 50%?*

A 50% water change will not reduce nitrate levels by 50%. Only continuous regular water changes will achieve a lasting reduction.

● *Why do some test kits show their results in different scales?*

Some manufacturers have chosen to measure the nitrogen ion (NO_3-N), while others measure total nitrate (NO_3). To convert NO_3-N to NO_3 multiply by 4.4. Conversely, to translate NO_3 to NO_3-N divide by 4.4. Levels in this book are always quoted as total nitrate NO_3. To avoid confusion, always check the scale on the test kit before purchase.

The third method, **denitrification**, is certainly very effective but requires a separate filter compartment. Here, an anaerobic (oxygen-free) environment is created through which the aquarium water is slowly trickled (not to be confused with aerobic trickle filters). Anaerobic bacteria then feed on the nitrates, converting them firstly to nitrous oxide and finally to free nitrogen gas.

Flow rates through the denitrification filter have to be carefully monitored; too fast and nitrates are converted back to nitrite, too slow and deadly hydrogen sulphide with its distinctive rotten eggs smell is produced. Commercial denitrification units are available, and many "total systems" have them integrated as standard. It is also fairly easy to construct one from plastic waste pipe.

Of course, there is nothing to stop the aquarist practising all methods of nitrate reduction as a precautionary measure and it would be wise to aim for total nitrate (NO_3) levels of less than 25 parts per million (ppm) in the fish-only tank and below 10ppm in the invertebrate aquarium. When all these forms of nitrate reduction are tried without success, then the aquarist must seriously consider de-stocking the tank.

◤ *By compartmentalising the filter box, the length of the filter is effectively increased, giving the anaerobic bacteria more time to process the water travelling through. Input water must be mechanically filtered to eliminate particulate matter that might cause clogging.*

DENITRIFICATION FILTER

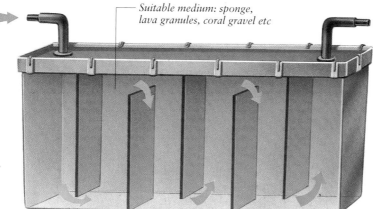

Pre-filtered water in

Suitable medium: sponge, lava granules, coral gravel etc

Treated water out to aquarium

Maturation

Of all the events to take place in the life of a marine aquarium, the initial maturation of the biological filter must rank as the most important. The filter rids the aquarium of metabolic waste products quickly and efficiently. Failure to set it up correctly results in a swift build-up of ammonia and nitrites, which are extremely toxic and can result in the death of livestock within hours. To avoid this tragic scenario it is vitally important that, before any livestock are introduced, the aquarium becomes home to several species of "friendly" aerobic (oxygen-loving) ammonia-consuming bacteria from the genus *Nitrosomonas*. These bacteria also produce waste products called nitrites, slightly less toxic to livestock, but still dangerous. These are consumed by other bacteria from the genus *Nitrobacter*. These too produce a waste product consisting of far less harmful nitrates, which may be broken down by yet another species of bacteria under anaerobic (oxygen-free) conditions.

These bacteria are not peculiar to the marine environment. In fact they occur in virtually all land and aquatic environments where there is organic matter to be decomposed. They make up part of what is known as the nitrogen cycle.

Maturation Methods

Once the newly set up aquarium is operational, several methods can be employed to introduce and encourage bacteria to establish themselves in the appropriate filter media. The first and most common method is the proprietary maturation fluid, added in measured doses, either over a period of days or in one large dose, depending on the constituent parts and manufacturer's instructions. The arrival and multiplication of the bacteria can be monitored by using an ammonia and nitrite test kit.

Once all traces of ammonia and nitrite have disappeared, it can be assumed that the *Nitrosomonas* and *Nitrobacter* bacteria have gained a firm foothold and the first livestock can be introduced. The maturation process can take anything up to 28 days to complete; although all systems are different and some may be ready much sooner, or sometimes take a little longer.

Living bacterial cultures are commercially available as an almost immediate maturation start-up. These cultures contain the correct species of bacteria in huge quantities, ready to take up immediate residence in the biological media. To preserve the high numbers of bacteria the culture bottles are stored in

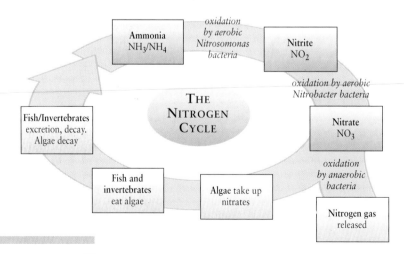

THE NITROGEN CYCLE

Ammonia NH_3/NH_4 → *oxidation by aerobic Nitrosomonas bacteria* → Nitrite NO_2

Nitrite NO_2 → *oxidation by aerobic Nitrobacter bacteria* → Nitrate NO_3

Nitrate NO_3 → *oxidation by anaerobic bacteria* → Nitrogen gas released

Fish/Invertebrates excretion, decay. Algae decay

Fish and invertebrates eat algae

Algae take up nitrates

◀ The nitrogen cycle describes the sequence of chemical reactions by which nitrogen circulates through an ecosystem, in this case the marine aquarium. In the aquarium the target is to remove as much from the system in the form of nitrogen gas and prevent the build-up of harmful ammonia and nitrites.

◀ Nitrosomonas *bacteria shown at a magnification of ×500.*

◀ Nitrobacter *bacteria shown at a magnification of ×60,000.*

Maturation of the Biological Filter

(Graph: LEVELS ppm (mg/l) on y-axis ranging 2 to 12; DAYS on x-axis ranging 6 to 48)

Ammonia

Nitrites

Nitrates

Initial maturation complete – safe to begin adding livestock

◀ *Approximate representation of the changes in levels of toxic compounds during initial maturation. First ammonia builds up, is converted to nitrites and these to nitrates. Ammonia and nitrite levels should be zero before fish are introduced.*

● What is the most reliable and safest maturation procedure?

... Proprietary maturation fluids have a number of advantages. Even though it means waiting a little while for the bacteria to establish, the whole process can be monitored with test kits to prove that the environment is safe for livestock. It is also impossible for disease or contamination to be introduced from another source.

● Is it possible to encourage a tank inoculated with maturation fluid to establish more quickly?

In some cases, raising the temperature to 32°C (90°F) can speed the whole process up and might be a useful alternative for tanks that seem to be reluctant to mature. Reduce the temperature slowly to a more reasonable 25°C (77°F) before any livestock is introduced.

● Can living bacterial inoculations survive storage in warm conditions?

Bacteriologists tell us that storage under such conditions will vastly reduce the bacteria count and cause the product to become very unreliable. The products should be refrigerated.

● Do Nitrosomonas and Nitrobacter bacteria inhabit the filters only?

No. They live on the rocks, glass and algae; in fact almost any surface that is well oxygenated and reasonably stable. By removing all the rocks from an established aquarium and replacing them with new ones, the biological filtration capabilities of the tank would be reduced. The same applies to rocks that are removed to be cleaned.

refrigerated conditions and remain viable for three months only. Bacteriologists insist that this is the most efficient way of preserving the cultures for immediate livestocking purposes.

Another method that has been used since the early days of marine fishkeeping is to introduce a few damselfish into an immature system, thereby using their waste products to provide an ammonia/nitrite rich environment that bacteria will find attractive and hence multiply. Although damselfish are fairly tolerant they are not immune to the toxic effects of their own waste products and are quite likely to die as a result. Exposure to such toxins also increases the likelihood of them contracting diseases such as whitespot or *Oodinium* and immediately the aquarium has become a potentially hazardous and infectious place for future livestock. Damsels are also very territorial fish and if they survive the initial stress they may be very aggressive to further introductions. All in all, this is a method to be discouraged.

Living rock has also been a popular, if rather disappointing, alternative way of introducing the required bacteria. Most creatures that inhabit living rock are, however, very sensitive to ammonia and nitrite and die off rapidly within an immature tank. Given the current high price of living rock and the potential waste of livestock, this is another method that cannot be recommended.

Maturation with Black Mollies

If fish must be used to mature a tank, Black Mollies have proved to be a suitable, if unexpected, alternative. Black Mollies are man-made hybrids that carry through traits of some of their wild ancestors. Their ability to live and thrive in full marine conditions and to dispel the effects of high ammonia and nitrite levels make them suitable for maturation purposes. Care must be taken to "convert" them from freshwater to marine conditions and this is easily achieved by dripping marine tank water into their container at a rate of one drop per second. The overflow can be discarded and after 6–12 hours a molly will have been fully adapted to marine

● *How often should biological filters be cleaned?*

... Infrequently, just enough to keep them free from blockage by mulm and detritus. Always rinse sponges, sand, gravel and other media in water from their tank. Washing in mains water will kill the bacteria and destroy the filter.

● *Are nitrifying bacteria present in direct proportion to the amount of livestock?*

Yes. That is why every new addition will upset the biological balance temporarily until the bacteria can multiply to meet the extra amounts of biological waste products. Hence, stock the aquarium slowly.

● *What can be done if an aquarium fails to mature?*

If the set-up is operating properly and the water is not polluted by an external toxin, then all aquarium filters will eventually mature. Four weeks is not an unusually long time to wait for the last traces of ammonia and nitrite to disappear.

▲ *Black Mollies are mainly freshwater fish but can be acclimatized to the marine environment, where they can be useful for maturing a new tank.*

● *Can lights be left on while the tank is maturing?*

Yes. There is no logical reason why not. Previous thinking always recommended that the tank should be matured in the dark even though experience showed that it made little or no difference.

● *Can stocking begin with just a trace of ammonia and nitrite in the water?*

No. The filter is not fully matured and if livestock are introduced the ammonia and nitrite levels will soar to dangerous levels.

● *Is it possible for an established tank that is free of livestock to be kept biologically mature indefinitley?*

Yes, one drop per gallon of maturation fluid every week will keep it biologically active and ready for stocking.

conditions. (Converting back to freshwater is a reversal of the same procedure.) Mollies are non-aggressive and thrive on marine algae, thus making an unusual and useful addition to the saltwater aquarium if required. Not all species of molly are capable of this conversion and species other than the Black Molly should be avoided.

Seeding with Coral Sand

"Seeding" a tank substrate with coral sand taken from a fully mature system can help the maturation process quite rapidly by introducing a living bacterial culture. Used in conjunction with maturation fluids, it can prove very successful. Care should be taken that the pH and specific gravity of both tanks match, otherwise the bacteria could suffer and die, so the whole point of the exercise will have been defeated. Caution must be exercised if the tank from which the seeded gravel is taken has ever suffered disease or been medicated. Many diseases have resting stages lying dormant in the gravel, immune to medication. These are likely to spring to life in a new, unmedicated environment and cause problems with livestock.

From time to time, the fishkeeping market seems to become inundated with granules, powders, potions and kits making varied claims on their abilities to mature a marine tank from 24 hours to 3 weeks. The aquarist may want to try one of these products. However, it is wise to remember that bacteria can only reproduce at a particular rate and exaggerated claims beyond the capabilities of nature often result in bitter disappointment for the newcomer. Therefore, always check the progress of maturation using ammonia and nitrite test kits and never introduce livestock until the readings from both kits are zero (the Black Molly method is, of course, exempt from this rule).

Most medications are perfectly safe and do not harm nitrifying bacteria. An exception to this are antibiotics that will destroy all bacteria, severely damaging or even destroying the biological filter and thereby causing further distress to the livestock.

Water Change Methods

THE WATER CHANGE IS PROBABLY THE SINGLE most important activity that the marine aquarist can undertake to refresh, revive, and preserve a valuable display of livestock.

Sea water mix is an incredibly complicated substance that undergoes rapid changes in the confines of the aquarium. Unless regular replenishments are introduced, the mixture can cease to remain in its desired form, leading to stressed livestock, possible disease and death. It will not have gone unnoticed that water is a heavy and awkward substance that offers absolutely no incentive to move copious quantities of it about, especially if a painful backache is all that can be expected as a result! But three main methods of water changing are available to make things easier for the hobbyist.

Temporary

If a suitable drain point is relatively close at hand (within 30ft (9m) approximately) then an aquarium pump and length of canister filter hose can reduce the workload considerably. Once the pump has been used to empty the required amount from the tank, it can then be employed to replace the new water back into the aquarium. Although a powerhead could be used, a hobby pump will be far more efficient, especially if long runs of piping are envisaged.

● *Is there any useful advice that needs to be followed when using the temporary water change method?*

Yes. **1** Purchase a pump that is of good quality and reliable with sufficient capacity for your needs. **2** Always cover the intake of the pump to prevent livestock being sucked in. **3** Purchase good quality hose with no kinks and store it in coils, similar to a garden hose (kinks will severely reduce the water flow or even stop it altogether). **4** Use only aquarium-quality pumps and hose to avoid pollution.

● *How can an even temperature be assured in the semi-automatic water mix container?*

A miniature pump or airstone can be left in the container to aid circulation (averaging out temperature) and mix the new water with salt.

● *Is it important to store freshly mixed sea water in a special container?*

Yes. Not all vessels are suitable as many leach toxins into the water. A food-grade container is the best choice and every effort should be made to secure one.

● *Can a sea water mix be stored indefinitely?*

It would be advisable to use a freshly mixed solution within 48 hours, avoiding contamination from bacteria, algae or airborne toxins (e.g. cigarette smoke).

◥ *Mark the water level on the side of the tank before you begin to empty it, so that you can gauge the exact amount of water to be replaced.*

TEMPORARY WATER CHANGE

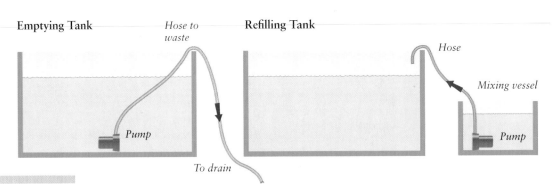

Emptying Tank — Hose to waste — Pump — To drain

Refilling Tank — Hose — Mixing vessel — Pump

Semi-Automatic

This method is similar to the temporary water change arrangement but some of the fixtures and fittings are permanent. For example, the waste pipe will be made of rigid ABS piping and installed tidily with brackets. A waste feed can be taken from a valve positioned on the downpipe to a trickle filter, canister filter or an equally convenient point.

A container used to house the replacement water is placed either next to the aquarium or in an unobtrusive place some distance away. With this configuration, small but very regular water changes can be undertaken with very little effort. In spite of the fact that only small amounts of water may be exchanged at any one time, it would still be worthwhile adding a heater to the replenishment vessel, set to the same temperature as the heater in the main show tank. This will prevent temperature fluctuations in the tank caused by quantities of cool water being introduced with every change.

Automatic

If space, budget and enthusiasm for the perfect arrangement were no object, then an automatic water change system would be the ideal option. A permanent waste pipe is still required but it will carry only a drop or two of aquarium water every second. A dosing pump connected to a float switch will be needed to replenish the lost water without flooding the system. The rate at which water evaporates from the tank has to be taken into account if salinity levels are not to rise dramatically out of proportion. A conductivity controller will be needed in order to add the correct amount of freshwater back into the system, maintaining complete equilibrium.

The container of fresh sea water mix can be hidden to suit the overall arrangement. As water replacement is relatively slow, a heater will not generally be necessary.

◆ *Automatic water change arrangements can reduce much of the hard work associated with essential maintenance. A trickle filter below the tank is not strictly necessary as long as there is a permanent drain facility. Reservoir levels must be monitored regularly.*

AUTOMATIC WATER CHANGE

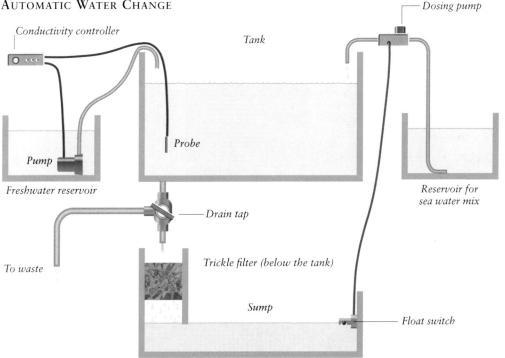

Conductivity controller

Tank

Dosing pump

Probe

Pump

Freshwater reservoir

Reservoir for sea water mix

Drain tap

To waste

Trickle filter (below the tank)

Sump

Float switch

Water Circulation

THE TREMENDOUS BENEFITS OF ADEQUATE water activity within the marine aquarium are all too often ignored by the majority of aquarists. This is all too understandable when there are so many other elements like lighting and filtration apparently requiring far more attention. In the vast majority of aquaria (particularly reef aquaria) the water is often barely moving and the livestock seems lifeless and unnatural in appearance. This is, of course, in total contrast to normal conditions in the wild.

The shallow waters of the coral reef are areas of exceptionally strong, sometimes violent, water movement. This is brought about by waves traversing many miles of deep ocean, then suddenly finding space restricted on a rising sea bed. In most cases, the outer reefs bear the brunt of these forces producing strong surges in, around and over the colonies of animals, while local eddies and disturbances are responsible for random turbulence. Sessile invertebrates and many fish are well adapted to these natural forces and often require such conditions to thrive.

The Benefits of Water Movement

The two main types of water movement reproduced in the tank are *surge* and *turbulence*. Surge is the movement of water backward and forward across the reef as if caused by wave action. It will push sea fans one way and then the other, almost at right angles. Turbulence is a more random movement of water in all directions causing eddies and isolated disturbances. It will make soft and leather corals gyrate in all directions.

By creating medium to powerful surge and turbulence within the aquarium, a host of advantages will become apparent:

Carbon dioxide (CO_2) will be dispersed far more quickly. As it has a tendency to acidify the water, causing the pH to drop, having less of this gas in the tank will eliminate one cause of pH crash.

Oxygen (O_2) will be encouraged to enter the water more readily and raise the pH slightly. This is because dissolved oxygen tends to make the water more alkaline and a higher pH results. As an additional bonus, reasonable levels of both CO_2 and O_2 will encourage greater health and vigour in fish and invertebrates.

Unwanted gases such as nitrogen (produced as a result of

◀ *The polyps of this* Clavularia *ripple in the current. Like its neighbour the clam* (Tridacna crocea) *it is enjoying the multiple benefits of surging tankwater.*

denitrification taking place on and within the rocks etc.) and ammonia are removed much more rapidly where circulation is brisk, especially at the surface water.

Uniformity of temperature – the constant and frequent mixing of water eradicates "hot" and "cold" spots.

"Dead" spots where water has a tendency to stagnate are less likely to occur.

Animal waste products are removed quickly and efficiently especially from sessile invertebrates. Conversely, nutrients and fresh supplies of the elements found in saltwater are brought into contact with livestock on a more frequent basis.

Detritus is prevented from accumulating, drawn swiftly into solution to be removed by the filters.

Physical stimulation of surge and turbulence benefits the health of most livestock.

Creating Water Movement

A number of very strong pumps will be needed to move aquarium water. Resistance from rocks and decoration tend to restrict the flow considerably. At least two pumps are required for a 3ft (90cm) tank, three for a 4ft (120cm) tank, four for a 5ft (150cm) tank, five for a 6ft (180cm) tank and so on. This may seem excessive in the larger aquaria, but providing a realistic surge in a 100–250 gallon tank is by no means an easy task!

Some experimentation with locations is going to be necessary to achieve the best results. Pointing the outlets at each other provides good random turbulence patterns and a variety of currents. Rotating the flow, in a whirlpool fashion, is probably best avoided unless an element of opposition can be supplied to break the pattern up. Although livestock need to feel the benefit of extra current, it is unwise to point the outlet of a pump at any particular animal directly. This will not replicate surge nor turbulence, merely a battering that may not be appreciated!

Circulating pumps can be controlled with an electronic surge device. A microchip can be set to a specific on/off pattern or a random sequence. Most have the added advantage of a feeding timer so that all pumps can be switched off for around 5 minutes to allow livestock to be fed in calm conditions. Turn-on is automatic; an ideal feature for those of us with less than perfect memories!

● *Should the flow pattern be altered at night?*

... Yes. Most corals and fish go into a resting mode in the dark, and calm conditions are appreciated. Some circulatory pumps can be switched off altogether; connecting them to the lighting circuit is a good idea.

● *Surely filter pumps supply enough circulation?*

Experience has shown that this is not so. Most tanks have a circulation that is sluggish to say the least! *never* switch off pumps operating biological filters, or connect them to surge devices unless used in the feeding mode only!

● *Can you list some species that benefit from extra circulation, and some that do not.*

Xenia spp., pulse corals, anemones, hard corals, soft corals, gorgonians, clams, sea fans, polyp colonies, sponges and sea squirts all benefit. Mushroom corals, seahorses, pipefish, sharks, cardinalfish, rays and some species of algae prefer quieter conditions.

◀ *A surge controller will automatically regulate several circulating pumps.*

▶ *The ideal circulating pump, or powerhead, should run with minimum noise, be energy-efficient and be designed so that it does not clog easily. Maintenance should be a straightforward task.*

● *Will using so many powerheads account for a great deal of electricity?*

Most pumps have a very small electrical consumption of between 4–20 watts, so even four or five pumps will cost very little to run.

Aquarium Decoration

ATTRACTIVE DECORATION IS OF PARAMOUNT importance to the presentation of any marine display; the wrong choices can make the most expensive set-up look like a heap of underwater rubble. Although many choices are purely subjective, there are also practical considerations such as how safe are the rocks, are they likely to affect water quality adversely, and will they complement the livestock? All rocks affect marine water to some extent, but a few may prove toxic in a saltwater environment!

Tufa Rock: This is the most popular rock for the marine aquarium. It naturally occurs around hot springs where the water is calciferous; it can also be found along ancient seabeds. It is supplied to the horticultural and aquatic industries for use where alkaline conditions are necessary. Tufa rock is soft, easy to work and will buffer the pH of any aquarium where it needs to remain in the region 7.5–9.0. It displaces large amounts of water but, in all, this is an excellent choice for the marine aquarium.

Lava Rock: Natural volcanic rock is not recommended for the marine aquarium as it contains heavy metals and toxic substances.

The lava rock supplied to the aquatic trade is often a by-product of the smelting industry, sold as totally inert and safe. However, there have been reports of toxic impurities in lava rock, and a reputable source of supply should always be used. Safe lava rock makes excellent homes for invertebrates and fish alike. It is light, porous, displaces very little water, and locks together well into safe structures. On the negative side, lava rock is very expensive, has dangerously sharp edges and is usually incapable of being worked. It has no pH buffering ability whatsoever and may even be slightly acidic.

Limestone: Limestone is a very hard rock of a particularly alkaline nature and well suited to the marine aquarium. However, it displaces massive amounts of water and its collection may not be sound from a conservation point of view.

Slate: Slate is inert and may be used without fear of toxicity. It looks rather unnatural, is heavy and displaces a lot of water.

Barnacle Shells: Giant barnacle shells are very decorative as well as providing good homes for small fish and invertebrates. They are usually scraped from the bottom of boats

Synthetic coral

Barnacle shells

Tufa rock

during regular maintenance, so their collection causes no harm to living reefs.

Coral/Synthetic Skeletons: Dead coral skeletons may look attractive, but they formed part of a living reef at one time and were collected alive to be dried in the sun. A growing number of marine aquarists are beginning to question this practice, particularly since synthetic corals (made in moulds using safe resins) are widely available. Sea whips and sea fans are also best purchased in synthetic form as these last longer and are much easier to clean.

Living Rock: (See pages 50–51)

Sandstone: Decorative sandstone with attractive sand-blasted shapes and varying colour striations is an interesting choice for people who want something unusual. However, it will discolour badly as micro-algae colonize the surface.

Petrified Wood: Petrified wood is safe to use, but will displace valuable quantities of water with little decorative return.

Other Decorative Items: Ceramic jugs and vases can be used to create special underwater effects and are safe to use. A creative flair will be needed to make the scene convincing – plastic toys and novelties rarely look so. They may not even be safe, as some plastics and dyes are toxic in saltwater. New natural rocks and synthetic decorations are becoming available all the time The golden rule is to make sure that they are safe for saltwater use.

● *How can I make a "reef wall" ?*

Construct a solid base of tufa rock flattening the bottom of each rock to prevent instability. Extend the height of the wall with fairly large pieces of lava rock, firmly locked together. The height should be approximately equal to the base measurement for maximum safety.

● *Can tufa rock from a copper-treated tank be reused in an invertebrate tank?*

No. The copper will have been adsorbed by the rock and can easily be discharged back into the water, posing a real threat to all invertebrate livestock.

● *Is it best to buy large or small pieces of tufa rock?*

Generally buy the larger pieces as they can always be broken up. Structures made of small lumps are prone to collapse.

● *What is a coral diorama?*

This is where a dry, illuminated box is constructed at the rear of the aquarium and filled with decorative items such as sea whips, shells, rocks and barnacles etc. The effect can be quite convincing when viewed through the aquarium as it provides greater depth to the scene. To maintain the illusion, the rear glass needs to be kept free of algae at all times.

● *Will sharp rocks damage the base of an aquarium?*

There is always a possibility that the bottom of an aquarium could be cracked if sharp rocks are used as the basis of a "reef wall". Reduce the risk by using softer rocks such as tufa.

● *How can rocks and decoration retain their natural appearance?*

All rocks and decoration are subject to discoloration as they are colonized by algae. The original features can be restored by soaking in a bleach solution for 24 hours. *All* traces of bleach must be removed by thorough rinsing under running water before being replaced into the aquarium. Bleach is very toxic and will cause harm to all livestock should any remain to pollute the water. A safe, if somewhat impractical, alternative is to clean the rocks by boiling them.

● *Could cleaning rocks harm the welfare of the aquarium?*

Yes, nitrifying bacteria live on the surfaces of rock, providing a source of additional valuable filtration. Cleaning will destroy the colonies and leave the aquarium prone to surges in ammonia and nitrite until they have been re-colonized.

Lava rock

Dead, cured coral

Living Rock

LIVING ROCK, AS IT HAS COME TO BE KNOWN, is simply pieces of limestone or other calciferous rock that has spent some time in the sea, and has become home to various invertebrates and algae. The quality of the rock is measured by just how many species are to be found on, or in, each piece. The more species, the higher the grade and the greater the price – in theory at least! High-grade living rock should support at least some of the various species of crab, shrimp, anemone, tubeworm, starfish, sponge, sea squirt, barnacle, encrusting algae (and some other forms of algae), polyps and molluscs.

Purchasing Living Rock

In most instances, the aquarist will be expected to purchase living rock to order, without a chance to examine it. Always insist on a full written description of what to expect; if it falls below specification, consumer laws in many countries will protect the buyer. Any experienced retailer will be able to order living rock from a specialist importer. In this way, the rock should be transported swiftly from the point of collection, straight to the customer, with no delay. Living rock generally travels "dry" (without water but still damp) in strong plastic bags to reduce freight charges. This method is acceptable as long as there are no delays en route. It is sold by the pound or kilogram of dry weight.

It is essential to collect living rock from the retailer as soon as it is delivered, or the same day. Under these conditions it should remain packed until the purchaser takes it home. If it cannot be collected the same day, the retailer will have little choice but to put it into a tank, and some of the livestock may migrate into rocks that are not going to be purchased. In addition, extra stress will be caused to animals and plants as they are transferred from one tank to another unnecessarily.

● *Do any pests accompany living rock?*

... Yes, and this is one of its major drawbacks. Mantis shrimps, pistol shrimps, bristleworms, carnivorous snails and nudibranchs are all found in abundance within living rock. Ridding the rock of all these pests is not easy and requires long periods of isolation where each pest can be physically removed.

● *What is "cured" living rock?*

During shipping, many animals and algae that have made their home in or on the rock will die. To avoid ammonia surges in the showtank as the animals and plants decompose, the rock is housed in isolation tanks until pollutants pose no further threat. The rock is then said to be "cured".

● *Can living rock be an aid to filtration?*

Yes. Limestone is extremely porous, and denitrification can take place in these internal areas. The external surfaces are easily colonized by species of aerobic bacteria and the oxidation of ammonia and nitrites can be performed here. Of course, other types of rock can perform the same function.

● *Living rock is said to form the basis of the "Berlin" filtration method, is this correct?*

Yes. In conjunction with a powerful and extremely efficient protein skimmer, living rock provides a home for nitrifying and denitrifying bacteria to perform the main biological filtration function.

● *Do all the lifeforms survive being shipped?*

No. The more desirable creatures and plants are fragile and tend to die off, whereas the hardier pests normally survive quite happily. Very often, living rock is an expensive disappointment being no more than sea-worn pieces of rock.

● *Is it wise to introduce large quantities of living rock into an already well-stocked aquarium?*

Owing to the almost inevitable surge in ammonia, no. If extra living rock must be introduced, it should be done over a considerable period of time with single pieces being added on each occasion.

On arrival at its final destination, the rock should be withdrawn immediately from the travelling bag and placed into a pre-matured aquarium. It will displace a good deal of water, so remove enough in advance to avoid an overflow. Any mulm, detritus and fouled water in the bottom of the bag should be discarded as it will be very polluted. As far as possible, position the pieces so that the "living" sides are outward facing. It is usually unnecessary to feed living rock until the vari-

First-class living rock, as seen here, should contain an abundance of sessile invertebrates as well as crustacea and algae. Rocks that are merely sea-worn and barren are not good value for money.

ous lifeforms have established themselves. After that, many sessile invertebrates will appreciate live rotifers or the juices from a thawed cockle or mussel.

The Need for High Water Quality

By introducing living rock into a pre-matured aquarium, any rise in ammonia (caused by the unavoidable deaths of animals and algae) can be dealt with. If the rock is introduced into an immature system, the ammonia levels will surge and result in the death of even more livestock. Living rock will only thrive in an aquarium with very high water quality and intense lighting. It is not at all suitable for aquaria housing mainly fish.

Micro and Macro Algae

ALGAE ARE EXTREMELY ANCIENT PLANT-LIKE organisms dating back almost to the dawn of life. Being so ancient, algae have adapted to suit practically every situation where moisture and light are available. From hot water springs to arctic waters, from snowfields on the highest mountains to steaming tropical rainforests, algae have developed to take advantage of almost every niche.

Tropical oceans are no exception and many species of micro and macro algae are to be found on reefs and in lagoons. The terms "micro" and "macro" should, perhaps, be explained at this point. Micro algae consist of a single cell or small groups of cells joined together; these may live as free-swimming phytoplankton or be rock-encrusting. Macro algae are much larger and take on a distinctly plant-like structure that is easily recognizable, *Caulerpa* species for example. These are the algae that most marine aquarists regard as decorative.

Algae never flower, and are always associated with water. They do not possess the internal framework that enables their terrestrial cousins to stand erect. Algae usually flop

➤ Caulerpa prolifera, *as the name suggests, is a fast-growing rampant species that is easy to keep, but needs regular harvesting to keep it under control.*

Popular Species of Algae

Caulerpa prolifera – rampant and easy to grow.

Caulerpa brachypus – similar to *C. prolifera* but with smaller blades. It demands high water quality.

Caulerpa racemosa, C. sertularioides, C. taxifolia, C. mexicana and *C. cupressoides* – fast growing and ideal for the beginner, but can overwhelm sessile invertebrates.

Acetabularia spp. – a delicate cup-like species demanding good lighting and high water quality.

Valonia ventricosa – commonly called Sailor's Eyeballs. Can become a nuisance by growing in among sessile invertebrates but is easily removed with a fingernail.

Rhodophyceae – a group of decorative red algae that are very slow growing.

Calcareous Algae

Codiacea spp. – delightful red algae that are slow growing

Halimeda spp. – attractive cactus-like algae that grow quickly in optimum conditions.

Pencillus capitatus – Resembles a shaving brush but is very difficult to culture.

🔺 *Red and pink calcareous algae will encrust rocks, glass, pumps, and virtually any available surface given favourable conditions. They can be encouraged by good water quality and sufficient levels of calcium.*

● *Do algae add any by-products to the water?*

... Yes, they add oxygen during the hours of daylight as part of the photosynthesis process and carbon dioxide at night. Normally the oxygen would be highly beneficial to the fish in particular, but if the aquarium is overstocked and there is a lush growth of algae, production of carbon dioxide at night could prove very stressful and in some cases fatal to livestock. Good water circulation will help to alleviate this problem.

● *What are ideal conditions for non-calcareous algae?*

Tank – in excess of 20 gallons (91 l; 24 US gallons); ammonia nil; nitrite nil; nitrates adjusted to suit livestock and not particularly elevated for algae growth; water changes 15–25% every fortnight; filtration any of the accepted methods. Calcareous algae require conditions as suggested for hard corals on page 151.

● *Do different algae require different types of lighting?*

Yes. In general, green calcareous algae prefer the highest intensities and other green algae require at least moderate light. Brown and red algae will tolerate low levels but are usually slow growing as a result.

● *What is "algae harvesting" and why do it?*

"Harvesting" simply means to thin out and remove. Many *Caulerpa* species benefit from this procedure because it encourages younger growth, and it is also a useful method of restricting species that would otherwise grow out of control. Look for the mature growths and remove them, leaving the younger vigorous shoots to grow. Where conditions are favourable, regular harvesting may be necessary.

● *What is "die-back", and how can it be avoided?*

Sometimes a whole crop of algae dies for no apparent reason. The blades go pale and any toxins that are bound up in the plant are released, causing potential pollution. There are several reasons for this disaster. The first is lack of sufficient light of the right quality; the second (more common) reason is deteriorating water quality triggering the plant to self-destruct. Sometimes the algae simply become too old to survive, this can be avoided by regular harvesting. If die-back does occur, remove all the dead algae as soon as possible. The holdfasts, where the plant has been secured to the rocks may still be green and can be left to regenerate when conditions have been improved.

about when removed from water. Exceptions are the calcareous algae, which extract bicarbonates from seawater to create a structure that is rigid in or out of water. These species are more difficult to keep and propagate.

Macro algae reproduce in three main ways: by "runners"; by spores released into the water; and by regeneration of small pieces that have broken away from the main plant, attaching themselves in a different location.

Although many macro algae appear similar to terrestrial plants, the names usually attributed to their parts are nearly always incorrect. Terrestrial leaves are equivalent to algal blades, the "stems" are the stipes and the "roots" are the holdfasts, which act as points of anchorage only and provide no nutrition for the algae, even though they may bury deep into the substrate. Like plants, algae photosynthesize, combining carbon dioxide

and water using the energy of light to produce usable nutrients, with oxygen as a byproduct. Generally speaking, the deeper in the water the species lives, the less green pigment it contains, usually appearing red or brown to take more advantage of the limited source of light.

Macro algae also absorb nutrients through their tissues, in the form of nitrate, nitrite, ammonia and iron. Therefore, a healthy patch of fast-growing algae like the many *Caulerpa* species can help to control unwanted toxins, although it would take a substantial amount of growth to be fully effective.

Many marine algae are quite tolerant of wide temperature ranges. Tropical species will thrive at non-fluctuating levels between 23–29°C (73°–85°F) depending on the requirements of other livestock. In the fish-only tank algae can make a colourful and

● *Why do calcareous algae go white and die?*

... Calcareous algae require optimum water conditions and often fail to thrive where this cannot be provided. However, it is also quite normal for them to lose their green pigment during the hours of darkness, when they may appear pure white.

● *How can herbivorous fishes such as tangs and larger angels be supplied regularly with fresh algae?*

Culture one of the rampant species in a separate, small, but well-lit tank and introduce it as a food source at regular intervals. Some invertebrates such as sea urchins require algae as a major part of their diet and this should also be provided.

● *Are fish medications tolerated by marine algae?*

Many treatments are harmless to algae but exposure to copper-based preparations can prove fatal.

● *How should newly purchased algae be introduced into a tank?*

Marine algae dislike changes in osmotic pressure brought about by rapid fluctuations in specific gravity. Therefore, introduce algae as you would a fish or invertebrate. Float the bag in the aquarium for 10 minutes, then introduce a cupful of tankwater every 5 minutes. After 40 minutes the algae can be removed from the bag and positioned.

● *Is it possible to have an algae-only showtank?*

Yes. Marine algae-only aquaria have become popular in many countries. With well over 20 species commonly available to the hobbyist, the total effect can be stunning.

interesting alternative to invertebrates so long as water quality is kept at a reasonably high level. Many herbivorous fish appreciate this desirable source of nutrition and will rapidly deplete any available stocks. A selection of algae also makes a very useful and attractive addition to the invertebrate aquarium. However, you will need to give some thought to achieving the correct mix of other species to live alongside them. Algae that grow rampantly will soon engulf and smother corals despite regular, hard pruning. Some algae species are almost impossible to eradicate completely once they have become established. The slower growing, more manageable calcareous algae and the red and brown species prove much more acceptable. They also tend to do much better in the invertebrate aquarium than in the fish-only aquarium because of the higher water quality.

Pencillus capitatus, *also commonly known as Neptune's shaving brush, is a calcareous algae that is quite rigid. It is difficult to maintain in captivity, requiring optimum water conditions and lighting as well as high levels of calcium.*

Caulerpa sertularioides is *commonly available and an ideal subject for the marine aquarium.*

Gracillaria sp. *is a slow-growing and very attractive red algae. Its holdfasts often regenerate new growth on freshly introduced living rock. Good water-quality is essential if specimens are to remain healthy.*

Fish/Fish Compatibility

FISH COMPATIBILITY CHART

Fish must be allowed every opportunity to co-exist peacefully in the confines of the aquarium. Use this chart to plan a tank of compatible livestock.

PUTTING INCOMPATIBLE FISH TOGETHER RANKS with overstocking and overfeeding as one of the major causes of failure to keep marine fish successfully. Incompatibility takes three general forms. The first scenario is that one or more dominant fish bully an unrelated species. As the harassed fish becomes more and more stressed, it is likely to succumb to disease which, if infectious, will spread to the rest of the livestock.

The second scenario is that territorial claims will create disharmony among the livestock. Although size may be a factor, even small fish can be very territorial and make larger species distinctly uncomfortable. If two members of the same species of an extremely territorial nature are introduced into the same aquarium, then the resultant disputes can be extremely serious, leading to the death of the defeated party and in all probability a badly injured victor. Occasionally, after an initial squabble, a male and female fish may form a pair bond and share a tank harmoniously thereafter, but the inexperienced fishkeeper should not try to set up such a partnership. The third form of incompatibility may seem obvious, but many fish go "missing" because they are eaten by a tankmate. A predatory fish is often introduced as a relatively harmless juvenile, but within a short time it will eat fish almost half its own size! Predators can only be trusted with species of the same size or larger, so habits should be established *before* purchase.

● *Is the order of introduction important?*

... Yes, sensitive, non-territorial fish must be given a chance to settle peacefully and should be introduced first. Dominant, territorial fish must be left until last, but it would be unwise to mix fish with such extreme temperaments.

● *How can I establish that all fish in a proposed community will be compatible?*

Before a single fish is introduced into a new aquarium, a fish stocking plan must be drawn up. This will outline the eventual complete stock and the order in which they are to be introduced. General family compatibility can be seen from the chart, but there are no hard and fast rules. *Never* buy fish on impulse. Alter your plan only when the implications have been investigated.

● *Is there a maximum stocking level?*

Yes. During the first six months fish should be stocked slowly at a rate of 1in (2.5cm) of fish length for every four gallons (18 l; 4.8 US gallons) nett. In the subsequent six months, stocking levels can be increased to an absolute maximum of 1in (2.5cm) of fish length for every two gallons (9 l; 2.4 US gallons) nett. Make all calculations on adult sizes to give the fish every opportunity to grow to their full potential.

● *What can be done if fish that are incompatible are mistakenly introduced into the same aquarium?*

New introductions may receive close inspection from the established community and this is quite normal. What is unacceptable is when this interest becomes naked aggression – fin-nipping, biting and relentless chasing. If this occurs, remove the victim as quickly as possible and transfer it to an isolation/quarantine tank or, by prior arrangement, return it to the retailer.

Compatible in most cases

Caution required

Incompatible in most cases

LIONFISH
MANDARINFISH
MORAY EELS
PINE-CONE FISH
PORCUPINEFISH
PUFFERFISH
PYGMY BASSLETS
RABBITFISH
REMORAS
SEAHORSES & PIPEFISH
SHARKS & RAYS
SQUIRRELFISH
SURGEONFISH
SWEETLIPS
TRIGGERFISH
TRUMPETFISH
WRASSES
WRASSES (DWARF)

Fish/Invertebrate Compatibility

IT IS VERY LIKELY THAT ANY MARINE AQUARIST with an invertebrate tank will want to add some suitable fish for further interest, colour and a little realism. However, not all fish are suitable as many graze on, or even eat, invertebrates. More importantly, treatments for sick fish are tolerated very poorly by invertebrates and some (e.g. copper-based medications) are lethal to all invertebrates.

It is advisable to choose those fish that are disease resistant and not so large that their waste products will distress invertebrates. Invertebrates produce very small amounts of waste compared with fish and when they are exposed to high quantities of biological waste they tend to react very badly. If possible, fish should be chosen as juveniles and introduced into the invertebrate aquarium at that stage.

FISH IDEAL WITH ALL INVERTEBRATES

Anemonefish	Gobies
Angelfish, Dwarf	Jawfish – *deep substrate*
Blennies	*required*
Cardinalfish	Mandarinfish
Damselfish	Pygmy Basslets
Firefish	Wrasses, Dwarf
Grammas	

FISH GENERALLY COMPATIBLE (but only with care)

Catfish – *become progressively destructive with age*	Seahorses and Pipefish – *preferably species tank*
Hawkfish– *shrimps may be at risk*	Squirrelfish – *crustaceans at risk*
Sea Basses – *not all species safe with invertebrates*	Surgeonfish – *can be difficult to treat for disease in the presence of invertebrates*

FISH NOT COMPATIBLE WITH INVERTEBRATES

Angelfish – *may be safe when very young*	Pufferfish
Batfish	Rabbitfish
Boxfish	Remoras
Butterflyfish	Sharks and Rays
Filefish – *some smaller species may be suitable*	Sweetlips – *safe when young, thereafter very destructive*
Groupers	Triggerfish – *very destructive*
Lionfish – *crustaceans and small fish at risk*	Trumpetfish
Moray Eels – *safe only when young*	Wrasses – *safe when very young, progressively destructive with age*
Pine-Cone Fish	
Porcupinefish	

● *Is it possible to add one or two invertebrates to a mainly fish tank?*

... This is not to be encouraged as invertebrates will find the fish waste products too much to cope with, and generally need higher water quality than fish do to survive.

● *Are there any rules governing fish stocking in the mixed fish/invertebrate aquarium?*

Yes, fairly strict ones. Fish stocks must be kept as low as possible. Generally, 1in (2.5cm) of fish length for every 6 gallons (27 l; 7 US gallons) nett of water must be regarded as the absolute maximum if invertebrate health is to be preserved. The tank should be stocked very slowly, ideally at a rate of one fish each month.

● *Is a fish plan necessary as well?*

Yes. The fish must be compatible with invertebrates and with each other as well. *Never* buy fish on impulse. Follow a carefully considered stocking plan and do not alter it unless the full implications of an unknown fish have been investigated.

● *Are there any very hardy invertebrates?*

No, there are no invertebrates that could truthfully be regarded as hardy; all are sensitive in varying degrees. However, hermit crabs will often tolerate poorer water quality than their relatives, and can survive the effects of some fish medications.

🔺 *Seahorses need somewhere to attach their tails, and all too often they choose a suitable gorgonian. If they attach themselves to the same gorgonian time after time, the invertebrate will "strip" as this one has done.*

◀ *A shoal of firefish* (Nemateleotris magnifica) *is an ideal addition to the invertebrate aquarium. Firefish in general thrive in the more "natural" environment of the mixed tank.*

Reef Tanks – *Substrate or not?*

As reef tanks grew in popularity during the late 1980s and early 1990s, there was much debate on whether they should have a substrate or not.

The Advantage of a Substrate

Introducing a substrate can create a natural effect instantly, making those animals that come into contact with it that much happier. KH, pH and calcium levels are all buffered more efficiently, especially when fresh coral sand is used. Other substrate materials can also be considered, such as white quartz or silica sand. These can be of a very fine grade and set off the whole scene beautifully. A substrate also performs a useful and practical function by cushioning and spreading the weight of heavy rockwork; sharp edges tending not to be such a threat to the base glass.

The Case Against

As reef aquaria demand optimum water conditions, any build up of detritus on the base is undesirable and media that might trap such potential pollutants is best disposed of. A

▲ *Like other substrate dwellers, the Blue-Cheek Goby* (Valenciennea strigata) *spends much of its life sifting the substrate for food particles.*

clean base can make use of a bottom-scouring device much more effectively. A bottom-scourer is a perforated pipe that runs the base length of the aquarium at the very back; water is pumped along the pipe, exiting from the small drilled holes. The resultant agitation forces any detritus into suspension and ultimately into the mechanical filter to be discarded. As a bonus, any areas of slow moving, stagnant water are also eliminated, with fresh water reaching all parts of the aquarium. Taking this procedure one step further, some marinists construct a platform out of rigid lattice-work plastic on which all the rockwork is placed. Any detritus or other waste falls through the platform and into the gap created between the platform and the base, where it is flushed away by a strong water flow.

It may worry some marinists that a glaring piece of glass on the base would look unnatural, but it might be regarded as a

Silica sand

▼ *Substrate materials (shown actual size) are readily available and can be used to great effect.*

White quartz   *Coral sand*

60

● *Will some animals suffer because of the lack of substrate?*

... Yes, livestock that rely on burrowing, or spend their days sifting the substrate sand would all find a substrate-free zone very difficult to live with. These may include, sea pens, jawfish, some gobies and sand anemones.

● *Will bristleworms help to aerate and disturb a deep substrate?*

Yes, but bristleworms in any great numbers can present a real threat to fish and invertebrates as they go in search of food (see Invertebrate Pests pages 198–199).

● *Can a deep substrate act as a denitrification filter?*

Being largely anaerobic, it is possible that suitable denitrifying bacteria will occupy certain areas and begin to reduce nitrates. Unfortunately, the aquarist will have no control over the procedure and denitrification might easily degenerate into the production of toxic hydrogen sulphide gas. It would be far preferable to have a relatively shallow substrate of 0.5–1in (1.25–2.5cm) and a separate denitrification unit instead.

➥ *A bottom-scouring facility is becoming increasingly popular with reef-tank enthusiasts, and justifiably so. Any device that can rid the aquarium quickly of unwanted detritus and mulm will help maintain a stable environment with high-quality water.*

positive opportunity to introduce yet more invertebrates. *Xenia*, sponges and algae will all grow and spread happily on the glass surface, making it appear not only perfectly natural, but attractive as well. By disposing of an existing bulky substrate, more room will be created for extra water, a vital commodity. It may only prove to be a few gallons but useful nonetheless. An unexpected dividend is that amphipods, bristleworms and other burrowing pests are deprived of hiding places and those caught in the open can easily be syphoned away.

Conclusions

While a substrate might be attractive to the eye, in practice several drawbacks present themselves. The buffering effect that the calcareous material in the substrate may have on pH, KH and calcium is short-lived perhaps lasting only a few months, and requiring regular renewal if the effect is to be maintained. Alternative media such as silica sand can deposit unwanted nutrients into the water in the form of silicates for the encouragement of nuisance algae. Also, burrowing animals have to deposit their spoil somewhere, and that is usually over the corals!

BOTTOM-SCOURING DEVICE

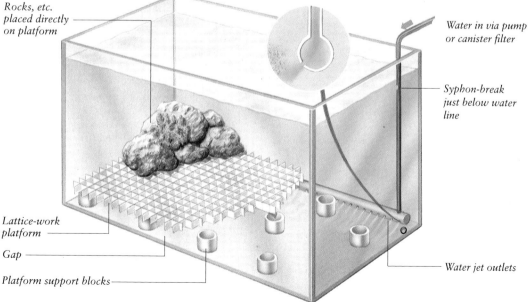

Water jets angled down at 45°

Rocks, etc. placed directly on platform

Water in via pump or canister filter

Syphon-break just below water line

Lattice-work platform

Gap

Platform support blocks

Water jet outlets

Aquarium Maintenance

SUCCESSFUL FISHKEEPING AND PROPER REGULAR maintenance go hand in hand. Many hobbyists spend hours each week on maintenance procedures well in excess of those realistically required, claiming that much of the pleasure is in the regular upkeep. Far from being a chore, the caring aquarist regards maintenance as an opportunity to restore and revitalize, making sure that everything is as good as it can be and that the health of all the animals is preserved and extended.

Maintenance is not constant and unnecessary meddling with the tank set-up, as this may prove harmful to the inhabitants. It is a logical system of regular activities designed to keep the aquarium fully functioning. Regular water changes with high quality water are fundamental to proper maintenance. As livestock continuously alter the physical composition of seawater by their biological functions, it is vital to renew and replenish all the life-supporting compounds, while diluting the undesirable or potentially toxic ones. Only regular water changes can achieve this completely. What constitutes a sufficient water change will vary from tank to tank. The exact proportion of water to be replaced will be influenced by the amount and the type of livestock kept. A heavily stocked fish-only aquarium will need larger, and probably more frequent, water changes than an invertebrate system with just a few fish.

Testing

Test kits are an essential part of the aquarist's maintenance programme. They are the only reliable way to determine the state of the water; it is impossible to make accurate judgements by just looking (see Testing and Water Conditions pages 16–19). Make sure that test kits are stored correctly away from heat and moisture, and that the shelf-life has not expired by the time you want to use it. Improper storage will lead to inaccurate results, which could indirectly cause the loss of valuable livestock.

✓ AQUARIUM MAINTENANCE CHECKLIST

DAILY
1 Check livestock – number and general health
2 Check temperature
3 Empty protein skimmer waste
4 Check all equipment is working properly
5 Remove any uneaten food after feeding
6 Enter observations into aquarium log
7 Check water flow to denitrification filter
8 Top up water in osmolator reservoir
9 Top up fresh and salt water reservoirs in automatic water change systems
10 Adjust ozonizer output, if required

EVERY OTHER DAY
1 Top up evaporated water
2 Remove algae from front glass
3 Clean pre-filters in systemized tanks

WEEKLY
1 Clean cover glasses, if fitted
2 Remove any "salt creep"
3 Add trace elements, pH buffers and vitamin supplements, etc., if necessary

FORTNIGHTLY
1 Change 15–25% of water, depending on how heavily the aquarium is stocked
2 Test for ammonia, nitrite, pH, nitrate and specific gravity in well established tanks; more often in new set-ups
3 Replace filter floss in canister filter
4 Disconnect fluorescent tubes when cool, clean with plain water and dry thoroughly
5 Clean probes of electronic meters and controllers with a brush, check for damage

● *Is it true that a nitrate filter fitted to an aquarium can substantially reduce the need for water changes?*

No. While high levels of nitrate are undesirable, they are certainly not the only substances to cause toxicity problems. Infrequent water changes will allow these substances to build up to dangerous levels and the only reliable solution is to dilute them back to safe limits with regular water changes.

● *Should an algae magnet be removed from the tank when not in use?*

Yes. Most algae magnets are prone to rusting or corrosion of the magnetic core which may prove toxic to livestock. In addition, the internal half can house harmful anaerobic bacteria, which can be confirmed by smelling it. If the odour is similar to rotten eggs then the magnet is best stored away from the aquarium!

● *Disabled aquarists can find many maintenance tasks very difficult to perform. Is it possible to employ someone to do it on a regular basis?*

Yes. Many aquarium shops provide a maintenance service and a few telephone calls to local retailers will give a good idea of prices. However, it is vital that you get a signed maintenance agreement from the person or company outlining exactly what they are going to do on each visit. This must also be accompanied by proof that they are properly insured in the event of an accident or breakages. If these assurances cannot be given, then any risk is likely to remain with the aquarist.

● *Will using reverse osmosis water for water changes and evaporation top-up make that much difference?*

Yes. Reverse osmosis (RO) water is denuded of around 95% of toxins in mains water, which may encourage disease in fish and premature death of invertebrates; not to mention the greater likelihood of nuisance algae. Although the initial cost of a unit may be high, this can easily be recouped as no other resins and remedies need be purchased to reduce nitrates, phosphates and other undesirable substances.

● *Does it make sense to position a marine tank in the dark alcove of a hallway, hoping to brighten the area up. Truthfully, most people ignore it and it gets very little attention, what should be done?*

The tank should be moved into the lounge or other well-frequented room. Placing an aquarium in an inhospitable location is always a mistake. Most people would not want to crouch uncomfortably in a draughty hallway for more than a few minutes, no matter how attractive the tank may be! An aquarium on full show to a regular 'audience' is far more likely to receive proper maintenance, not to mention appreciation!

● *Is it necessary to keep any spares in the event of an equipment failure?*

Yes, they can literally be a life-saver. Keep a spare heater, battery-powered airpump, airstones, impellers and any pumps used to operate trickle filters, etc. It may be a little too optimistic to expect equipment to fail when aquarium retailers are open!

MONTHLY
(More often, if required)
Rake through the coral sand substrate.
Syphon off any detritus

BI-MONTHLY
1 Replace any airstones, including protein skimmer diffusers
2 Change carbon
3 Clean protein skimmer
4 Remove excess algae (this may need to be done more often, or less often, than bi-monthly)
5 Check all electrical connections

Safety: *Salt water and electricity are a lethal combination. Always fit a plug-in residual circuit breaker (RCB) to the main power supply.*

EVERY THREE MONTHS
1 Clean pump impellers, pipework, internal housing, and check for wear
2 Clean out all canister filter hoses with suitable hose brushes
3 Change air filter pads in air pumps and check diaphragm for wear
4 Clean the internal quartz sleeve of the ultraviolet sterilizer

EVERY SIX MONTHS+
1 Replace ultraviolet sterilizer tubes
2 Renew fluorescent tubes and other lighting if required
3 Change damaged or worn pump impeller assemblies
4 Renew non-return air valves

Holiday Preparation

EVERY MARINE FISHKEEPER HAS RESERVATIONS about leaving their prized aquarium behind while they go away on holiday. Worries about the safety of the tank can, in extreme circumstances, completely cancel out the benefits of a holiday! However, with advance planning, the aquarium can be left for up to 2–3 weeks quite safely, and with a minimum of supervision.

Initial Arrangements

First find a competent friend, relative or neighbour who would be willing to visit the aquarium at least once a day and perform a few simple tasks. It will not be necessary for them to become an expert, merely to feed the livestock, check for any fatalities and make sure that the system is functioning normally.

Do not leave these arrangements to the last minute, but invite the person to visit on a normal day when you can answer questions and show them how the system works. Keep in mind that this person will, understandably, not be as knowledgeable nor as enthusiastic as the owner.

Explain the Key Issues

Feeding: It is a good idea to prepare a measured amount of food for each day; label it with the date when it is to be used and seal it in a small package. Frozen foods can be stored in the freezer, whereas flake or other dried food packets can be left close by the aquarium in an airtight plastic box. Reduced feeding will decrease the load on the filtration system and maintain a higher water quality for a longer period of time. Even with half their normal feed, livestock will not suffer over a period of several weeks.

'It is vitally important to assure the stand-in that *no extra food* will be necessary. You might want to hide the extra food, or even use an automatic feeder, dispensing only flake

● *Is it possible to buy reverse osmosis water?*

... Many marine aquarists do not possess a reverse osmosis filter unit but are able to purchase supplies of processed water from an aquatic retailer.

● *What can be done if there is a power cut while the owner is away?*

A tank that is correctly set up and stocked will usually come to no harm if power is restored within 24 hours. Helpers should be told not to feed during a power cut and not to worry if it is predicted to be a short one. If a major power failure exceeding 24 hours is likely, then the emergency expert may have to be called to remove livestock temporarily to a safer environment.

● *How close to a holiday can livestock still be introduced?*

Up to a month, but no closer. It is vital to make sure that all livestock are settled and healthy long in advance of being left alone.

● *Should a helper perform any water tests in the absence of the owner?*

Only if they are fully confident that they can carry them out properly and interpret the results correctly.

● *Is it wise to attempt to bring back livestock from a tropical reef location while on vacation?*

Generally no. Most countries will not let livestock be removed from their shores without proper export permits. Livestock confiscated at Customs usually die due to lack of care. Even if living organisms could be brought back, they would need to be correctly packed with oxygen, which most people could not hope to locate. All in all, it would be best to observe the creatures in the wild and bring back happy memories instead of dead fish! Making a video or taking photographs will prove longer lasting and more satisfying in the end.

✓ EQUIPMENT CHECKLIST

Reduce the likelihood of a mechanical or electrical failure by replacing any item suspected of being faulty. Use the following checklist to help identify potential problems:

✓ **Heating** – Replace old or unreliable heaters or thermostats.

✓ **Lighting** – If spotlamp bulbs are near the end of their lives (mercury vapour lasts 6–12 months, metal halide lasts 12–18 months) then replace them, especially if valuable corals are kept. Fluorescent tubes with very blackened ends are likely to fail. Check the end caps for cracking and signs of disintegration owing to the constant heat. The same applies for the plastic nuts, bolts and clips holding the tubes in place as they can become very brittle after a while. Consider using a domestic timer to control lighting.

✓ **Power Heads** – Clean the impeller and water pathways.

✓ **Air Uplifts** – Replace airstones.

✓ **Air Pumps** – Replace diaphragms, and air filter pads.

✓ **Protein Skimmers** – Replace wooden air-diffusers; clean all component parts and renew worn airline tubing to prevent clogging.

✓ **Non-Return Air Valves** – Check for efficiency and renew if faulty.

✓ **Ozonizers/UV Sterilizer** – Check connections for any signs of deterioration. Replace ultra-violet bulbs if nearing the end of their useful life (usually six months).

✓ **Cable Tidies/Plugs** – All electrical connections should be inspected for loose, burned or frayed wires. If in doubt, call on the services of a qualified electrician.

✓ **Canister Filters** – Change media such as activated carbon and filter floss as close to the date of departure as possible. Clean impellers and clear detritus/algae from the interior of hoses with a suitable hose brush.

✓ **Trickle Filters** – These come in all shapes and sizes but all water pathways should be checked, pre-filters cleaned/replaced, hose connections checked and pumps cleaned.

✓ **Undergravel Filters** – Rake through compacted sand and syphon off any detritus.

---

food. Do test automatic feeders for reliability by installing and using them for at least a week before departure. Follow the manufacturer's instructions carefully as moisture can cause the flake to become damp and fail to dispense properly.

Fatalities: Explain to your helper that dead fish or corals pollute the system causing the death of other livestock. If discovered, they must be removed immediately. Describing the appearance of dead or dying coral may require some effort, whereas a dead fish should present few problems. Leave instructions on how to dispose of the body. If any of your fish or invertebrates are venomous, then warn your helper of the danger.

A Fully Functioning System: Provide a short checklist explaining what each item should be doing when it is behaving normally (not *why*, otherwise confusion will set in).

A Helping Hand: In case anything goes badly wrong, your helper needs the telephone number of a very experienced person willing to visit the tank and take any necessary action. That person will nearly always be a reliable aquatic retailer with whom an arrangement will have been made well in advance. Make sure any call-out fees for visits have been agreed beforehand to prevent disputes later. A diagram of the system, including a list of livestock and water parameters, should be lodged with the expert as part of your holiday preparations.

Water Changes

Never underestimate the importance of good water quality; it can help livestock to survive when all else has failed (during a power cut, for example). Change approximately 20% of the water one week before departure and another 20% as close to the leaving day as possible. Use the highest quality water available such as that filtered through a reverse osmosis unit.

Moving House

RELOCATING AN AQUARIUM WHILE MOVING house is not a guaranteed safe procedure but if it is well planned in advance and the move can be completed in 18 hours or less, then there is every reason to expect success. Two things take priority: the livestock and the biological filter. Fish, invertebrates, algae and bacteria have a "survival time limit" and livestock needs a stress-free move if disease is to be avoided later.

Livestock

It is essential to pack livestock properly to ensure maximum survival time, using two or more strong polythene bags placed one inside the other to hold the animal in the water securely. The air trapped inside the bag will maintain the package in a rigid state so that the animal may move freely and not become trapped or injured in a floppy container. Bear in mind that sharp rocks and fishes with spines will pierce a single bag quite easily, causing leaks, collapse of the bag and possibly unnecessary deaths. Up to four bags may be used to pack sharp objects, with a double layer of newspaper placed between each layer as an extra safety precaution.

Having sealed up the animals, the bags can be placed in a polystyrene box and the air spaces filled with crumpled newspapers to preserve as much heat as possible and prevent the bags from moving. Polythene bags, elastic bands and polystyrene transporter boxes can all be obtained from an aquatic retailer, usually as a goodwill gesture, but do offer to make a contribution if only out of politeness. A correctly packed animal can stay healthy in normal air and water for 12–18 hours, but if the journey is to be a particularly long one in low temperatures, chemical heating packs available from camping shops can be positioned at the base of each polystyrene box and covered with a thick layer of newspapers.

▲ *Multiple polythene bags packed correctly with livestock and protected with layers of newspaper.*

Beware of introducing too many heating packs or letting them come into contact with livestock bags as serious overheating could result. You may want to check for leaking bags halfway through the journey, but more frequent inspections will let out too much heat and cause stress to livestock.

The Biological Filter

Oxygen-loving bacteria can survive for some time in transit and, even after a move lasting 18 hours, a correctly packed biological filter will still be able to support livestock. Bag *all* filter media, whether it be sand, gravel, sintered glass or plastic shapes in the same way as the livestock and pack it in polystyrene boxes. Make sure there is just enough original tank water to keep it submerged.

On Arrival

Once the destination has been reached, the tank can be set up using 50–75% of the original water, topped up with a fresh mix. Run the aquarium, complete with biological filter until it is up to operating temperature and the water is clear. A proprietary living bacterial culture (*not* maturation fluid!) can be added to boost the filter (see Maturation page 40), after which the livestock can be floated in the usual way before release. Leave the lights off during the whole procedure and do not feed for the rest of the day. A light feed can be given on the following day if tests show no trace of ammonia or nitrite. Readings should be regarded as temporary until the filter bacteria multiply back to full strength.

Preparing checklists will have to be tailored to individual circumstances, but the importance of planning cannot be overemphasized.

Labelling the contents of each bag as you seal it will help to avoid any confusion when the box is unpacked at the point of destination. A sturdy polystyrene box will help to keep the temperature stable.

● *Are there any useful guidelines for successful packing?*

1 In general, pack only one animal in each bag; an exception to this are mated pairs of fish which should occupy the same bag to preserve the pair bond.

2 36 hours before the move, cease feeding the livestock to prevent fouling of the bag water.

3 A teaspoon of zeolite granules placed in the bag will help adsorb any ammonia from the travelling water.

4 Improve water quality by performing several water changes in the days preceding the move.

● *Would it be better to try to obtain pure oxygen to fill out the livestock bags?*

Retailers use pure oxygen to prolong survival times, but it can be a very dangerous gas in untrained hands and is best avoided if the user is not fully aware of its potential dangers.

● *Are there less expensive alternatives to using chemical heating packs?*

Heating packs tend to be effective and long-lasting, but an alternative is to fill plastic bags with warm water and use them in the same way, being careful not to let the heated bags come into contact with the livestock bags.

Nuisance Algae

NUISANCE ALGAE AFFECT MOST MARINE aquaria at one time or another. They pose complicated problems with no simple or quick solutions. Slime (or smear) algae are not true algae, and scientifically are known as cyanobacteria. In fact, along with bacteria, they form a kingdom, the Monera. They are one of the first forms of life known to exist on Earth. Their rapid growth and resilience enables them to smother an otherwise attractive aquarium in a slimy skin, not dissimilar to an underwater oil slick! Colours may range from rust red, through green to black.

Filamentous algae are true algae but no less troublesome. Like slime algae, they are capable of completely smothering sessile animals. Not only do they look unsightly but, unchecked, can cause the death of livestock.

The reason why nuisance algae should plague one tank while leaving another almost identical set-up untouched is not completely understood, but the appearance of algae is a perfectly natural occurrence and most tanks will have at least one small patch. Water quality is probably the single most important factor in controlling algae; where water quality has been allowed to deteriorate, nuisance algae are far more likely to proliferate. Rivers, lakes and coastlines that are stricken by pollution often suffer algae plagues too.

Improving Water Quality

Most domestic water supplies contain high levels of nitrates, phosphates and sulphates (among other impurities) and these encourage nuisance algae to multiply unchecked. It would be wise to filter all mains water in an effort to rid it of contaminants. Most highly recommended for overall efficiency is a reverse osmosis filter. A deionizer is a second-best choice, and nitrate-removing resins are a useful cheaper alternative.

Salt mix may also contain undesirably high

● *Are nuisance algae toxic to fish and invertebrates?*

... Not in the accepted sense of the word. However, as a result of photosynthesis, massive growths can deprive livestock of vital oxygen during darkness, leading aquarists to attribute (wrongly) any deaths to "toxic" algae.

● *While a problem tank is under treatment, can anything else boost recovery?*

Reduce feeding and if the tank is overstocked, remove some fish. Frequently syphon off, or physically pull away, as much of the offending algae as possible.

● *Can mains water be used to replace evaporated aquarium water?*

Use only the purest water produced by a reverse osmosis filter, distillation or deionization. By using nutrient-rich water, the pollutants are increased in concentration.

● *Why do nuisance algae tend to be more prominent during the Spring and Autumn?*

Reasons are poorly understood. It may be connected to the change in quality of daylight.

levels of nitrates and phosphates. Check this by mixing a sample of distilled water and salt mix to a specific gravity of 1.021. A relevant test kit will reveal any contamination.

Many of the impurities supplied through mains water can also be generated within the aquarium itself. Fish, and to a lesser extent invertebrates, pollute the tank water with waste products. Many of these are dealt with by the tank filtration, but dissolved solids will still build up to undesirable levels if regular water changes are not performed to dilute them. Most aquarists should aim to replace 15–20% every fortnight. This may seem excessive but it is the only way to keep the water pure and to prevent nuisance algae from gaining a foothold in the first place.

◀ *Filamentous algae, also known as hair algae or green thread algae, will overgrow marine invertebrates, ultimately choking them to death.*

➤ *These red slime algae (cyanobacteria) are tolerable in small patches but as they begin to spread they become harmful aquarium pests.*

● *Are the bubbles rising from slime algae dangerous?*

No, these are harmless oxygen bubbles produced by photosynthesis within the algae.

● *Will growths of macro-algae deprive the nuisance algae of their nutrients?*

All too often nuisance algae smothers the macro-algae as well. In addition, decorative algae do not do well in deteriorating water quality and will not grow fast enough to utilize sufficient nutrients.

Limiting the Other Factors

It is important that maximum stocking levels are strictly observed and that tanks are not stocked too quickly. Both will result in a swift deterioration of water quality and a chance for algae to gain the advantage. Overfeeding has much the same effect and liquid invertebrate food can prove highly polluting. If nuisance algae are already a problem, do not introduce more stock into the tank until they are under control. Also, be sure to avoid any form of algal fertilizer; healthy tanks will support fine growths of macro- and micro-algae without the need for extra nitrates.

Being so adaptable, nuisance algae can survive under most forms of lighting and it would be a mistake to begin altering lighting systems without improving water quality. Ultraviolet radiation will have very little effect on nuisance algae but it will improve the tank set-up as a whole to reduce the risk of disease. (see Ultraviolet Sterilizers page 33).

Some reports suggest that maintaining very high redox levels (in excess of 450 mv) has helped rid tanks of slime algae, but this can usually be explained by residual ozone escaping into the main aquarium proving toxic to the algae (as well as to fish and invertebrates). On the whole, this is probably not a safe or realistic alternative. Nor is it viable to expect your fish to eat nuisance algae. Some herbivorous fish will browse on filamentous algae; unfortunately they usually prefer decorative algae species (for the same reason that slugs prefer flowers to weeds, no doubt).

Chemical Control

Combating algae with chemicals is the very last resort and a sign of desperation. Tests have shown that success is nearly always temporary and that fish and invertebrates can suffer from side effects produced by the additional chemicals in the water. The best and most reliable way to combat nuisance algae has always been to keep water quality extremely high. If this goal is pursued vigorously, a gradual improvement is nearly always the reward; even badly affected tanks can be transformed within a few months.

Fish Health

OF LATE THERE HAS BEEN A MOVEMENT against using the phrase "fish diseases" in favour of "fish health". And rightly so, since "fish diseases" is a negative phrase implying that it is almost inevitable for fish to contract an ailment; it also deflects attention away from the fact that, as caring hobbyists, we should be providing the best possible conditions as a prevention against such diseases.

Bearing all this in mind, it has to be said that marine fish are far more likely to experience some form of ailment than their freshwater counterparts, mainly due to the fact that the marine environment is so much more difficult to maintain.

Prevention

Preventing disease is obviously far more desirable than having to treat a sick fish and in most cases there is little or no extra effort required; whereas an infected aquarium is going to need special care and expensive medications. The main causes of marine fish ill-health fall into three categories: overstocking, overfeeding and stress. It could be argued that the last category occurs as a direct result of the first two, but there are many other unrelated causes of stress including bullying, bad handling, poor compatibility with other tankmates, etc. What, then, are the best ways to prevent disease?

Stocking *Always stock slowly* – the quicker a tank is stocked, the greater the risk of disease, especially in a newly matured tank.

Feeding Feed no more than the fish can consume in a few minutes. Remove any excess without delay. There are very few instances of fish dying because they are underfed, so do not be afraid to feed very sparingly.

Stress Marine fishes are easily stressed, ultimately leading to a rapid breakdown of their natural immune systems and the subsequent contraction of disease. Apart from the causes

● *How safe are copper-based medications?*

... Used properly, very safe. However, it is important to maintain the correct level of copper in the water. Too much and the fish could be poisoned; too little and the disease organism will not be eradicated. A copper test kit is essential to monitor accurate dosages.

● *What is a freshwater dip?*

As the phrase implies, it is quite literally a dip into freshwater. This can be a useful way of giving immediate relief from parasitic infections. Freshwater kills the parasites clinging to the fins, body and gills but does little or no harm to the fish if the water is prepared to exactly the same temperature and pH of the tank from which it is taken. Immersion times vary between 20 seconds and 2 minutes, depending on the constitution of the fish involved. If the fish begins to look distressed, remove it back to the original tank water immediately. Any small, clean aquarium can be used as the fish need never be allowed out of the catching net. One or two dips each day can prove very effective against many diseases.

● *How can fish be treated for whitespot in a mixed fish/invertebrate aquarium?*

With great difficulty. The most effective remedies are based on copper, which is lethal to invertebrates, even in minute quantities. Experience has shown that alternative remedies designed especially for this situation do not work nearly as well as is claimed and the fish are best removed to a separate hospital tank (see pages 74–75) where copper can be used safely.

● *At what point should copper medication be stopped?*

Follow the *whole* course of treatment as recommended by the manufacturer, even if the fish looks fully recovered halfway through the programme. If the fish is still suffering after a complete course, a second course and/or increased dose might be necessary. In this case, consult the manufacturer or an expert for advice.

of stress already mentioned, stress can be brought about by high nitrate levels, unstable water conditions, loud external noises (slamming doors, loud music, tapping on the glass, etc.) and toxic fumes within the room (heavy smoking, carpet cleaners, paint fumes, insecticides, etc.).

Early Signs

Nearly all diseases will be signalled at an early stage by a change in the behaviour of the fish. A depressed appetite is usually a clear sign, as is hiding or sudden shyness. This may be accompanied by more dramatic symptoms such as flicking or scratching against rocks, swimming erratically, rushing around the tank in a frenzy or an inability to maintain swimming equilibrium.

A good fishkeeper will know the normal behaviour of the fish and recognize these early warning signs so that swift action can be taken. Action without delay is important as many marine diseases can become dangerous within 24 hours, making treatment progressively more difficult.

Diseases

There are four main types of diseases: parasitic; bacterial; fungal; and viral. Often, one disease will complicate another. It is not often discussed, but fish can suffer from most of the same physiological diseases as humans or other animals. Heart, kidney, liver and intestinal problems are bound to occur from time to time, along with a whole host of other disorders. The point to bear in mind is that if a fish is ill, it may not be one of the common aquarium diseases; sometimes there is no effective treatment and a distressed fish may have to be destroyed humanely. If in doubt, seek expert advice from a veterinarian specializing in marine fish.

COMMON MARINE AQUARIUM DISEASES

Whitespot
Cryptocaryon irritans

Symptoms: flicking and scratching against various surfaces, small (1mm) white spots covering fins and body.
Comments: this is a highly infectious disease that spreads rapidly and needs an equally rapid medicinal response.
Treatment: copper-based medications to kill the vulnerable free-swimming stages of the parasitic lifecycle. Using an ultraviolet sterilizer in the tank can help to control the disease at the same stage.

Oodinium or Marine Velvet
Amyloodinium ocellatum

Symptoms: flicking and scratching against surfaces, rapid breathing, very small spots peppering the body producing a "velvet" appearance in the worst cases.
Comments: perhaps the most infectious and deadly of all marine diseases. Swift treatment is essential but some strains of this disease

◆ Whitespot *(sometimes called marine "ich")* *afflicting a Regal Tang* (Paracanthurus hepatus).

can be extremely resistant to medication.
Treatment: a proprietary copper-based
medication to kill the vulnerable free-
swimming stages of the parasitic lifecycle.
Once again, using an ultraviolet sterilizer in
the tank will destroy the free-swimming
parasites.

Black Spot

Symptoms: small (1mm) black spots on the
body. Fish will flick and scratch.
Comments: spots are not usually so
numerous as those connected with whitespot,
neither are they so deadly. Surgeonfish seem
to be particularly vulnerable.
Treatment: a proprietary copper-based
medication or one based on Trichlorofon.

Gill and Fin Flukes

Symptoms: rapid breathing, flicking and
scratching, cloudy eyes, white patches on the
skin; worm-like attachments are sometimes
visible but not always.
Comments: another very infectious disease
that can quickly become fatal; if the gills are
infected the fish will suffocate.
Treatment: a freshwater bath for immediate
relief and proprietary anti-fluke medications.

Head and Lateral Line Erosion Disease
(HLLE)

Symptoms: erosion of the lateral line and the
formation of pits in the skin; very similar to
freshwater hole-in-the-head disease.
Comments: the condition of the fish
gradually deteriorates and often results in the
death of the fish if water conditions are not
vastly improved.
Treatment: No real proprietary cure. This
disease is a direct result of poor environmental conditions, which will have to be
investigated and improved.

Finrot

Symptoms: erosion of fins and fin rays,
reddened areas, particularly at the base of
fins, lethargy and depressed appetite.

▲ Oodinium *seen here as white "powder" along the
back of this Lionfish* (Pterois volitans).

▲ *A Striped Sailfin Tang* (Zebrasoma veliferum) *with
a severe case of Head and Lateral Line Erosion. Happily
this fish recovered.*

 Finrot leaves the fin ragged and torn.

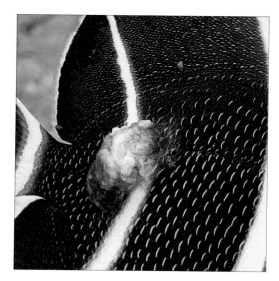

 Lymphocystis *(Cauliflower Disease), seen here on a French Angelfish* (Pomacanthus paru), *can affect the body or fins; even the most serious symptoms rarely cause distress to the fish.*

Comments: in very bad cases the body of the animal can also begin to rot as well.
Treatment: immediate improvement of environmental conditions, and proprietary bacterial medications.

Marine Fungus
Ichthyophonus spp.

Symptoms: fish darken markedly, depressed appetite, listlessness, sandpaper appearance of the skin.
Comments: this is not particularly common and requires careful diagnosis but is a good example of a fungal disease.
Treatment: very difficult, as proprietary anti-fungal medications are not always effective. Food soaked in Phenoxetol can be effective, *if* the fish is eating. Improve environment.

Cauliflower Disease
Lymphocystis spp.

Symptoms: warty clumps of miniature "cauliflowers" form on the fins and body.
Comments: this viral disease often looks a great deal worse than it really is. Although rarely fatal, secondary infections may occur.
Treatment: there is no proprietary medication. A freshwater dip may help. Normally, if optimum water conditions are maintained and the fish is under very little stress, its immune system will eventually defeat the virus.

Q&A

● *Must diseased fish always be isolated?*

... If they are suffering from an infectious disease, the whole tank including healthy tankmates will have to be treated. Isolate the sick fish only if it is being bullied or stressed by other fish.

● *Fish are still scratching and flicking after treatment has been completed and all other signs of disease are gone, why?*

Many diseases, particularly parasitic ones, leave scarring on the skin and gills that may take some time to heal and disappear. This often causes irritation long after the disease has gone.

● *Many sources recommend scraping or cutting off Lymphocystis "cauliflowers" with a scalpel; is this correct?*

Such procedures can be very dangerous to the fish, and owner! Secondary infections are often encouraged by the damage done with the scalpel and considering the relatively harmless nature of the disease, such drastic actions are completely unnecessary.

● *Can a veterinarian be consulted?*

By all means. However, most vets know very little about diseases of marine fish and may cause more harm than good. Specialist marine vets do exist and these can be traced by contacting your national veterinarian association.

Quarantine

THE TRADITION OF MAINTAINING A TANK exclusively for quarantine purposes has declined over recent years. Marinists are under the impression that the fish they see displayed for sale have already been screened for disease and acclimatized to the aquarium environment. While this may be true in some cases, most retailers lack the space and resources to provide a full quarantine service, and newly imported fish are often put on sale immediately. In these circumstances it falls to the aquarist to shoulder more responsibility for protecting the existing showtank stock from a potential disease carrier, as well as doing everything possible to increase the survival chances of the new arrival.

Quarantined fish tend to adapt to showtank conditions better in the long term. The owner can use the quarantine period (when the new arrival is not competing with tankmates for food) to condition the fish to aquarium foods and allow it to "feed-up", creating a greater resistance to illness once introduced to the showtank. It also allows the owner a "decision window" whereby, if the wrong species has been chosen, arrangements can be made to return or rehouse it. (see Fish/Fish Compatibility pages 56–57)

Setting Up a Suitable Tank

A 12 gallon (55 l; 14 US gallon) tank would accommodate one or even two small fishes (damsels, basslets, etc) at a time, while larger fish (groupers, large angels, etc) will need a tank with a capacity of approximately 20 gallons (90 l; 24 US gallons) or more for each fish. A fully functioning biological filter that has been well matured beforehand is vital. Whether the option is for undergravels or perhaps a large external canister housing biological media, any fish will be put at grave risk if the filter has not been prematured, preferably with a proprietary maturation fluid. Other designs such as trickle, wet and dry, or powered sponge filters are, of course, perfectly acceptable.

There has been much debate over whether such items as protein skimmers, ozonizers, activated carbon or ultraviolet sterilizers are necessary as these may impede the efficiency of various medications. While this may be true of the first three items, an ultraviolet sterilizer will only aid the destruction of free-swimming disease organisms and is to be highly recommended.

Maintain, as far as possible, the same water parameters in the quarantine tank as in the

● *How long should a fish be kept in a quarantine tank?*

... Once the fish is cured and/or eating correctly, allow another 3–4 weeks before introducing it into its final home. This is particularly important where a mixed fish/invertebrate tank is concerned as infected fish are extremely difficult to treat.

● *Does regular maintenance need to be carried out on a quarantine tank?*

Apart from removing uneaten food, no, not really. Filters of vacated tanks should be cleaned and water completely changed ready for the next client.

● *Is it possible to quarantine invertebrates?*

A few, such as octopus and cuttlefish, can be acclimatized to aquarium foods in a quarantine tank but others can be installed immediately.

● *Once all the fish have been acquired, should the quarantine tank be used as a second showtank?*

Absolutely not, you may need to use a quarantine tank on a later occasion, and in the meantime it can double as a hospital tank if a fish requires special treatment. Remember to keep the biological filter active by adding a few drops of maturation fluid every other day.

main showtank. In this way there will be very little shock in transference as temperature, specific gravity and pH will all be identical. As with any fishtank, a quiet site must be found. One that is free from loud bangs, music or vibration. All these will create stress and encourage subsequent ill-health.

To help elude injury in a relatively confined space, a blunt, soft rock should be used such as tufa. The aim is not to create a coral wall, but just enough sheltering places to make the fish feel comfortable, provide sufficient swimming space and retain as much volume of water as possible. Too much rockwork may also encourage a specimen to hide continuously, making it very difficult to assess its health by masking clear observations. Syphoning off uneaten food will also be an arduous task. The base of the tank should be free of substrate to enable any detritus to be syphoned away every day. Ensure that black paper or plastic is positioned below the tank glass as the dark colour will have a significant calming effect on the fish.

Illumination is not critical and one or two fluorescent tubes over a tank will keep lighting sufficiently subdued to reduce stress but light enough to observe the subject. In most cases a combined heater/stat would suffice but a heating mat and external thermostat will avoid any risk that the fish may burn itself against an unguarded element.

Introducing the Fish

Once a fish has been purchased, introduce it into the quarantine tank in the usual way and leave it to settle down until the following day when a little food may be offered. If it is not eaten within a few minutes, simply syphon it out with as little fuss as possible.

Build up a prophylactic dose of a copper-based medication to 0.25 mg (1.1 mg/gallon) over the next few days and test frequently with an accurate copper test kit; do not rely on guesswork as an overdose of copper can be fatal. This protection against many of the commonest diseases will allow the subject to settle in its new surroundings without the threat of illness. Should disease break out, increase the dosage level to 0.5 mg (2.2 mg/gallon). This will be effective in most cases against whitespot, *Oodinium*, flukes and fungal diseases. The fish should be feeding boldly within two or three days and be settled by the end of a week.

A quarantine tank need not be an unattractive feature. As an added advantage, quarantining forces the aquarist to slow down the rate that the showtank is stocked, since the fish pass through the process one at a time.

Marine Fish

This section provides practical information on the care of some of the most commonly available tropical marine fish. The vast majority can be successfully accommodated within the home aquarium to provide a peaceful and stunningly colourful display. Some of them will make ideal choices and are relatively straight-forward to care for. Others are more unusual and need special conditions, but the enthusiastic fishkeeper may feel that they are worth the extra trouble. A few species are not recommended for a domestic tank, and suitable warnings are given.

The facts and tips offered here will arm the beginner and experienced hobbyist alike with much of the knowledge required to become a successful fishkeeper.

▶ *The Spotted or Pacific Boxfish* (Ostracion meleagris) *see page 109.*

What is a Marine Fish?

FISH ARE SOME OF THE MOST ADAPTABLE animals on this planet. They occupy practically every watery niche Mother Earth has to offer: saltwater, freshwater, brackish water, hard water, soft water, cold water, temperate seas, tropical seas, arctic seas, lakes, rivers and lagoons. Marine fish, those that survive and multiply in saltwater, inhabit a relatively concentrated medium, containing a host of dissolved substances, the commonest of which by far is sodium chloride or common salt. The presence of so much salt makes it difficult for organisms to survive in such an environment and fish have had to adapt. To understand these adaptations, we need to call on some simple physics.

Osmosis

Osmosis describes the process by which molecules in an aqueous solution can pass through a semi-permeable, biologically active, membrane, while the movement of other molecules due to size, shape or other reasons, is restricted. In fish, this process takes place across the skin covering the gills, body and gut. The smaller water molecules may pass freely through what is in effect a semi-permeable membrane while the movement of larger salt molecules is denied. It is important to bear in mind, however, that molecules are actively transported by the metabolism of the fish, which means that fish expend great amounts of energy to maintain osmosis.

Nature is always striving to keep things in a state of equilibrium and will use osmosis to dilute a concentrated solution, eg sea water, with a weaker solution such as freshwater, in an effort to balance the concentrations.

If we apply this process directly to marine fish, the weaker solution represents the fishes' bodily fluids and the stronger solution is the surrounding sea water. Water molecules will pass through the semi-permeable membrane

● *How does specific gravity (S.G.) change within the aquarium?*

... At any point where the saltwater interfaces with air, constant evaporation is taking place. However, only water molecules evaporate leaving the various salts behind to form an increasingly dense solution. It is essential, therefore, that top-up water must be freshwater (of appropriate quality) to redress the balance.

● *How can a steady specific gravity be maintained?*

This is generally achieved by using an accurate water level sensor; as the water level drops, a switch triggers a pump in a freshwater reservoir and replaces only the amount lost. In this way, specific gravity remains stable and illness-inducing stress on the osmo-regulatory systems of the livestock is reduced to an absolute minimum.

● *Would it be beneficial to reduce the specific gravity of aquarium water from 1.025 to 1.021?*

Yes. The higher the concentration of salts in the water, the harder the fish have to work to rid themselves of it owing to the increased intake of saltwater. If the salinity is lowered the metabolism of the fish is reduced with a consequent lowering of stress. Complete the task over a period of several weeks, allowing the metabolism of the fish to adjust slowly. Nearly all those species kept by the marine aquarist would be unhappy at a specific gravity of less than 1.018, or more than 1.028; 1.021 has proved to be a satisfactory universal level.

● *A newly introduced fish is lying on the bottom of the tank looking pale and breathing heavily, what has happened?*

The fish is suffering from an osmotic imbalance. Some fish adapt easily to rapid changes in salinity, while others become very distressed even when a long introductory period is observed. These fish should be left without disturbance, protected from other fish, and preferably with the tank lighting switched off. If in good health, the shocked fish will usually recover within 6–24 hours.

of the skin to dilute the sea water in a continuous process. Therefore, the marine fish has to drink saltwater constantly in an effort to replace that lost through osmosis, otherwise it would die of dehydration. As only the water is lost, this leaves a lot of salt in the body which is excreted through the kidneys and special cells in the gills.

This imbalance between the two fluids creates what is called osmotic pressure and the greater the salinity of the sea water, the greater the osmotic pressure within the fish, consequently, the harder the fish has to work to restore an osmotic balance.

Freshwater fish suffer the same osmotic imbalance but in reverse. The denser fluid is to be found within the fish and the less dense solution is the freshwater surrounding it. In this situation, the water molecules pass through the skin and into the denser bodily fluids causing the fish to excrete it at a high rate via the kidneys. The system used by either marine or freshwater fish to maintain an osmotic balance is called osmoregulation.

The Non-Conformists

Some fish species move effortlessly between freshwater and saltwater, well-known examples include salmon, flounders, scats and monos, as well as species of stickleback and goby. Certain species have developed special glands to excrete either salt or freshwater depending on which medium they happen to be swimming in at the time. Others have skins that are not semi-permeable and so the question of osmotic imbalance does not arise.

Brackish-water fish occupy an intermediate, often highly changeable environment, living neither totally in freshwater nor full-strength sea water. Most are quite happy moving between varying salinities in a short period of time, although relatively little is known about how their bodies cope.

◄ *The skin of a marine fish acts as a biologically active, semi-permeable membrane, transporting water molecules from inside the body to the denser saltwater surrounding it. In effect, it is nature's way of trying to dilute the ocean to achieve equilibrium!*

OSMOREGULATION IN MARINE FISH

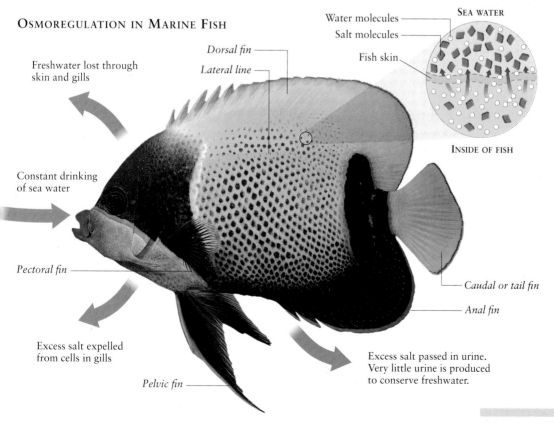

Water molecules
Salt molecules
SEA WATER
Fish skin

INSIDE OF FISH

Freshwater lost through skin and gills

Dorsal fin
Lateral line

Constant drinking of sea water

Pectoral fin

Caudal or tail fin

Anal fin

Excess salt expelled from cells in gills

Pelvic fin

Excess salt passed in urine. Very little urine is produced to conserve freshwater.

Surgeonfish (Tangs)

FAMILY: ACANTHURIDAE

SURGEONFISH, ALSO COMMONLY KNOWN AS tangs, are some of the most popular and widely available tropical marine fish on offer to the hobbyist.

They are easily distinguished from other fishes by an oval-shaped body with eyes set high up on a steeply rising forehead. The undulating dorsal and anal fins are mirror images of each other. In addition, there is a sharp, scalpel-like spine on each side of the caudal peduncle which may be erected and locked, providing an effective weapon in territorial disputes, or even against a careless aquarist. Hence the name Surgeonfish! Like many other coral reef fish, tangs come in a dazzling array of colour and patterning. Males and females are indistinguishable in most species.

In the wild, tangs may live in large and occasionally mixed shoals, grazing on the rocks and reefs for algae. As algae are generally found in areas of strong currents and highly oxygenated water, these fish are powerful swimmers used to battling tidal forces

The Powder Blue Tang (Acanthurus leucosternon) *is susceptible to whitespot and is best restricted to a fish-only aquarium.*

The Yellow Tang (Zebrasoma flavescens) *shoals naturally in the wild, but shoaling can only be replicated in the largest aquaria if serious fighting is to be avoided.*

while searching for food in niches denied to most other coral reef fish. Like athletes, they use the high levels of oxygen to keep strong muscles working efficiently.

Although most tangs shoal in large numbers, each individual requires its own feeding space and, temporarily, may establish a small territory. This trait continues in the aquarium

Tank Conditions and Care

HABITAT: Tangs are active fish that require plenty of swimming space. Access to night-time retreats toward the back of the tank is essential.

Tank size A tank of at least 4ft (120cm) in length and a volume of 45 gallons (205 l; 54 US gallons) gross.

pH	8.1–8.3
Temperature	25–26°C (77–79°F)
Ammonia	Zero
Nitrite	Zero
Nitrate	Less than 20ppm total NO_3
Specific Gravity	1.021–1.024
Dissolved Oxygen	6–7ppm

Water Changes 15–25% with high quality water every two weeks.

Filtration Efficient protein skimming and activated carbon filtration as standard.

Lighting An intensely-lit aquarium to encourage a good growth of macro- and micro-algae.

FEEDING: Once settled, tangs can be totally omnivorous, eating brineshrimp, mysis, squid and even flake foods. Their main diet is algae-based and this should be provided in abundance. If the aquarium is short of green algae, a good substitute is lettuce or spinach that has been dipped in boiling water for a few seconds to break down the cellulose content that the fish find indigestible.

HEALTH: Tangs are prone to *Oodinium* and whitespot, as well as some viral diseases such as Head and Lateral Line Erosion. These diseases are common with overstocking or where water quality is poor due to irregular maintenance.

Q&A

● *Are surgeonfish suitable for the beginner?*

... In many cases, yes. But they need the very highest quality stable water conditions, plenty of swimming space and a good supply of algae and suitable green foods. They tend to do much better in a well established aquarium, rather than a freshly matured one.

● *Do surgeonfish have any unexpected behaviour patterns?*

When newly introduced into an aquarium, a specimen may rest on its side and look very distressed. This is not uncommon and passes quite quickly. Darken the tank to prevent other fish from bothering it. To keep stress levels to a minimum, it is best to introduce tangs to their new home very slowly over a period of up to 40 minutes with all the lights off.

● *Are tangs suitable for the invertebrate tank?*

Owing to their susceptibility to disease, no. The most effective remedies for such diseases are copper-based, and lethal to invertebrates. Also, most invertebrate tanks have very little swimming space, and this may cause unnecessary stress.

● *Why are some tangs seen on sale with hollow, pinched-in bellies?*

Fish are not fed prior to being shipped to prevent them from fouling their travelling water. On arrival at their destination reputable importers will quarantine the fish for several weeks during which time they will be fed properly, and treated for any diseases. Fish that are not quarantined but put on sale immediately will not have a chance to recover and will be in poor condition with hollow stomachs and pale coloration. It would be very unwise to purchase any of these specimens.

environment and may lead to friction. As a general rule, only one specimen should be kept in a tank of 48in (120cm) or less. Juvenile Regal Tangs (*Paracanthurus hepatus*) may share the same aquarium but, even then, serious disputes may break out as the fish grow and space is at a premium. Despite this, tangs make excellent community fish when kept with other species of about the same size; they are generally peaceful and graze the rockwork taking little notice of tankmates.

As far as we know, all tangs are group spawners. A shoal may migrate to a particular spot on the reef, usually in the late afternoon, where the currents are deemed favourable, and individuals or small groups will dash vertically into the water column scattering eggs and sperm as they ascend. The fertilized eggs are epipelagic (floating) and join the plankton layer where they hatch. Development is slow and it may be months before the juveniles descend to join a shoal of the same species.

Surgeonfish are rarely bred in captivity, although some public aquaria and a few hobbyists with very large tanks have reported successful spawnings. So far, no fry have been reared to adulthood.

▲ *The Regal Tang* (Paracanthurus hepatus) *is one of the most stunning reef fish suitable for the marine aquarium, but high-quality water is essential.*

Popular Species of Surgeonfish and Tangs

maximum adult size

Yellow Tang 6in (15cm)
Zebrasoma flavescens
A brilliant yellow fish sometimes confused with a juvenile Blue Tang (*Acanthurus coeruleus*), which has additional blue markings around the eye and blue edging to the dorsal and anal fins.

Sailfin Tang 8in (20cm)
Zebrasoma veliferum
Body colour is brown with vertical stripes. Characterized by large sail-like dorsal fin.

Emperor Tang 8in (20cm)
Zebrasoma xanthurum
Colour ranges from purple to brown with a bright yellow caudal fin.

Regal Tang 4in (10cm)
Paracanthurus hepatus
Deep blue with black and yellow markings.

Lipstick Tang 10in (25cm)
Naso lituratus
Marked with red/orange around the lip area.

Pyjama Tang 6in (15cm)
Acanthurus lineatus
Marked with a striped pattern of yellow, blue and black. Peaceful and fairly easy to keep.

Powder Blue Tang may exceed 8in (20cm)
Acanthurus leucosternon
Light to royal blue, black face, yellow dorsal and white anal fin. Needs a large tank.

Achilles Tang 8in (20cm)
Acanthurus achilles
Brown body with red markings on caudal fin and caudal peduncle. Needs excellent conditions.

Goldrim Tang/ 8in (20cm)
Powder Brown Tang
Acanthurus glaucopareius
White cheeks with a yellow bar across the caudal fin and blue-edged dorsal and anal fins.

Zebra Tang 7in (17.5cm)
Acanthurus sohal
A rare and striking fish, with a blue and black striped body and orange scalpels.

Cardinalfish FAMILY: APOGONIDAE

CARDINALFISH BELONG TO A LARGE FAMILY, which includes approximately 200 species. Practically all make good aquarium fish, but only a few species are routinely imported; the Pyjama Cardinal *(Sphaeramia nematopterus)* and the Flame Cardinal *(Apogon maculatus)* are most often available from dealers.

They are easy to recognize as they have two separate dorsal fins held proud of the body at all times. Being nocturnal, they have large eyes to assist in locating their planktonic prey. However, they adapt well to the relative brightness of the aquarium.

Cardinals are mouth brooders. The fertilized eggs are held in their distended mouth for safety until the fry are ready to hatch, at which point they are released. Incubation may either be the task of the male, female or shared, depending on the species.

Most cardinalfish are not difficult to keep and are ideal for the beginner and experienced hobbyist alike. Although they will live as individuals, they are shoaling fish, so it is kinder to introduce them to the aquarium in small groups. Even in these restricted conditions, cardinals are peaceful fish although they are often not afraid to stand their ground when threatened by bullies of a similar size!

Tank Conditions and Care

HABITAT: The tank can be fish-only or mixed fish/invertebrate. For water conditions see Dwarf Angelfish page 116.

Tank size The smallest tank to consider would be 36in (90cm) in length and 25 gallons (114 l; 30 US gallons) gross volume.

FEEDING: Cardinals will generally accept all the usual marine fare, brineshrimp, lobster eggs, plankton, small pieces of mussel, squid and cockle. However, some individuals may refuse flake and other dried foods.

HEALTH: Cardinals are very disease-resistant.

 Pyjama cardinals (Sphaeramia nematopterus) *are much underrated fish owing to their largely inactive nature and relatively subdued colours.*

Q&A

● *Are cardinalfish suitable for the fish-invertebrate aquarium?*

... Yes, they will do no harm to invertebrates or algae.

● *Is it normal for cardinals to prefer the darker areas of the aquarium?*

Yes. It is a good idea to provide a part of the tank which has more subdued lighting particularly for the cardinals.

● *I want to make up a shoal of cardinals, how many should I choose?*

As a good general guide, choose one fish for every 12in (30cm) of aquarium length. So, if you have a 36in (90cm) aquarium, three specimens will be ideal; likewise five would do very well in a 60in (150cm) tank. To prevent any initial disputes, choose the smallest juveniles available and introduce the whole shoal into the tank all at once.

● *Will cardinals breed in the aquarium?*

Breeding is not common in captivity and, to date, very few fry have been raised to maturity.

Triggerfish

FAMILY: BALISTIDAE

TRIGGERFISH HAVE AN UNUSUAL BODY SHAPE, similar to an elongated diamond, and a range of colours and patterns from the dull to the outrageously gaudy. The dorsal fin is unique for a number of reasons. It can be carried flat within a groove in the body, totally concealing it, but it can also be raised and locked into place. This feature, the source of its common name, enables the fish to lock itself within a crevice, protecting it from predators.

The undulating motions of the rear dorsal and anal fins make triggerfish fascinating to observe. The pelvic fins have all but disappeared in most species, although a rudimentary stub may remain. Although they are not particularly strong swimmers, they are very manoeuvrable, swimming backwards to reverse into safe crevices while keeping a watchful eye on the world outside.

Triggerfish have powerful jaws and teeth, giving their prey – crabs, shrimps, sea urchins and starfish – little chance of escape. Crab shells and shrimp exoskeletons are crushed with ease; the triggerfish blow jets of water at urchins and starfish until they are dislodged onto their backs, exposing the soft body parts to be eaten.

Popular Species of Triggerfish

	maximum adult size
Undulate Trigger	8–12in (20–30cm)

Balistapus undulatus
A colourful but very aggressive species that will often require an aquarium on its own and can become very tame.

Bursa Trigger	6in (15cm)

Balistes bursa
An interesting smaller species, but it is not very colourful and can be aggressive.

Queen Trigger	10in (25cm)

Balistes vetula
A popular aquarium fish that is not as aggressive as some of its cousins.

Clown Trigger	10–12in (25–30cm)

Balistoides conspicillum
An expensive and much sought after fish owing to its beautiful markings.

Black Trigger	10in (25cm)

Odonus niger
May be rather dull to look at, but its peaceful nature makes it a good community fish.

Picasso Trigger	9–12in (22.5–30cm)

Rhinecanthus aculeatus
As bizarre and colourful as the name suggests! However, it can be very aggressive and needs to be kept with larger species.

Tank Conditions and Care

HABITAT: A fish-only system is essential as triggerfish will destroy any invertebrate neighbours.

Tank Size A 36in (90cm) tank could house one juvenile. An intermediate specimen would require an aquarium at least 48x18x15in (122x46x38cm). Mature triggerfish will need a minimum volume of 100 gallons (455 l; 120 US gallons).

pH	8.0–8.3
Temperature	25–26°C (77–79°F)
Ammonia	Zero
Nitrite	Zero

Nitrate Will tolerate 50ppm total NO_3 but much less is preferable.

Specific Gravity	1.021–1.024
Water Changes	20–25% every two weeks

Filtration Efficient protein skimming and activated carbon filtration as standard.

Lighting Will tolerate dim to highly illuminated conditions.

FEEDING: Triggerfish have insatiable appetites and will eat almost any live or frozen marine fare. Shrimp, crab meat, mussel, cockle, squid and all other substantial foods are eaten with relish. Take care not to overfeed.

HEALTH: They are extremely disease-resistant.

 A mated pair of Clown Triggerfish (Balistoides conspicillum) *living peacefully together is a very rare sight in the home aquarium. A single specimen is a safer option.*

In the wild, some triggerfish grow in excess of 20in (50cm); aquarium specimens reaching half that length. They are extremely territorial, and only one specimen should be kept per aquarium, or they may fight to the death. Fortunately, most triggerfish can be housed with larger fish quite successfully. Large angelfish, groupers, grunts, lionfish, rabbitfish, large wrasse and moray eels all prove ideal tankmates. However, triggerfish are known for their individual temperaments and there are no guaranteed suitable companions. Communities to include triggers are best made up of juveniles that can grow up together. Mature specimens are difficult to introduce peacefully.

Q&A...

● *Can triggerfish be recommended to newcomers?*

Triggerfish are relatively easy to keep and will tolerate less than perfect water conditions. However, this comparative toughness is reflected in a temperament that varies from irritable to highly pugnacious, depending on the species.

● *Can I keep them with invertebrates?*

No. Nothing is safe from their powerful jaws, a fish-only tank is essential.

● *Apart from being aggressive, do triggerfish have any other bad habits?*

Some specimens move sand and gravel around the tank and may even bite through airlines or electrical cables. Watch new fish for unsocial or dangerous behaviour. Take care if feeding by hand as they can inflict a nasty bite.

Filefish

FAMILY: BALISTIDAE
SUBFAMILY: MONACANTHIDAE

IF YOU HAVE EVER CONFUSED A FILEFISH WITH a triggerfish then you can be forgiven for the mistake since the two families are so closely related that some taxonomists think they should be regarded as one. Scientific arguments aside, closer examination will reveal that filefish are subtly distinctive fish. Their scales are rough and coarse to the touch, hence the popular names "file" fish or leatherjacket. A dorsal spine is usually carried erect and may be accompanied by a small second spine; the third, locking spine, characteristic of the triggerfish is missing. Although filefish do have teeth, they are unlike the sharper teeth of the triggerfish in that they are more suited to nibbling and browsing than crushing hard material.

Blending into the Background

Compared with many other coral reef fish, the filefish family is composed of unobtrusive species that hold little or no appeal for the aquarist in search of bold, striking colours and patterns. A rare exception is the Long-Nosed Filefish *(Oxymonacanthus longirostris)* with its bright orange spots set on a turquoise background. Unfortunately, most specimens rarely survive long in captivity either due to a refusal to feed or, possibly, because of the lack of an unidentified nutritional element in their diet. Another unusual species is the Tassel Filefish *(Chaetoderma pencilligera)* whose feathery appearance provides camouflage among the floating seaweeds of its natural home in the Indo-Pacific regions.

Filefish, unlike their triggerfish cousins, are nearly always peaceful and well-behaved in the community fish-only tank, and do well with other restrained species. Little is known about their breeding habits, and although some authorities claim to have noted sexual differences, these observations have yet to be confirmed.

Tank Conditions and Care

HABITAT: For tank and water conditions see Triggerfish page 84.

FEEDING: Any meaty marine fare – cockle, prawn, brineshrimp, mussel, squid, krill, mysis.

HEALTH: This family is very disease resistant, especially where water quality remains high.

● *Are filefish suitable for less experienced hobbyists?*

... Apart from Long-Nosed Filefish, rarely seen in the aquarium trade, the members of this family can be recommended as excellent aquarium subjects for the beginner.

● *How large do filefish grow?*

Depending on the species, filefish can be expected to attain 6–10in (15–25cm) in the aquarium under optimum conditions.

● *Are filefish suited to the invertebrate aquarium?*

No, they are not to be trusted. In the wild their natural diet is coral polyps.

● *Can I keep more than one filefish in a tank?*

Unless the tank is very large, it is best just to keep one in any collection.

● *Can you suggest a few suitable species?*

The Tassel Filefish (*Chaetoderma pencilligera*), the Red-Tailed Filefish (*Pervagor melanocephalus*), and the Filefish (*Monacanthus chinensis*). The most popular of these, the Tassel Filefish, grows to 7in (18cm) or more, and will need a large tank.

➤ *The Tassel Filefish* (Chaetoderma pencilligera) *is a much underrated species and the enthusiastic fishkeeper will appreciate its peaceful disposition and other desirable attributes.*

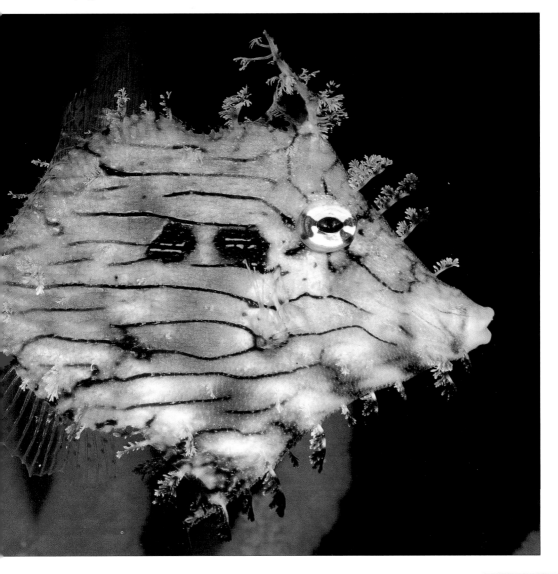

Blennies FAMILY: BLENNIIDAE

BLENNIES ARE FOUND ALL OVER THE WORLD, inhabiting temperate, sub-tropical and tropical waters. There are over 300 species in the family Blenniidae. Most of those suitable for the domestic aquarium are easily accommodated as the largest rarely reach 4in (10cm).

Blennies are nearly all bottom-dwellers and like to occupy a cave or burrow for protection. They tend to rest on horizontal surfaces where they can get a good view of the surrounding area. Their ability to move each eye independently makes it easier for them to spot predators and then escape from the vantage point to the safety of a burrow or crevice. Exceptions to this behaviour pattern include Scooter Blenny (*Petroscirtes temmincki*) and Sabre-Toothed Blenny (*Aspidontus taeniatus*). The Scooter Blenny's body is heavily camouflaged and freezes at any perceived threat. The

▲ *The male Scooter Blenny* (Petroscirtes temmincki) *uses its dorsal fin to flash at others of its own species as a way of communicating.*

Sabre-Toothed Blenny is free-swimming and mimics the coloration of the Cleaner Wrasse (*Labroides dimidiatus*). Once it has gained the confidence of another fish (which expects to be cleaned of parasites) the Sabre-Toothed Blenny tears off a piece of flesh instead, earning its nickname, the False Cleaner Wrasse!

Anyone intending to purchase a Cleaner Wrasse should ensure that its dangerous impersonator is not purchased by mistake (though it is rarely imported deliberately). The Sabre-Toothed Blenny is identified by its shark-like underslung mouth and is generally not as brightly coloured as a Cleaner Wrasse.

The Blenniidae is a relatively large family

Tank Conditions and Care

HABITAT: Most blennies flourish in the reef aquarium as well as in fish-only systems

Tank size	An aquarium of 25 gallons (114 l; 30 US gallons) or more would be fine.
pH	8.1–8.3
Temperature	25–26°C (77–79°F)
Ammonia	Zero
Nitrite	Zero
Nitrate	25ppm total NO_3 – lower if possible
Specific Gravity	1.020–1.024
Dissolved Oxygen	6–7ppm
Water Changes	15–20% every two weeks

Filtration Efficient protein skimming and activated carbon filtration as standard.

Lighting Moderate to brightly lit aquaria are tolerated well. Good water circulation is appreciated.

FEEDING: Nearly all blennies will readily take frozen or live brineshrimp as well as other finely chopped pieces of marine fare. Some fish will even eagerly take marine flake.

HEALTH: Although capable of contracting all the common marine diseases and ailments, blennies tend to suffer less than most fish species, making them excellent choices for all marine hobbyists.

▼ *The Midas Blenny* (Ecsenius midas) *is typical of the majority of blennies in its appearance and behaviour. This species needs plenty of small caves in which to hide.*

and species include substrate browsers as well as algae eaters and planktonic feeders. The latter are by far the largest group. They perch on a convenient outcrop and dart out for any tasty morsel that might drift by. Most blennies spawn in a cave or burrow. The males generally assume responsibility for guarding the eggs until they hatch. Subsequently, the larvae make their way into the surface plankton layers until they are large enough to descend to a niche on the sea floor.

Suitable blennies for the marine aquarium include: Bicolor Blenny (*Ecsenius bicolor*); Midas Blenny (*Ecsenius midas*); Redlip Blenny (*Ophioblennius atlanticus*); Banded Blenny (*Salarias fasciatus*); Scooter Blenny; Smith's Blenny (*Meiacanthus smithii*); Forktail Blenny (*M. atrodorsalis*); and Oualan Forktail Blenny (*M. oualanensis*).

● *Are blennies recommended for the beginner?*

... Yes, they are ideal for beginners, being some of the easiest fish to keep in a marine aquarium.

● *Can I keep more than one species of blenny together in the same tank?*

Most species of blenny are highly territorial and generally will not tolerate their own, or a similar species, in the confines of a domestic aquarium.

● *Should the aquarium be decorated in any special way to accommodate blennies?*

Yes. There should be plenty of rockwork, built up to provide high vantage points. Large barnacle shells are ideal for blennies to retreat into.

● *Do blennies get on with other fish?*

Invariably yes. Although blennies are inquisitive fish, they nearly always get on well with other species that will not be a threat to them.

● *Are they compatible with invertebrates?*

Blennies do no harm to sessile or other invertebrates. Indeed, some species (including the Scooter Blenny) will actually improve conditions for invertebrates by controlling plagues of smaller marine pests that might otherwise bother sedentary invertebrates.

● *Is breeding possible?*

A male and female pair will sometimes spawn in the cover of a barnacle shell. However, the fry are extremely difficult to rear, even though professional breeders have tried for some time.

Mandarinfish FAMILY: CALLIONYMIDAE

MANDARINS AND DRAGONETS FORM A SMALL family of bottom-dwelling fishes that are represented in all the world's oceans, tropical and temperate. Just two species of mandarins are greatly prized in the aquarium trade – Psychedelic Fish (*Synchiropus picturatus*) and Mandarinfish (*S. splendidus*).

Presented against a plain background, their colour and patterning would appear blatantly eye-catching, but in their natural habitat of mixed algae growths, the fish are ideally camouflaged. Due to their need to be camouflaged at all times, mandarins are rarely found on coral reefs and prefer warm tropical lagoons or surge zones (areas of high turbulence, for example a gap in a coral wall where the water surges through) overgrown with algae. Favourite foods include small crustaceans, micro-organisms, marine worms and some algae; all of which are consumed in a combined pecking/sucking action. Unwanted material is expelled through the gills.

Mandarins produce pelagic eggs that float in the plankton layers, hatch and develop before descending back to a suitable sea-floor habitat as juvenile fish. Mating is a gentle and graceful affair with both male and female rising in the water column, abdomen to abdomen. As the female releases her eggs, the male can be sure of efficient fertilization. Mating may take place with the same pair every evening at twilight for many months.

Tank Conditions and Care

HABITAT: A well-established invertebrate aquarium or a quiet fish-only tank that houses only seahorses, small blennies and gobies.

Tank size The smallest tank to consider would be 36in (90cm) in length and 25 gallons (114 l; 30 US gallons) gross volume.	
pH	8.1–8.3
Temperature	25–26°C (77–79°F)
Ammonia	Zero
Nitrite	Zero
Nitrate Will tolerate 25ppm total NO3 but levels should be as low as possible.	
Specific Gravity	1.021–1.025
Dissolved Oxygen	6–7ppm
Water Changes	15–20% every two weeks
Lighting Mandarins prefer the shadier areas of the aquarium.	
Water Circulation Good circulation is essential	

FEEDING: Feed mandarins regularly on live brineshrimp and rotifers. Small frozen foods are often taken as well. Extra feeding is especially important where specimens are introduced into an unestablished aquarium.

HEALTH: Mandarins are normally healthy, given good water conditions in an established aquarium.

● *Is it easy to tell the difference between males and females?*

Q&A ... Yes. The male has an extended first dorsal ray.

● *Can a pair be kept together?*

A male and female will often get on quite well together in a reasonably roomy aquarium and may even mate on a regular basis. However, keeping more than one mandarin of the same sex – particularly males – in an aquarium usually results in vicious fighting and serious injuries to both parties, and so is best avoided.

● *On transporting a mandarin home, the water was full of a clear, slimy substance. What is it?*

When under stress, mandarins shed their mucus coating. The slime is noxious to other fish and in the wild is used as a deterrent to predators. Therefore, avoid any rough treatment and never introduce them into an aquarium where they are likely to be bullied or pursued.

● *Should a tank housing mandarins be covered?*

Yes. When startled or in the throes of mating, mandarins can leap from the water.

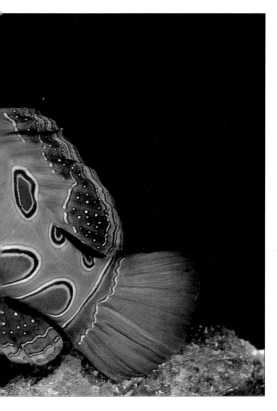

This beautifully marked Mandarinfish (Synchiropus splendidus) can easily be identified as a male owing to its extended first dorsal ray.

● *Some specimens have noticeably pinched-in flanks. Is this normal?*

No, this particular condition indicates that the fish has not eaten for some time and even though it may have recently begun feeding, it will take quite a while to regain a healthy, plump appearance, given the correct food. Fish seen in this condition are best shunned as the mortality rate is high.

● *Will a mandarin eat nuisance flatworms?*

Although there have been one or two reports of mandarins eating these flatworms, the majority will not consume them.

● *Given the choice between some very large and very small specimens, which would be best for an average tank?*

On the whole, smaller specimens definitely do better than larger ones. Individuals of 3–4in (7.5–10cm) may be suited to a very well established invertebrate aquarium in excess of 72in (180cm), but usually they cannot locate enough food to survive for long periods.

The Psychedelic Fish (Synchiropus picturatus) is not quite so readily available as its relative (S. splendidus), but nevertheless makes a fine colourful addition to a well established reef aquarium.

Butterflyfish

FAMILY: CHAETODONTIDAE

BUTTERFLYFISH … JUST THE NAME CONJURES UP pictures of delicate and beautifully coloured creatures flitting around the underwater coral garden. Although they are often confused with angelfish, closer observation will reveal the lack of a spine on the lower part of the gill cover. More subtle differences include a more ovate body shape, and a longer or very extended snout, ideal for probing deep into coral recesses in search of small crustaceans, marine worms and polyps. The snouts of some species are so well developed that in the case of the Long-Nosed Butterfly (*Forcipiger longirostris*) it accounts for roughly one third of the total length of the fish.

In the wild, butterflyfish form strong pair bonds and individual species will commonly defend large territories. This pairing behaviour is hardly ever carried over into the aquarium environment; however members of the same or very similar species may fight to the death if kept in the same aquarium. Some exceptions include *Heniochus acuminatus*, commonly known as Wimplefish; which although similar to Moorish Idol (*Zanclus canescens*) is much easier to keep.

Most butterflyfish are spectacularly marked and many possess a black spot on the dorsal or anal fin, while the real eye is camouflaged. The false eye spot confuses potential predators, which usually attack the eye in the first instance, and the butterflyfish escapes with nothing more serious than a torn fin.

These are not fish for beginners, but some species are relatively easy for the fishkeeper with some experience. They include such species (with maximum sizes) as: Dot-Dash Butterfly (*Chaetodon punctatofasciatus*) 4in (10cm); Sunburst Butterfly (*C. kleini*) 4in (10cm); Raccoon Butterfly (*C. lunula*) 6in (15cm); Vagabond Butterfly (*C. vagabundus*) 8in (20cm); Pakistani Butterfly (*C. collare*) 4in (10cm); Black Pyramid Butterflyfish

● *Can butterflyfish be kept with invertebrates?*

… No. Almost without exception these fish will consume or damage most invertebrates available to them in the aquarium.

● *Is it possible to keep various species of butterflyfish in the same tank?*

Species with very unlike markings and coloration will share an aquarium if it is large enough and if they are all introduced before any one species can become too territorial. This is best attempted by only the most experienced hobbyists.

● *Are butterflyfish suitable candidates for the fish-only community tank?*

Yes, as long as the tankmates are compatible and optimum water quality can be maintained. Many butterflyfish, once established, can hold their own with most other marine fish of a similar size. However, do not keep them with fish that might nip their fins.

● *Is it better to introduce butterflyfish into a freshly matured tank?*

No. It would be far safer to introduce butterflyfish into a well established tank as water quality is likely to be far more stable.

● *What should be done if butterflyfish lose their colour and adopt a blotchy pattern at night?*

Do nothing. This is natural night-time coloration. Many marine fish alter their colour and patterning at night to become less conspicuous as they blend in with their surroundings.

● *Is it possible to breed butterflyfish in captivity?*

So far, no. The breeding record with this family of fish is very poor indeed.

▶ *A shoal of Addis Butterflyfish* (Chaetodon semilarvatus) *in their natural Red Sea habitat. This peaceful shoaling behaviour is not carried over into the domestic aquarium.*

(*Hemitaurichthys zoster*) 6in (15cm); Wimplefish (*Heniochus acuminatus*) 7in (18cm); Long-Nosed Butterflyfish (*Forcipiger flavissimus*) 5in (12.5cm).

The following are classified as difficult to keep but possible with great care by an experienced marinist: Addis Butterfly (*Chaetodon semilarvatus*) 8in (20cm); Threadfin Butterfly (*C. auriga*) 6in (15cm); Falcula Butterfly (*C. falcula*) 5in (12.5cm); Copperband Butterfly (*Chelmon rostratus*) 6in (15cm).

Many species of butterflyfish do not do well in the aquarium and last only a few months. This is due to a reluctance to feed on standard aquarium food and their unusually high sensitivity to anything but superb water conditions: Meyer's Butterfly (*Chaetodon meyeri*); Eight-Banded Butterfly (*C. octofasciatus*); Ornate Butterfly (*C. ornatissimus*); Chevron Butterfly (*C. trifascialis*); Rainbow Butterfly (*C. trifasciatus*); Goldrim Butterfly (*C. xanthocephalus*). In recent years, most reputable importers and exporters are aware of the problems and have voluntarily banned these fish from the aquarium trade. However, less responsible sources will supply traders.

Tank Conditions and Care

HABITAT: There should be plenty of rockwork for hiding in and an adequate swimming area.

Tank size	48 x 15 x 18in (122 x 38 x 46cm) min.
pH	8.1–8.3
Temperature	25–26°C (77–79°F)
Ammonia	Zero
Nitrite	Zero
Nitrate	Less than 10ppm total NO_3 at all times
Specific Gravity	1.021–1.024
Dissolved Oxygen	6–7ppm
Water Changes	15–25% every two weeks is essential, using high quality nitrate-free water.
Filtration	Efficient filtration with protein skimming and activated carbon as standard.
Lighting	Medium to bright illumination

FEEDING: Many butterflyfish will accept the usual frozen and live marine fare such as brineshrimp, mysis, lobster eggs, sponge-based foods and small pieces of squid. Occasionally they may take marine flake food.

HEALTH: Butterflyfish are extremely sensitive to parasites, bacterial infections and other diseases brought about by poor environmental conditions and usually succumb very quickly.

Porcupinefish   FAMILY: DIODONTIDAE

WIDELY DISTRIBUTED THROUGHOUT THE tropical and temperate seas of the world, porcupinefish are generally larger than their cousins the pufferfish (page 134) with some specimens exceeding 36in (90cm).

Diodontids possess single fused incisor teeth in each jaw, and use them to crack the hard shells of crustaceans, their favourite food. Their scales have become modified into spines that may be held against the body and projected when the fish is threatened, or projected permanently, depending on the species. The spines make a formidable defence against the most determined predator, especially when the fish draws in water and puffs itself up much larger than its normal size.

In addition, porcupinefish have one final safeguard – a poisonous mucus that can be shed into the water. Enemies taking an unhealthy interest in a porcupinefish are soon deterred by the taste of a foul substance in the water. Unfortunately, this characteristic can be carried over to the confines of the aquarium where the results can be catastrophic!

● *Are porcupinefish suitable for the invertebrate aquarium?*

... No, they are very destructive and are best kept in a fish-only tank.

● *Do porcupinefish make good community fish?*

Yes, but only with fish of a similar size and a peaceful nature. Inflating in reaction to extreme aggression is very stressful for the fish.

● *Can two, or more, porcupinefish be housed together?*

In the confines of a normal domestic aquarium, they will normally fight. Similar fish, such as puffers and boxfish, should not be introduced into the same tank.

● *What should be done if poisonous mucus is shed into the aquarium?*

Remove the porcupinefish to another vessel or vacant aquarium and perform a 100% water change; install fresh activated carbon. The toxin takes effect very quickly, so the aquarist must be swift to prevent the total loss of all fish. Thankfully the shedding of mucus is not a common occurrence.

● *If the fish has to be netted and inflates with air, what should be done?*

Once inflated with air, porcupinefish will float on the surface of the water with gills exposed. If left long enough, the specimen will eventually suffocate. If netted carefully and gently, this scenario should not happen; however, if it does, gently tip the tail up so that the face of the fish is underwater. Porcupinefish do not like being inflated and will deflate at the earliest opportunity. Therefore, if its face is below water and there is no other conceived threat, it should deflate quite quickly and swim off.

● *Can porcupinefish breed successfully in captivity?*

This is unlikely. Reports of aquarium spawnings are rare and so far no larvae have been reared to adulthood.

Popular Species of Porcupinefish

	maximum adult size
Spiny Boxfish *Chilomycterus schoepfi* An attractive fish less inclined to inflate than other species.	12in (30cm)
Bridled Burrfish *Chilomycterus antennatus* A very peaceful fish, not difficult to keep.	6in (15cm)
Long-Spined Porcupinefish *Diodon holocanthus*	9in (22.5cm)
Common Porcupinefish *Diodon hystrix*	12in (30cm)
Masked Burrfish *Diodon liturosus* Could outgrow all but the largest aquarium and may be beyond the scope of the average fishkeeper.	20in (50cm)

The Spiny Boxfish (Chilomycterus schoepfi) fully inflated (left) and in its normal state (below). It is not a good idea to encourage a porcupinefish to inflate as it puts undue stress upon the fish and could well be considered cruel. It also teaches the fish to become a frightened animal rather than a relaxed, tame one. All porcupinefish are capable of inflicting a painful bite, especially when being fed by hand. It is best to use aquarium tongs to offer food.

Tank Conditions and Care

HABITAT: Rockwork is unnecessary, the more swimming space the better.

Tank size A reasonable guide to a suitably sized aquarium would be a 100 gallon (455 l; 120 US gallon) tank for a 9in (22.5cm) specimen.

pH	8.1–8.3
Temperature	25-26°C (77–79°F)
Ammonia	Zero
Nitrite	Zero

Nitrate 25ppm total N0₃ may be tolerated but much less is preferable.

Specific Gravity	1.021–1.024
Water Changes	15–25% every two weeks

Filtration Efficient filtration is essential owing to the amount of food consumed. A good protein skimmer and activated carbon must be used as standard.

Lighting Porcupinefish will tolerate subdued, moderate, or bright lighting.

FEEDING: Molluscs are greedily taken, especially if they still possess their shell. Opening the shell to extract the meat wears down their constantly growing teeth. In addition, all meaty marine fare such as shrimps, squid, lancefish, crab and lobster are readily accepted. Feed using aquarium tongs.

HEALTH: Diodontids are relatively resistant to disease. However, poor water quality often leads to eye infections whereby one or both eyes appear cloudy. If conditions are not improved, permanent blindness can result.

Hawkfish FAMILY: CIRRHITIDAE

● *Can I trust hawkfish in the invertebrate aquarium?*

... They may eat shrimps and other crustaceans and can even be tempted to eat cleaner shrimps. They will also perch on the branches of gorgonians, possibly causing damage.

● *Do hawkfish have any worrying habits?*

They have a tendency to jump out of the water. If the tank is not covered this could prove to be fatal!

● *Should I provide any special conditions?*

Yes, as hawkfish love to perch on high vantage points, several cured sea whips and sea fans should be provided for the purpose close to the top of the tank.

Tank Conditions and Care

HABITAT: For water and tank conditions see Dwarf Angelfish page 116.

FEEDING: Hawkfish are greedy fish – mysis, brineshrimp, live river shrimp, prawns, cockles, mussels, squid, krill and marine flake are all eagerly accepted.

HEALTH: Given proper water conditions, hawkfish are very disease-resistant.

▼ *The Long-Nosed Hawkfish* (Oxycirrhites typus) *is an opportunist predator with keen eyes and a large mouth!*

HAWKFISH ARE APTLY NAMED, PERCHING ON a high vantage point and swooping down on their prey. Many of the larger hawkfish, a few exceed 20in (50cm), enjoy a diet of small fish, while their smaller relations are very fond of shrimps and other crustaceans. Lacking a fully developed swim bladder, hawkfish tend to dash from one location to another, then sit motionless for long periods of time.

The pectoral fins have developed long and thickened rays, enabling the fish to perch firmly rather than being swept away by the current. In this position, their bodies sway from side to side in a comical fashion.

Most hawkfish exhibit no external sexual differences and, while it is known that they lay demersal (sinking) eggs, reproduction in captivity is very rare. Hawkfish are suitable for both beginners and experienced hobbyists alike. Unless you have a large aquarium, keep only one specimen as there is a likelihood of fighting if they are not a mated pair. Some specimens worth noting are Scarlet Hawkfish *(Neocirrhites armatus)*, Long-Nosed Hawkfish *(Oxycirrhites typus)*, Arc-Eye Hawkfish *(Paracirrhites arcatus)* and Spotted Hawkfish *(Cirrhitichthys oxycephalus)*.

Batfish FAMILY: EPHIPPIDAE

THE BATFISH IS UNMISTAKABLE, IF NOT IN colour, then certainly in shape. Their oval bodies and high fins have led to the nickname "discus of the sea". There are four species within the genus *Platax*, all found in the tropical regions of the Indo-Pacific. The Common Batfish *(Platax orbicularis)* and Red-Faced Batfish *(P. pinnatus)* are the two species most frequently imported, while Long-Finned Batfish *(P. tiera)* and Marbled Batfish *(P. batavianus)* are rarely seen even though they make fine aquarium subjects.

One feature shared by all four species is that they spend their juvenile lives in areas of mangrove, mimicking the coloration of dead mangrove leaves for protection. They feed on plankton and crustaceans, and are especially fond of jellyfish. Growth is rapid on this rich diet and most species reach 20in (50cm). So far, very little is known about their reproductive behaviour and experts have found no external sexual differences.

▲ *The Red-Faced Batfish* (Platax pinnatus).

● *Are batfish compatible with invertebrates?*

... Only when small (up to 2in). As they grow, the urge to nibble at invertebrates becomes stronger and eventually they can be extremely destructive.

● *Are batfish easy to keep?*

The Common Batfish *(P. orbicularis)* is quite easy and suitable for a beginner. The Red-Faced Batfish *(P. pinnatus)* is difficult and best left to experienced fishkeepers. The two remaining rarer species fall somewhere between the first two in terms of difficulty.

● *Are batfish compatible with their own kind, and other fish?*

Although they may be seen in large shoals in the wild, only single specimens may be kept in an aquarium if aggression is to be avoided. Batfish are peaceful with other species but avoid housing them with boisterous fish or those likely to nip fins.

Tank Conditions and Care

HABITAT: For water conditions see Porcupinefish page 95.

Tank size All batfish will require a large aquarium eventually! Mature specimens can grow to 18in (45cm) demanding plenty of swimming space and a minimum tank size of 72x24x24in (183x61x61cm).

Lighting Subdued to moderate illumination would be ideal.

FEEDING: Batfish can be fussy feeders, especially Red-Faced Batfish, which, when first imported, may only eat live brineshrimp. Once feeding, all species of *Platax* will accept frozen marine food. Try brineshrimp, mysis, squid, lobster eggs and shellmeat.

HEALTH: If the tank is too small, or the fish is subject to harassment, or if water conditions have deteriorated, batfish will succumb to whitespot and *Oodinium*.

Gobies FAMILY: GOBIIDAE

THIS EXTREMELY LARGE FAMILY (OVER 1,500 species) contains some of the most adaptable fish available to the aquarist. Gobies live in freshwater, brackish and marine environments. Some, such as the Neon Goby *(Gobiosoma oceanops)* have become cleaner fish while others have formed symbiotic bonds with invertebrates. Perhaps the best known of this group are those sharing a burrow with shrimps. The goby stands guard while the poor-sighted shrimp excavates their shared home. At the first sign of danger, the watchful goby disappears into the burrow, alerting the shrimp. Other species share burrows with a mate. If territories are established, they are usually quite small.

Many people confuse gobies with blennies. In nearly all cases, the goby is easily distinguished as it has fused pelvic fins forming a sucker-like disc which can be used to cling to vertical or smooth surfaces, allowing them to live in areas of high turbulence. Some gobies appear to have the usual two pelvic fins instead of this suction disc, but closer inspection reveals that the fins are indeed joined closer to the base. Unlike blennies nearly all species have two separate dorsal fins.

Habits and Behaviour
Gobies do not have a swim bladder and spend much of their time resting in a stationary position. Swimming excursions into open water are brief and jerky, mostly in the pursuit of small morsels of food drifting in the current. This is typical goby feeding behaviour, taking advantage of any passing food opportunity but not actually pursuing anything beyond the limits of safety.

Sexual differences are obvious in some species; for example, the Catalina Goby *(Lythrypnus dalli)* male has an extended first dorsal ray which is absent in the female. Other species are identical in all external respects. Several species have been bred in captivity. The most notable is the Neon Goby, now bred commercially in the United States. Gobies are mostly substrate spawners and the male guards the eggs until they hatch. The larvae drift into the plankton layers to develop there before returning to the sea floor.

Tank Conditions and Care

HABITAT: For tank and water conditions see Blennies page 88.

FEEDING: Gobies like to take food while it is drifting in the current and enjoy live foods such as brineshrimp, mysis and small river shrimp. Squid, bloodworm, chopped cockle, mussel, shellmeat and flake foods are also relished.

HEALTH: If water quality is good and the tank is neither overfed nor overstocked, then gobies suffer very little from diseases. However, in the first few weeks of aquarium life a close watch should be kept for whitespot and *Oodinium*.

● *Would a goby make a suitable beginner's fish?*

... Yes. Most species of gobies are quite easy to keep.

● *Will gobies share an aquarium?*

In many cases, yes, but temperaments vary. If you have seen them happily sharing the same tank at your dealer's, then they will probably be fine. The larger the tank, the less chance of territorial disputes.

● *Are gobies suitable for the invertebrate aquarium?*

Yes, but with two reservations. Very small gobies can easily fall prey to predatory anemones, crabs and some shrimps (Mantis and Pistol Shrimps, in particular). Other gobies spend most of their time taking mouthfuls of coral sand, sieving it for small particles of food, then passing it out through their gills. Unfortunately, this sand can be sprayed over sessile invertebrates causing them distress. The most common culprit is the Blue-Cheek Goby.

● *Are gobies compatible with other species of fish?*

Yes, on the whole they make excellent community fish providing they are not kept with larger fish that might see them as a potential meal or other very territorial species that may unduly harass them.

◆ *Thick strong lips indicate that the Blue-Cheek Goby (Valenciennea strigata) is a substrate sifter. They are often seen in pairs, side by side, searching the sand for particles of food. This is an excellent beginner's fish.*

● *Can a goby help improve my undergravel filter?*

Yes. Some species take mouthfuls of coral sand and sieve it through their gills. With this constant disturbance, the substrate will·never become compacted and detritus will be brought to the surface to be filtered off. If external filtration is used and a layer of coral sand covers the bottom, a goby can disturb it enough to prevent anaerobic activity.

Popular Species of Gobies

	maximum adult size
Neon Goby *Gobiosoma oceanops*	1in (25mm)
Catalina Goby *Lythrypnus dalli*	1in (25mm)
Lemon Goby *Gobiodon citrinus*	1.2in (30mm)
Yellow Goby *Gobiodon okinawae*	1.2in (30mm)
Orange-Spotted Goby *Valenciennea puellaris*	4in (10cm)
Blue-Cheek Goby *Valenciennea strigata*	7in (18cm)
Sulphur Goby *Cryptocentrus cinctus*	4in (10cm)

◀ *Neon Gobies (Gobiosoma oceanops) often have a favourite perching place to which they will return time and time again. They use it to watch out for food or a potential mate.*

Grammas  FAMILY: GRAMMIDAE

 ● *Are grammas suitable additions to the invertebrate aquarium?*

... Yes, but Royal Grammas suffer from whitespot and, since copper-based medication is lethal to invertebrates, the tank should have an ultraviolet sterilizer as a precaution.

● *Are grammas peaceful fish?*

The Royal Gramma is usually peaceful, and although the Black-Cap Gramma may prove aggressive, this can be avoided if there is plenty of space and rockwork.

● *Can I keep more than one type of gramma together?*

Yes. Although territorial, Royal and Black-Cap Grammas can be kept together as breeding trios so long as they are introduced as juveniles all at the same time, and given enough space.

◀ *The Royal Gramma* (Gramma loreto).

GRAMMAS, ALSO KNOWN AS FAIRY BASSLETS, are mainly confined to the Caribbean. The family includes some of the most popular marine fishkeeping favourites; Royal Gramma (*Gramma loreto*) growing to 3in (7.5cm), Black-Cap Gramma (*G. melacara*) growing to 4in (10cm), and a fish so rarely seen in captivity that it has no common name, *Gramma linki*. Grammas are secretive fish, making use of the maze of rockwork crevices

Tank Conditions and Care

HABITAT: For tank and water conditions see Dwarf Angelfish page 116.

FEEDING: Most grammas will take live and frozen brineshrimp and mysis readily as long as it is kept suspended in the current; rarely will they scoop food from the substrate. Even flake foods can be acceptable if presented correctly.

HEALTH: Should water conditions be allowed to deteriorate, or the grammas are unhappy with their surroundings, whitespot and *Oodinium* could be a problem.

to travel from one location to another without having to cross open water. Their highly territorial nature demands that they lead solitary lives, although a truce is usually called for breeding. All grammas are predatory plankton feeders, so they will take full advantage of any nutritious animals drifting past them in the current and any small crustaceans or marine worms to be found among the rockwork.

The Royal Gramma has been observed performing its spawning ritual many times in the aquarium. The male builds a nest of algae into which he invites passing females to lay eggs before he passes through to fertilize them. The female is then chased off and the nest guarded solely by the male until the eggs hatch and the larvae drift off into the plankton layers to feed and develop. So far, limited quantities of Royal Gramma and the Black-Cap Gramma have been reared by commercial hatcheries and made available for sale. The hobbyist, however, has encountered greater difficulty in raising fry to adulthood.

Squirrelfish FAMILY: HOLOCENTRIDAE

COMMONLY FOUND IN THE TROPICAL AND sub-tropical waters of the Indo-Pacific and Atlantic Oceans, squirrelfish are shy, shoaling animals that spend most of their time beneath shady rock overhangs and in reef caves. They are almost all nocturnal feeders and do not venture from their shadowy retreats until night has fallen.

Although they will eat smaller plankton, squirrelfish prefer to feed on crustaceans and small fish which they snap up in their cavernous mouths. Their large eyes aid nighttime vision, and indicate that these are highly predatory fish.

Squirrelfish are predominantly red, varying in subtle tones from pale pink to deep salmon. Some are marked with horizontal bars. Red aids camouflage under water. It is one of the first colours in the spectrum to be filtered out, while the blue wavelengths penetrate further. Under blue light, red appears black, masking the squirrelfish, which deliberately position themselves where mostly blue light can reach them.

Squirrelfish are shoaling spawners, scattering their fertilized eggs to develop in plankton layers. As yet, there have been no reports of any successful captive rearings.

Tank Conditions and Care

HABITAT: For tank and water conditions see Triggerfish page 84.

Lighting — Provide shady areas for retreat

FEEDING: Live or frozen shellmeat, crabmeat, shrimp, mussel, squid and cockle are eagerly taken as they fall through water, but some individuals are reluctant to take food from the substrate.

HEALTH: Holocentrids are remarkably disease resistant in high-quality water. However, they suffer from eye problems if water conditions deteriorate or if the lighting is too high in ultraviolet content.

● *Are squirrelfish suitable for the inexperienced hobbyist?*

... Yes. They are quite easy to keep and reasonably forgiving of fluctuations in water quality and conditions.

● *Can I keep more than one squirrelfish together?*

Yes, especially in a large aquaria. Squirrelfish are at their best when kept in groups of five or six, or even more, but check that stocking ratios are not exceeded.

● *Are squirrelfish suitable for the community tank?*

They may eat smaller fish, shrimps and other crustacea. In a tank with fish of their own size or larger they grunt if they feel threatened.

● *Should I be careful when netting these fish?*

Yes. Squirrelfish have very sharp fin rays and some species possess spines on the gill covers which will become entangled in coarse nets.

● *Which species are ideal for the aquarium?*

Common Squirrelfish (*Holocentrus diadema*) 8in (20cm); White-Tip Squirrelfish (*H. rufus*) 6in (15cm); Long-Jaw Squirrelfish (*H. ascensionis*) 10in (25cm); Big-Eye Squirrelfish (*Myripristis murdjan*) 10in (25cm); Red-Orange Squirrelfish (*M. vittatus*) 6in (15cm).

◀ *The Common Squirrelfish* (Holocentrus diadema).

Wrasse FAMILY: LABRIDAE

Of all the fish kept by aquarists world-wide, the wrasses, encompassing over 400 species, are easily the most numerous. Only a fraction of these are available to the hobbyist, but the choice is still wide and attractive.

Labrids range in size from approximately 4–6in (10–15cm) to the monster Napoleon Wrasse (*Cheilinus undulatus*) reaching 7ft (2.1m). Within the aquarium, the ultimate size and sheer speed of growth can come as something of a shock. For example, African Clown Wrasse (*Coris formosa*) may regularly be found on sale as a tiny but highly colourful 1in (2.5cm) specimen. However, within a few years, depending on conditions, it may have attained 8–14in (20–35cm)!

Many juvenile wrasse act as cleaner fish and these may be recognized by their distinctive red and white livery. As they grow into sub-adults and adults, several species form an intricate hierarchy presided over by a

These attractively marked juvenile Twinspot Wrasse (Coris angulata) *will soon have to be separated if fighting is to be avoided.*

"supermale". His coloration is different from that of the rest of the group, which consists not only of females but subordinate males. Marine scientists have found these groups to be fascinating subjects for investigation and much work has been done to study these complicated social interactions. As the family Labridae is so vast, it is difficult to generalize, but it would be fair to say that most wrasse are opportunistic feeders. Not only will they browse suspended plankton but they will also scavenge the bottom and rocks for marine worms, crustacea and just about anything edible, although algae does not appear to be the favourite diet of any particular species. Many of the larger species have formidably sharp teeth; beware of feeding them by hand!

Tank Conditions and Care

HABITAT: Larger wrasse can only be safely housed in a fish-only system.

Tank Size A fish-only aquarium of at least 45 gallons (205 l; 54 US gallons) for juvenile or small fish; mature specimens will require in excess of 100 gallons (455 l; 120 US gallons) gross volume.

pH	8.0–8.3
Temperature	25–26°C (77–79°F)
Ammonia	Zero
Nitrite	Zero
Nitrate Most species will tolerate 50ppm total NO₃ but less than 15ppm is desirable to avoid disease.	
Specific Gravity	1.020–1.025
Water Changes 15–25% every two weeks in a heavily stocked tank.	
Filtration Efficient protein skimming and activated carbon filtration as standard.	
Lighting	Moderate to bright
Water Circulation	Brisk

FEEDING: Larger wrasse are greedy feeders and will accept flake foods, marine pellets, frozen and live shrimps, cockles, mussels and any other meaty marine fare.

HEALTH: Larger wrasse tend to be fairly disease-resistant and will only suffer when water conditions deteriorate.

Popular Species of Wrasse

	maximum adult size
Cuban Hogfish *Bodianus pulchellus*	8in (20cm)
Spanish Hogfish *Bodianus rufus*	10in (25cm)
Twinspot Wrasse *Coris angulata*	15in (37.5cm)
African Clown Wrasse *Coris formosa*	14in (35cm)
Clown Wrasse *Coris gaimardi*	14in (35cm)
Birdmouth Wrasse *Gomphosus coeruleus*	10in (25cm)
Harlequin Tuskfish *Choerodon fasciata*	14in (35cm)
Thalassoma spp.	6–14in (15–35cm)

● *Are wrasse suitable fish for the beginner?*

... In the main, yes. Most species have manageable temperaments, are easy to keep and make good community fish.

● *Do wrasse require any special conditions?*

Yes. Many wrasse like to bury themselves under coral sand at night, and when frightened or disturbed. Therefore, 2–3in (5–7.5cm) of fine coral sand should be provided as a substrate. A few species hide in rock crevices and spin a mucus cocoon around themselves every night and there should be sufficient rockwork to allow for this behaviour.

● *Which of the larger wrasse are suitable for the invertebrate aquarium?*

Ultimately none! Larger wrasse quickly become a nuisance, attacking corals and crustaceans in a bid to satisfy their huge appetites.

● *Can I mix the larger wrasse with large fish of other species?*

Large wrasse are very active fish, always on the lookout for a quick meal. Slow-moving species, such as lionfish, have been known to have spines, skin, fins and eyes attacked quite badly. Wrasse are more suited to the company of active fish such as the larger angelfish, triggerfish and tangs.

● *Can I keep two or more large wrasse together?*

No. In most cases they will fight until one, or both, are dead.

● *Is it possible to breed larger wrasse?*

Very experienced aquarists have been trying to breed larger wrasse but success appears to be some way off.

● *How can I recognize a healthy specimen?*

Wrasse should be seen to be active, although newly imported specimens may hide under the sand for up to a day but usually no longer. They should have clear eyes, with no signs of ragged fins or blemished bodies. Healthy wrasse will always feed greedily.

Dwarf Wrasse FAMILY: LABRIDAE

IF ASKED TO NAME ONE GROUP OF FISH WITH beautiful markings, a generally peaceful nature, lively and active personalities, easy to feed, compatibility with invertebrates and disease resistance, most hobbyists would have difficulty in identifying one fish successfully, certainly not a group! But such a group does exist and they are called dwarf wrasse. This might be a new term to many aquarists; it refers to members of the wrasse family that grow no larger than 4in (10cm), an ideal size for the domestic aquarium.

Cleaner Wrasse

The Common Cleaner Wrasse *(Labroides dimidiatus)* spends its whole life performing grooming duties, but it is not widely known that many juvenile wrasse also act as cleaner fish. These are generally recognized by their distinctive red and white, or blue/black and white livery. One theory to explain their helpful behaviour is that it gives the very young fish an opportunity to mix safely with larger, and potentially predatory, species in relative safety. Whatever the true reason, it certainly works very well as juvenile wrasse are commonly seen on the reef in full view and in open water. While cleaning parasites from larger fish, dwarf wrasse are mainly supplementing their regular diet of plankton, marine worms and small crustaceans.

Nearly all wrasse, and particularly the dwarf species, take refuge during the hours of darkness in a soft, sandy substrate, sometimes burying themselves up to 3in (7.5cm) beneath the surface. This strategy for safety should, as far as possible, be provided for in the aquarium by supplying a few inches of coral sand on the base of the aquarium. If there is none available, the fish do not appear to be unduly stressed, once they are confident as to their security, as long as there is plenty of rockwork within which to hide.

◄ *The Common Cleaner Wrasse* (Labroides dimidiatus) *is far more sensitive than other dwarf wrasse. It needs the highest quality water conditions.*

Popular Species of Dwarf Wrasse

	maximum adult size
Coloured Cleaner Wrasses *Labroides* spp	4in (10cm)
Common Cleaner Wrasse *Labroides dimidiatus*	4in (10cm)
Parrot Wrasses *Cirrhilabrus* spp	3in (7.5cm)
Dwarf Parrot Wrasse *Cirrhilabrus rubriventralis*	3in (7.5cm)
Golden Rainbowfish/Banana Wrasse *Haliochoeres chrysus*	4in (10cm)
Fourspot Wrasse/Banana Wrasse *Haliochoeres trispilus*	4in (10cm)
Green Wrasse *Haliochoeres chloropterus*	4in (10cm)
Pyjama Wrasse *Pseudocheilinus hexataenia*	3in (7.5cm)
Dragon Wrasse *Novaculichthys taeniorus*	2.5in (6cm)
Fourline Wrasse *Larabicus quadrilineatus*	4in (10cm)

● *Do dwarf wrasse make good community fish?*

... Yes. Easy-going temperaments make them good community fish and very compatible for the fish-invertebrate aquarium.

● *Can two or more wrasse be mixed in the same aquarium?*

In most cases, no. Two wrasse of the same species will usually fight until one, or both, are dead. Even unlike species cannot be trusted and usually end up in a vicious dispute.

● *How can a healthy specimen be recognized?*

Dwarf wrasse should always be active. They must have clear eyes and unblemished bodies, and no signs of ragged or clamped fins.

● *Should a settling-in period be allowed for when a fish is first purchased?*

Yes. Some specimens will dive straight into the sand or lie gasping and shocked on the bottom. Leave the

lights out until the fish recovers and resist the urge to intervene. In a healthy fish this stage should last no longer than a few days.

● *How can a dwarf wrasse be distinguished from a larger species?*

It cannot be, unless the subject is identified first! For example, many species of wrasse are imported as tiny juveniles with attractive coloration. These include African Clown Wrasse *(Coris formosa)* and Twin-Spot Wrasse *(C. angulata)*. Both can be found on sale at around 1in (2.5cm) in length, however, within a few years they can achieve up to 15in (37.5cm)!

Tank Conditions and Care

HABITAT: For tank and water conditions see Dwarf Angelfish page 116.

FEEDING: Dwarf wrasse are greedy feeders and take flake, brineshrimp, mysis, lobster eggs; in fact, almost any marine fare will suffice.

HEALTH: Wrasse rarely contract serious diseases where water conditions are good, and may live for many years. But Common Cleaner Wrasse are susceptible to illness when water conditions are less than perfect.

➡ *Widely available, the colourful and peaceful Pyjama Wrasse* (Pseudocheilinus hexataenia) *can be recommended as an ideal marine fish for a beginner.*

Firefish

FAMILY: MICRODESMIDAE

● Are firefish suitable for beginners?

... Yes, they make ideal choices. for fishkeepers at all levels of the hobby.

● Can firefish be introduced into the invertebrate aquarium?

Yes, they harm neither invertebrates nor algae.

● Can firefish be kept in a shoal?

Yes, although there may be some bickering among individuals if conditions are cramped or there are not enough bolt-holes.

● Do firefish have any predators within the aquarium?

Yes, bristleworms can be a problem, as can hermit crabs. When a firefish "locks" itself into a favourite bolt-hole for the night, nothing will cause it to release itself. Bristleworms and hermit crabs simply eat them alive! The best solution is to remove all bristleworms and keep the crabs well-fed!

▲ The Purple Firefish (Nemateleotris decora) is a beautiful species and an ideal choice for the invertebrate aquarium. All firefish are excellent jumpers, but the risk of fatalities can be minimized by covering the tank.

FIREFISH USED TO BE GROUPED SCIENTIFICALLY with blennies, then gobies and now, more accurately, with wormfish (Microdesmidae). Only three species are kept by the hobbyist: Firefish (Nemateleotris magnifica), Purple Firefish (N. decora) and the much rarer N. helfrichi. All firefish have elongated bodies with extended first dorsal fin rays, which they flick up and down at will. This is a signalling device to warn other firefish to maintain a respectable distance, and a "locking" mechanism when the fish retreats into its bolt-hole.

Retreating to a Bolt-hole

In the wild, the common species may be seen in great numbers, hovering close to a rocky outcrop, facing into the current and feeding on drifting plankton. Each individual fish has its own bolt-hole from which it will not stray far. At the first sign of danger, the fish disappears into the rockwork. This practice is carried over into aquarium life. If the aquarium contains a bully that is constantly upsetting the firefish it may refuse to appear altogether. Even in quieter circumstances individual fish may be nervous and need the company of other confident fishes to encourage them out.

They breed by scattering pelagic (floating) eggs into the current where they drift along to develop into small fry. No fry have yet been raised in captivity.

Tank Conditions and Care

HABITAT: For tank and water conditions see Dwarf Angelfish page 116.

FEEDING: Firefish eat almost all small marine fare. Frozen and live brineshrimp are a particular favourite, while lobster eggs, marine flake and small pieces of cockle, mussel and squid are also readily accepted.

HEALTH: In a good aquarium environment, firefish are disease-resistant.

Moray Eels FAMILY: MURAENIDAE

MORAY EELS BELONG TO THE MURAENIDAE OF which there are approximately 100 species to be found worldwide in tropical and temperate waters. They have no swim bladder and no pelvic or pectoral fins and rely for locomotion on the movement of continuous dorsal and anal fins running the whole length of their body. Size is solely dependent on species; Snowflake Morays *(Echnida nebulosa)* rarely exceed a manageable 12in (30cm) in the aquarium, whereas Spotted Morays *(Gymnothorax favagineus)* can reach in excess of 36in (90cm). Morays can reach huge lengths in the wild, some well in excess of 8ft (3m). They usually live in a crevice or cave, big enough to accommodate their bulk.

Morays are extremely short-sighted and rely on a well-developed sense of taste to detect prey. They gape and lunge forward, drawing in streams of water to "taste the scent" of anything nearby. Feeding usually takes place at night with prey generally consisting of other fish and crustaceans. However, if the opportunity arises, a daytime foray is rarely foregone. They have a formidable array of needle-sharp teeth and very strong jaws, and are best kept with fish too large to be eaten and those (such as lionfish) that can protect themselves.

● *Is a moray a good choice for a newcomer to the hobby?*

... On the whole they are quite forgiving as far as water quality is concerned. However, the beginner should be aware of how large the species grows, and the danger to tankmates.

● *Are there any safety rules that need to be followed?*

Yes. Moray eels are consummate escape artists and a securely covered tank is essential. They can inflict a nasty bite, and should be fed using aquarium tongs.

▲ *The Snowflake Moray* (Echnida nebulosa) *protrudes from its lair to "taste" the water for prey.*

Tank Conditions and Care

HABITAT: Plenty of rockwork forming caves and crevices should be provided.

Tank Size An aquarium should be at least three times the ultimate length of the species kept. A 24in (60cm) fish will require a 72in (180cm) tank.

pH	8.0–8.3
Temperature	24–26°C (75–79°F)
Ammonia	Zero
Nitrite	Zero

Nitrate   Will tolerate 50ppm total NO₃ but much less is preferable.

Specific Gravity	1.019–1.026
Water Changes	15–25% every two weeks

Filtration Efficient filtration, with protein skimming and activated carbon filtration is essential.

Lighting Subdued lighting is ideal but eels will adapt to moderate or bright conditions.

FEEDING: Most morays will accept almost anything edible. Meaty marine fare is relished–frozen mussel, shrimp, squid, lancefish and cockle.

HEALTH: Morays are very disease-resistant, even in less than perfect water conditions.

Jawfish <small>FAMILY: OPISTOGNATHIDAE</small>

JAWFISH CAN BRING GREAT INTEREST TO THE aquarium substrate. They dig burrows for protection and hover above them gathering food carried by the current. At the first sign of danger, the fish retreat, tail first. Some species disguise the burrow entrance with a rock. Particularly when jawfish are newly introduced, it is important that tankmates are non-aggressive leaving them in peace.

Jawfish are found in most of the shallow tropical, and some of the temperate, seas of the world. They occupy flat, sandy expanses where few other fish live. Some species form colonies, allowing mating under safe conditions, without straying far from the burrow.

All species of jawfish have large heads with a gaping mouth. They are mouthbrooders; one of the pair holds the fertilized eggs in its mouth until they are ready to hatch. The eggs not only fill the oral cavity but protrude some way out! The Caribbean species *Opistognathus aurifrons* has been bred in commercial quantities by fish farms in America.

Species vary in size tremendously, but the popular Yellow-Headed Jawfish *(Opistognathus aurifrons)* and Blue-Spotted Jawfish *(O. rosenblatti)* rarely exceed 4in (10cm).

▼ *A healthy Yellow-Headed Jawfish* (Opistognathus aurifrons) *is always alert.*

Tank Conditions and Care

HABITAT: For tank and water conditions see Dwarf Angelfish page 116.

FEEDING: Brineshrimp, mysis, chopped squid and other small marine fare is preferred. Large specimens will accept live river shrimp. Introduce food close to the fish and allow it to drift into range. Tankmates can be fed simultaneously at the other end of the aquarium to prevent the jawfishes' food from being "stolen". Often they would rather starve than stray from safety!

HEALTH: They are sensitive to stress caused by poor water conditions or lack of a burrow. In such cases they suffer from whitespot, *Oodinium*, fin rot and fungal diseases.

● *Are jawfish recommended for the beginner?*

... No. They generally require special understanding and experience.

● *Do jawfish require a burrow in the aquarium?*

Yes, jawfish without a burrow become stressed and succumb to disease. They need to burrow in substrate 3–5in (7.5–12.5cm) deep, ideally made up of equal parts coral sand, coral gravel and crushed shells.

● *Do jawfish have any unexpected habits?*

Yes, they jump out of the aquarium for no apparent reason! It is imperative to secure the tank with close-fitting cover glasses.

● *Are jawfish compatible with invertebrates?*

Yes, but their digging activities might prove an inconvenience as rockwork in the tank could be undermined and sessile invertebrates covered with excavated substrate.

Boxfish FAMILY: OSTRACIIDAE

AS THE COMMON NAME IMPLIES, THESE FISH have rectangular bodies, the result of a unique arrangement of hard skeletal plates just under the surface of the skin. This "armour" is not the only defence of the boxfish. Most can release a potent toxin, repulsing predators. In the wild, both parties can swim away from the toxin, but within the aquarium it can kill the predator and boxfish alike.

In the wild, boxfish will eat almost anything. They browse the reefs and sandy areas searching for small crustaceans, marine worms and, surprisingly, large quantities of algae. Their strong, beak-like teeth enable them to remove pieces of rock to reveal small prey sheltering beneath. They are also capable of blowing jets of water at sandy areas to reveal any tasty morsels.

The Spotted Boxfish (*Ostracion meleagris*) has a distinct male and female form; the female is almost entirely black with white spots; the male is more colourful with flanks of blue with yellow spots. In other species, however, the sexes are impossible to distinguish. Breeding is almost unknown in captivity and no fry have been reared to date.

It is easy to see how the Cowfish (Lactoria cornuta) *came by its common name.*

● *Can a newly purchased boxfish poison itself and its companions?*

... Normally boxfish release their poison under two extreme conditions: if they are badly stressed due to bullying, bad handling or trauma; or if they develop a severe or fatal disease. Keep a careful watch, and at the first sign of distress, remove to a quarantine tank.

● *What do I do if toxin is released into the tank?*

Isolate the boxfish immediately into a separate aquarium and carry out a very large water change in the main tank – 100% if possible.

● *Are boxfish compatible with invertebrates?*

They have ravenous appetites and will peck at tubeworms and other sessile invertebrates that look like a potential meal.

Tank Conditions and Care

HABITAT: For tank and water conditions see Triggerfish page 84.

FEEDING: Boxfish have large appetites and will devour almost any standard marine fare with relish. Try brineshrimp, mussel, cockle, clam, shellmeat, lancefish and mysis. Algae should also be offered wherever possible.

HEALTH: Given good conditions, boxfish are relatively disease free. In poor or deteriorating water conditions, however, they can succumb to whitespot, *Oodinium*, skin and eye diseases. Being poor swimmers, boxfish may be victimized by inquisitive tankmates, resulting in body wounds and ragged fins.

Popular Species of Boxfish

	maximum adult size
Blue Boxfish *Ostracion cyanurus*	6in (15cm)
Spotted Boxfish *Ostracion meleagris*	18in (45cm)
Cube Boxfish *Ostracion cubicus*	18in (45cm)
Blue-Spotted Boxfish *Ostracion tuberculatum*	18in (45cm)
Cowfish *Lactoria cornuta*	16in (40cm)
Hovercraft Boxfish *Tetrasomus gibbosus*	16in (40cm)

Sweetlips  FAMILY: HAEMULIDAE

● *Do they need special conditions?*

Sweetlips cannot tolerate surges in ammonia or nitrites. They like large areas of soft, sandy substrate where they can forage for food, much as they do in the wild. They will grow to 18in (45cm) – too large for all but the most committed hobbyists.

● *Do they make good community fishes?*

Sweetlips are excellent community fishes with a very placid nature. However, they dislike being housed with bullies or very boisterous species.

● *Can sweetlips be kept with invertebrates?*

Juveniles will be very well behaved, but as they mature they will grow progressively more destructive.

Tank Conditions and Care

HABITAT: For tank and water conditions see Triggerfish page 84.

FEEDING: Sweetlips are substrate feeders. All frozen and fresh meaty marine fare is greedily accepted, including cockle, mussel, squid, lobster and crab meat, shellmeat, shrimp and krill.

HEALTH: Given the right environment, sweetlips should remain healthy. However, they are quite sensitive fish and if conditions are poor will readily succumb to whitespot, *Oodinium* and other diseases.

Popular Species of Sweetlips

	maximum adult size
Yellow Sweetlips *Plectorhynchus albovittatus*	9in (22.5cm)
Harlequin Sweetlips *Plectorhynchus chaetodontoides*	18in (45cm)
Oriental Sweetlips *Plectorhynchus orientalis*	16in (40cm)
Panda Sweetlips *Plectorhynchus picus*	24in (60cm)
Yellow-Banded Sweetlips *Plectorhynchus lineatus*	14in (35cm)

SWEETLIPS ARE PART OF THE HAEMULIDAE, which also includes grunts, snappers and porkfish. They are nearly always brightly coloured, especially in the juvenile stage when they swim with an endearing style that is hard to resist. They also have a peaceful disposition. Sweetlips differ from their close relatives largely in dentation only, although they gain their common name from the development of large, fleshy lips.

Sweetlips are shoaling fish, spending much of their daylight hours in the shelter of reef overhangs; when dusk falls they venture off to the sandy areas where they search for crustaceans and marine worms.

Unlike many other reef fishes, sweetlips and their allied families are born either male or female and cannot change sex in later life. A shoal will come into "season" and the males and females will mate regularly for several months, allowing their fertilized eggs to develop in the anonymity of the plankton layers. Breeding information is of little use to the aquarist as it is only relevant to adult fish kept in large shoals and enormous tanks.

▲ *This juvenile Harlequin Sweetlips* (Plectorhynchus chaetodontoides) *may be offered for sale as a charming polka-dot fish, but it will eventually lose all of its interesting markings and become a drab brown adult.*

Catfish FAMILY: PLOTOSIDAE

CATFISH ARE NOT NORMALLY ASSOCIATED with the sea, and indeed there are only a few species that live in full marine conditions permanently. The best known of these, and the most suitable for the marine aquarium, is *Plotosus lineatus* – the Saltwater Catfish. In common with their freshwater and brackish water cousins, Saltwater Catfish have distinctive barbels around the mouth.

Juvenile specimens of *P. lineatus* possess some extremely interesting behavioural characteristics. A shoal of them will remain very close together and if danger threatens, will form a ball-like clump with their heads at the centre and their tails waving about on the outside resembling the tentacles of an anemone – which may quite possibly be the intention! In addition, they are equipped with venomous spines preceding the dorsal and pectoral fins which must be respected at all times, since the sting is dangerous and extremely painful.

At about 4–5in (10–12.5cm) the individual fish disperse and live mostly solitary lives. The cream and brown striped markings, so attractive in the juveniles, fade to a dull uniform brown and the fish become largely inactive, except to feed.

Saltwater Catfish are known to deposit non-adhesive, demersal (sinking) eggs into the cracks and crevices of rocks in shallow water or, more usually, within a nest of debris, algae, sand and gravel. The male guards the nest and the eggs hatch in about 7–10 days. The large yolk-sac is absorbed in a further 10 days and the fry become free-swimming to feed immediately on anything small enough for them to eat (newly hatched brineshrimp would suffice in captivity).

Females are sexually mature at about 6in (15cm) in length and full maturity is reached in approximately three years. Most specimens live for more than seven years.

Are catfish compatible with invertebrates?

... Only when very young. As they grow, they become very destructive.

Can just one juvenile be kept?

No, they tend to pine away and die. Shoals of at least 8–12 are recommended until the fish reaches maturity.

Do catfish hold any drawbacks?

Yes. They grow up to 12in (30cm), and become unmanageable in the aquarium. A sting from a mature specimen could hospitalize an adult for several weeks, so the aquarist should take precautions, even with juveniles! If stung, hold the affected part under very hot water for a few minutes to help alleviate the pain, then seek medical advice.

Saltwater Catfish (Plotosus lineatus) *are very desirable as juveniles.*

Tank Conditions and Care

HABITAT: For tank and water conditions see Wrasse page 103.

FEEDING: Catfish will eat almost any marine fare, including flake and tablet foods.

HEALTH: There are no major disease problems with marine catfish.

Angelfish   FAMILY: POMACANTHIDAE

VIVID COLOURS SET IN UNIQUE PATTERNS ON large, impressive fish have inspired "regal" names for these fish: King, Queen, Emperor and Majestic Angelfish are just a few that spring to mind. Whether you are a person who is drawn to larger species, or not, no-one can fail to be impressed by the sheer grandeur of this group of fish.

While the largest dwarf angels (see page 115) reach a maximum adult length of about 5in (12.5cm), no such restrictions exist on their bigger cousins; indeed, some species are capable of reaching 24in (60cm) in the wild. Fortunately the more desirable aquarium fish fall into the maximum growth range of 6–12in (15–30cm), even though they may be found well in excess of this in their natural habitat. Larger angels are found throughout the world's tropical seas, with many of the popular and easy to keep species coming

◄▲ ◄▼ *The juvenile Emperor Angelfish* (Pomacanthus imperator) *shown above is dark blue with distinct white markings. Given excellent water conditions and a suitable diet, it will develop into the stunning creature below. Size plays little part in the colour-change process, age is the most important governing factor.*

● *Is it safe to mix large angelfish?*

Generally speaking, no. Angels of the same species that are not a mated pair will nearly always fight to the death of the weakest. Angels of different species with radically dissimilar colours and patterns may sometimes mix, but there is no guarantee that an initially harmonious relationship will last either.

● *Are mated pairs ever seen on sale?*

Hardly ever. If you are offered a pair, exercise the utmost care as they may not remain a pair once moved to different surroundings!

● *If an angelfish is seen in juvenile livery, how long will it take to change to adult coloration?*

As a broad guide, a 2.5in (6.25cm) juvenile should change within 14–18 months. Given the right conditions, all angels change colour eventually. Size is unimportant, although age is. If a specimen delays changing colour, it is a sure sign that water conditions are poor. An improvement will continue the maturing process.

● *Could any suitable tankmates be suggested?*

Large angels can be very aggressive and fully dominate an aquarium, so tankmates must be chosen with the greatest care. There is no magic formula but they seem to do better with fish that are not easily upset.

Groupers, tangs, boxfish, grunts, lionfish, moray eels, puffers, rabbitfish, sweetlips, triggerfish, larger wrasse and mature butterflyfish may all prove acceptable. Any tankmates should be at least the same size, or larger.

● *Is it true that Caribbean species might be susceptible to Indo-Pacific fish diseases and vice-versa?*

There is no conclusive proof that this is true. Aquarists can mix healthy specimens together without fear.

● *Can larger angelfish be kept with invertebrates?*

No. While very small juveniles might be kept in a mixed tank for a short period, they will become progressively destructive with age.

● *How will I recognize suitable specimens?*

They will have a good colour and be alert. There will be no serious blemishes on the skin or fins and the eyes will be clear and bright. Settled fish will always eat greedily and a prospective purchaser should always witness this before buying.

Popular Species of Angelfish

The adult Blue-Ring Angelfish (Pomacanthus annularis) is an impressive, if fairly sensitive fish.

	maximum adult size
Species in which juveniles resemble adults	
Scribbled Angelfish *Chaetodontoplus duboulayi*	8in (20cm)
Queen Angelfish *Holocanthus ciliaris*	18in (45cm)
King Angelfish *Holocanthus passer*	18in (45cm)
Rock Beauty *Holocanthus tricolor*	24in (60cm)
Species with black/yellow juvenile markings	
Grey Angelfish *Pomacanthus arcuatus*	20in (50cm)
French Angelfish *Pomacanthus paru*	12in (30cm)

Species with blue/white juvenile markings	
Majestic Angelfish *Euxiphipops navarchus*	10in (25cm)
Blue-Faced Angelfish *Euxiphipops xanthometapon*	15in (37.5cm)
Blue-Ring Angelfish *Pomacanthus annularis*	16in (40cm)
Emperor Angelfish *Pomacanthus imperator*	16in (40cm)
Koran Angelfish *Pomacanthus semicirculatus*	16in (40cm)

Tank Conditions and Care

HABITAT: A fish-only aquarium shows off these dramatic looking fish to best advantage. Rocky outcrops are desirable for night-time shelter.

Tank size Larger angels require an aquarium of 48x15x18in (122x38x46cm) as a minimum to allow for growth and swimming room. As a general rule, house the fish in a tank at least four times the expected adult size in captivity.

pH	8.1–8.3
Temperature	25–26°C (77–79°F)
Ammonia	Zero
Nitrite	Zero
Nitrate Below 25ppm total NO$_3$ can be tolerated but 5ppm or less is far better.	
Specific Gravity	1.021–1.024
Dissolved Oxygen	6–7ppm

Water Changes 20–25% every two weeks with high quality nitrate-free water is essential.

Filtration Efficient biological filtration as well as protein skimming and activated carbon are all indispensable.

FEEDING: Live and frozen brineshrimp as well as mysis, squid and sponge-based foods are all eagerly accepted. Some algae are desirable on a regular basis.

HEALTH: Newly imported specimens often suffer from Lymphocystis, a viral disease producing white cauliflower-like growths on the skin and fins. It is rarely fatal and indicates a breakdown in the immune system due to stress or shock. Once the immune system recovers, the fish normally cures itself. Medications usually prove ineffective. Aid recovery by keeping the water quality high.

from the Caribbean as well as the Indo-Pacific region and the Red Sea.

A great number of species possess distinct juvenile and adult stages defined by a totally different coloration and patterning. In these cases, the juveniles are usually dark blue with white vertical bars or circular patterning, or alternatively black with yellow vertical bars. This difference in coloration serves as a form of camouflage and as a method of deflecting aggression from adult angelfish until maturity is reached. Juveniles have been seen to act as cleaner fish, removing parasites from other, often larger, fish and the blue/white or black/yellow livery is universally recognized by coral reef fish as a "cleaner" signal. When a fish matures, usually between 1–2 years, the immature colours gradually change and the fish takes its place within the adult angel community. Some angels, such as the King Angelfish *(Holocanthus passer)* and the Queen Angelfish *(H. ciliaris)* are very colourful as juveniles and in comparison change far less dramatically as they develop their full adult coloration.

Life in the Wild
Large angels browse the reefs for algae, marine worms, crustaceans, and sponges as well as taking passing plankton. They will also scavenge on dead animals if not too threatened by other fish in attendance.

Angels can be seen singly or quite often in pairs where a strong male/female bond has formed. They almost always spawn at dusk, producing pelagic eggs (free-floating on the surface) that develop in the upper plankton layers. As yet, breeding in the aquarium has proved a very rare occurrence and raising larvae to maturity has eluded most experts.

Experience has shown that fish acquired as juveniles rarely reach their full potential size within the aquarium. Growth rates are usually 50–75% of those in the wild. Such restrictions are not harmful to the fish in any way but they do enable big fish to exist comfortably within the necessary restrictions of the aquarium.

Generally speaking, keeping larger angelfish requires skill and experience. However, some species are much more difficult to keep than others. For example, French Angelfish *(Pomacanthus paru)* would be regarded as relatively easy to keep, but Bandit Angelfish *(Apolemichthys arcuatus)* and Regal Angelfish *(Pygoplites diacanthus)* should be regarded as extremely difficult. Most species fall into an intermediate category; given scrupulous attention to water quality, they have the possibility of a long and healthy life.

Dwarf Angelfish

FAMILY: POMACANTHIDAE
GENUS: CENTROPYGE

THE "LIVING JEWELS OF THE REEF" DWARF angels have won the hearts of marine aquarists the world over with their interesting and endearing behavioural patterns, manageable size and superb coloration.

Although there are no hard and fast rules, it is generally accepted that a dwarf angelfish is one that grows to a maximum length of 5in (12.5cm) or less. This means that practically all the species termed "dwarf" belong to the genus *Centropyge*. A number of the larger pomacanthids, on sale as juveniles, may look like dwarf angels, but the hobbyist can receive a nasty shock when they grow to adult size. A good example of this is Rock Beauty *(Holocanthus tricolor)*. It is frequently

◆ *The Coral Beauty* (Centropyge bispinosus) *is a very desirable fish that varies in intensity of coloration, depending on where it was collected in the wild.*

Popular Species of Dwarf Angelfish

	maximum adult size
Lemonpeel Angelfish *Centropyge flavissimus*	4in (10cm)
Herald's Angelfish *Centropyge heraldi*	4in (10cm)
Cherub Angelfish *Centropyge argi*	2in (5cm)
Fireball Angelfish *Centropyge acanthops*	2in (5cm)
Coral Beauty *Centropyge bispinosus*	3.5in (8.75cm)
Eibl's Angelfish *Centropyge eibli*	4in (10cm)
Bicolor Angelfish *Centropyge bicolor*	5in (12.5cm)
Flame Angelfish *Centropyge loriculus*	4in (10cm)
Potters Angel *Centropyge potteri*	4in (10cm)

offered for sale when it is only 1.5–2in (3.75–5cm), but unfortunately has a potential adult length of well over 10in (25cm)!

Dwarf angels are represented in all the world's oceans, although only a fraction of the total number are found in the tropical Atlantic. Depending on the species, they may be observed in the wild as individuals, in pairs or in small groups grazing the reefs for food – algae, small worms and crustaceans, and various sponges.

In common with large angelfish, the dwarf species nearly always spawn at dusk, producing pelagic eggs (free-floating on the surface) that hatch out and develop as larvae in the plankton layer.

Like many of the larger angels, members of the genus *Centropyge* vary in their suitability as aquarium fish. Some species, for example the Cherub Angelfish *(C. argi)*, are extremely easy to keep, while others have a specialized diet and are not recommended for aquarium life. Multibarred Angelfish *(C. multifasciatus)* are a good example of the second type. Most centropygids fall somewhere between these two extremes and a marinist with some experience will be able to keep them successfully.

▼ *The Fireball Angelfish* (Centropyge acanthops) *is an ideal species to share the invertebrate aquarium.*

Tank Conditions and Care

HABITAT: The tank can be fish-only or mixed fish/invertebrate.

Tank size The smallest tank to consider would be 3ft (90cm) in length and 25 gallons (114 l; 30 US gallons) gross volume.

pH	8.1–8.3
Temperature	25–26°C (77–79°F)
Ammonia	Zero
Nitrite	Zero

Nitrate Less than 20ppm total NO_3 for fish only; 5ppm or less in a mixed aquarium.

Specific Gravity	1.020–1.024
Dissolved Oxygen	6–7ppm

Water Changes 15–25% every two weeks with high quality, filtered water.

Filtration Efficient protein skimming and activated carbon filtration as standard.

Lighting   Will adapt to almost any intensity.

Water Circulation Good circulation is essential, though areas of slack current are appreciated.

FEEDING: Brineshrimp and mysis, live and frozen. Frozen squid, sponge and flake foods should also be offered. Most species feed quite readily in the aquarium.

HEALTH: Given good water quality, dwarf angels are generally disease resistant. However, poor conditions are not tolerated well and may trigger parasitic and bacterial infections.

● *Will dwarf angels tolerate variable water conditions?*

... No. Most require stable and optimum water quality for a healthy, long life. Most losses occur as a result of poor water conditions.

● *Can more than one dwarf angel be kept in the same tank?*

In general, no. Most dwarfs will not tolerate the company of their own species or other centropygids in the same aquarium, even if the tank is very large. There are exceptions which include mated pairs and very dissimilar species.

● *Do dwarf angels make suitable companions for other fish?*

Very often, yes. Centropygids are usually well behaved with both smaller and larger fish of a dissimilar shape and coloration.

● *Can they be kept with invertebrates?*

On the whole, invertebrates are quite safe in the presence of these fish. Some dwarfs may be tempted

▲ *The Flame Angelfish* (Centropyge loriculus) *is one of the most attractive dwarf angels, and it is not difficult to keep. Its desirability means it commands a high price.*

to peck at tubeworms or anemones but most are well suited to the mixed fish/invertebrate aquarium.

● *Is it wise to introduce a dwarf angel into a newly matured aquarium?*

No, for two reasons: (1) the water quality is usually not stable enough, and (2) there will be insufficient amounts of micro- and macro-algae, as well as micro-organisms on which to browse and maintain a healthy diet.

● *What should be looked for in a healthy dwarf angel?*

Apart from a high degree of alertness, the body should be full and free from blemishes and both eyes perfectly clear. Fish with split or ragged fins are best avoided, as are unnaturally pale specimens. Witness a good appetite before purchasing.

● *Can dwarf angels be bred?*

Only by experienced aquarists specializing in this area. Raising fry has proved to be a rare occurrence, although it is possible.

Damselfish FAMILY: POMACENTRIDAE

THESE VERSATILE, COLOURFUL AND EXCITING fish are, on the whole, inexpensive and good value for money. Damsels are found in great variety and quantity in all the world's tropical seas. Because of this profusion—and because some species have a distinct juvenile, sub-adult, adult and even aged coloration—there is some confusion about their taxonomy. Taxonomists have described three or four species, where in reality only one existed.

Most damselfish live in community groups around a "safe" area such as a coral head; at the first sign of danger, the whole group retreats into the rockwork. Each individual has its own particular crevice in which to withdraw and also spend the night, the most secure places being reserved for the dominant fish of the group.

Community Hierarchy

Being naturally territorial, a group of damsels lends itself easily to a hierarchical system and most communities form a distinct pattern of dominance. It is usually a large dominant male that mates with the attendant females. He may invite one or several females to spawn on a rock that he has previously cleaned and guards the eggs ferociously, even from very large potential predators.

After hatching, the larvae drift up into the plankton layers to develop and feed on smaller organisms. Within 1–2 months they become juvenile fish, able to migrate back down to the reef and join a community of an identical species.

Damsels feed on small planktonic animals and plants brought to them on a favourable current. They rarely go hunting for food. However, some species "farm" patches of algae which they guard fiercely from poachers. They tend the patches with great care and skill, only feeding on small amounts, so enabling the algae to self-sustain.

Popular Species of Damselfish

	maximum adult size
Blue Damsel *Abudefduf cyaneus* Fairly aggressive	2in (5cm)
Black Neon Damsel *Abudefduf oxyodon* Aggressive, especially when mature	3in (7.5cm)
Sergeant Major *Abudefduf saxatilis* Pugnacious	2in (5cm)
Green Chromis *Chromis caerulea* Fairly peaceful	2in (5cm)
Blue Reef Chromis *Chromis cyanea* Peaceful	2in (5cm)
Yellow-Tailed Damsel *Chromis xanthurus* Can be aggressive,	2in (5cm)
Humbug *Dascyllus aruanus* Aggressive	2.5in (6.25cm)
Domino Damsel *Dascyllus trimaculatus* Aggressive	2.5in (6.25cm)
Yellow-Backed Damselfish *Paraglyphidodon melanopus* Reasonably peaceful	2.5in (6.25cm)
Beau Gregory *Stegastes leucostictus* Very aggressive	3in (7.5cm)

Tank Conditions and Care

HABITAT: For tank and water conditions see Dwarf Angelfish page 116.

FEEDING: Damsels will eat a variety of marine fare, whether live, frozen or dried. Choose brineshrimp, mysis, lobster eggs, plankton, small pieces of squid, cockle and mussel. Flake foods are also readily accepted.

HEALTH: Most damsels are very resistant to disease given reasonable water conditions.

● *Are damsels recommended for the newcomer?*

... In general, yes. They are not indestructible, but being less sensitive than many marine fish, they will tolerate a certain amount of accidental mismanagement.

● *What are their advantages and disadvantages?*

Most damsels are robust, colourful, active, interesting and affordable. On the negative side, they can be aggressive and territorial. Some individuals will dig actively and may harm undergravel filter efficiency or undermine rockwork.

● *Will damsels of a different species share a community tank?*

Most will when they are young but compatibility also depends on the size of tank, rockwork, other inhabitants and the temperaments of the individuals involved. Generally, the more mature a damsel gets, the more aggressive it becomes.

● *Is it best to keep a group of damsels?*

Not necessarily. Fighting in the aquarium is common and a dominant pair may be all that survives of a group. There are exceptions to this behaviour including such peaceful species as Green Chromis and Blue Reef Chromis.

● *Can a tank filter be matured with some damsels?*

This is not an approved practice; it is far better to mature a filter with a proprietary brand of maturing fluid. The high levels of ammonia and nitrite occurring during maturation cause stress in the fish which makes it deliberately cruel! If they survive (and not all do), territories will have been established making it very difficult for further fish to be introduced. If the damsels succumb to disease due to stress, subsequent additions will be more prone to that disease.

● *Are damsels compatible with invertebrates?*

Yes, they invariably behave very well in a mixed fish-invertebrate aquarium.

● *Are damsels safe with other species of fish?*

Generally, yes. But they should not be kept with shy or sensitive species, or large fish that might eat them.

● *When stocking a new aquarium, when should damsels be introduced?*

Owing to their territorial nature, damsels should be introduced close to last.

◄ *Blue Reef Chromis* (Chromis cyanea) *may safely be kept singly or in groups. They do, however, demand excellent water quality, unlike many other damsels.*

Clownfish (Anemonefish)

FAMILY: POMACENTRIDAE

WITHOUT DOUBT, THE CLOWNFISH IS THE most popular marine fish in captivity today. The name conjures up an image of a brightly coloured fish frolicking among the tentacles of an anemone. This image represents one of the best-known examples of mutual cooperation in the underwater world. For the aquarist, the natural relationship between the anemone and the clownfish has come to symbolize the very essence of the marine fish-keeping hobby.

There are some 26 species of clownfish recorded, 25 of which are in the genus *Amphiprion* and one in *Premnas*, the Maroon Clownfish *(Premnas biaculeatus)*. Of the total number, about half are commonly available in the aquatic trade; the other species are rarely in the trade as they live in

▲ *Clark's Anemonefish* (Amphiprion clarkii) *is a fine choice for beginners and experts alike. Once an anemone has been adopted, the fish will defend it vigorously.*

isolated locations, either protected by legislation or inaccessible to collectors.

No clownfish species ever grow excessively large; in the wild 5in (12.5cm) is usually the maximum; commonly kept aquarium specimens rarely exceed 3.5in (8.75cm). Diet in the wild is usually made up of various zooplankton and algae drifting in the current. Species rarely stray far from the safety of their adopted anemone in search of food and consequently rely heavily on the passing water to bring them an adequate diet.

All species of clownfish form a relationship with an anemone and this had been thought

● *Are clownfish suitable for the newcomer to the hobby?*

... Yes. Although they cannot be termed "hardy", most species respond well to reasonable care.

● *Must clownfish be kept with an anemone?*

No. In fact, anemones are extremely sensitive creatures requiring the best water and lighting conditions and are not easily managed by newcomers to the hobby. Luckily, clownfish usually survive quite happily without an anemone.

● *What should a healthy fish look like?*

Clownfish should always be active and alert. There should be no signs of marked skin or split fins. Eyes must be clear and bright. Avoid any specimens swimming erratically or sulking in a corner. Tank-bred fish may lack the intensity of colour of specimens in the wild and the white marking may not be complete; this is nothing to worry about if the individual is otherwise in good health.

● *Can clownfish be housed in a community tank?*

Yes, they are good community fish and generally very peaceful toward tankmates.

● *Are all clownfish wild-caught?*

No. Although clownfish are in no way an endangered species, tank-bred specimens are now freely available and you should ask for these wherever possible.

● *Can clownfish be kept with* Condylactis *anemones?*

Not really. This anemone is a Caribbean species and clownfish are not found in the Caribbean; therefore the relationship would not be a natural one.

● Amphiprion frenatus *and A.* ephippium *both appear to have the common names Fire Clownfish and Tomato Clownfish, is this correct?*

Yes, in many countries these common names have become interchangable for both species. This highlights the unreliability of common names. It is best to use scientific names wherever possible.

● *How can a true pair be established?*

Buy two juvenile clownfish at approximately 0.5in (1.3cm) – they will both be males. As they mature, the most dominant individual will develop into a female and a pair bond will be formed.

◀ *The Maroon Clownfish* (Premnas biaculeatus) *is a less sensitive species that will thrive without an anemone in the aquarium. The female is often three times larger than the diminutive male, but true pairs are rare.*

to be symbiotic but is now more properly described as commensal. Commensalism may be seen as a first step toward true symbiosis, whereby two partners draw an advantage from living in close association but are not fully reliant on each other as in symbiosis. In this case, the anemone provides a safe home for the clownfish, which, in return, protects the anemone from would-be predators owing to a highly developed territorial nature. However, many anemones are quite capable of surviving successfully without their clownfish partners, debunking the theory that the relationship is fully symbiotic.

Popular Species of Clownfish

	maximum adult size
Common Clownfish *Amphiprion ocellaris*	2in (5cm)
Maroon Clownfish *Premnas biaculeatus*	4in (10cm)
Fire Clownfish *Amphiprion frenatus*	3in (7.5cm)
Clark's Anemonefish *Amphiprion clarkii*	4in (10cm)
Tomato Clownfish *Amphiprion ephippium*	3in (7.5cm)
Pink Skunk Clownfish *Amphiprion perideraion*	2in (5cm)
Skunk Clown *Amphiprion akallopisos*	2in (5cm)
Black-footed Clown *Amphiprion nigripes*	2.5in (6.25cm)

The question of how members of the family Pomacentridae can survive the stinging tentacles of an anemone without being devoured has yet to be fully resolved. Put simply, the theory favoured by most researchers in this area relies on the fact that composition of clownfish mucus is based on sugar rather than protein, so the anemone fails to recognize the fish as food and does not fire its nematocysts or stinging cells (see anemones page 158). As work proceeds on this topic, a definitive answer may become available in the near future.

Breeding in the Wild

Clownfish lay their eggs on any flat surface close to, or preferably under, the protection of the host anemone's tentacles. The eggs are mainly cared for by the male and always hatch in complete darkness after some 7–10 days. Hatching occurs in a natural rhythm directly connected with the phases of the moon. The larvae – for they are not as well developed as fry in the true sense – then migrate upward to the plankton layers of the sea to feed and develop. Many will not survive this stage but of the small number that do, a place must be secured under the protection of a suitable anemone back on the reef floor as quickly as possible.

● *A clownfish will not go into the anemone supplied for it, why not?*

... This happens from time to time and the reasons are not fully understood. Patience is necessary as they usually take up residence eventually.

● *Can clownfish be kept in shoals?*

Clownfish are by nature very territorial and may resent the presence of other clownfish in the same tank. There are no specific rules, however, some clownfish will live quite happily together, others may fight to the death! In all cases, clownfish will not "shoal" in the scientific sense of the word.

● *Are clownfish long-lived?*

Yes, some have been kept in captivity in excess of eighteen years!

Many large anemones of the genera *Stoichactis* and *Heteractis* are capable of hosting numerous clownfish (although only one species will occupy each anemone) but of these, there can be only one breeding female, the rest will form a hierarchy of males. The female will only breed with the most dominant male but if she should die or be removed for any reason, the dominant male will change sex to become a breeding female and the other members of the male hierarchy will each step up one. This ability to change sex to suit prevailing conditions is not uncommon in the marine environment and is a means by which the species can guarantee continued existence.

The most commonly kept clownfish, and arguably the most popular fish in the hobby today, is the Common Clownfish. Some authorities claim that this fish is really two species – *Amphiprion ocellaris* and *A. percula*. However, the evidence is far from conclusive and it is likely that the two species are one and the same. Clownfish show a great deal of variety in their colour and pattern, depending on location, and it would seem logical to assume that, all other things being equal, the Common Clownfish should be known by a single scientific name. For our purposes this will be *Amphiprion ocellaris*.

Tank Conditions and Care

HABITAT: For tank and water conditions see Dwarf Angelfish page 116.

FEEDING: Brineshrimp and mysis, live and frozen, is greatly appreciated as a staple diet. Occasionally vary with flake, squid and other meaty foods of a suitable size.

HEALTH: In poor conditions, clownfish are susceptible to whitespot, *Oodinium*, and other parasitic diseases. Bacterial diseases are more common in newly imported wild fish. Copper medications are usually helpful but good conditions are the key to long-term success.

▶ *A group of healthy Common Clownfish* (Amphiprion ocellaris) *pictured in a dealer's sale tank. From this, the fishkeeper can easily choose a stunning individual fish, or pair, for the best display possible.*

Pygmy Basslets   FAMILY: PSEUDOCHROMIDAE

EVERY MARINE AQUARIUM REQUIRES A TOUCH of brilliant colour and pygmy basslets provide it in abundance! Found throughout the tropical Indo-Pacific and Red Sea regions, this family supplies numerous popular species to the marine aquarium trade.

Pseudochromids are highly territorial and solitary by nature. They live within the maze of passageways to be found within established coral reefs and rarely stray into open water for any reason. These fish are built for acceleration and will chase morsels of food drifting in the current or trying to evade capture with great swiftness. Intruders into their territory are also seen off with great ferocity and at high speed!

Pygmy basslets possess needle-sharp teeth which are used both for defence and in the capture of prey. Some of the larger specimens are capable of giving the unwary fishkeeper a nasty nip, should a finger be mistaken for an intruder or a piece of food!

Among the popular and easily kept species are: Flash-Back Gramma *(Pseudochromis diadema)*, False Gramma *(P. paccagnellae)* and Strawberry Gramma *(P. porphyreus)*. Aquarists looking for species offering more of a challenge might try Neon-Back Gramma *(P. dutoiti)*, Sunrise Dotty-back *(P. flavivertex)* or the rarer *P. fridmani*, *P. aureus* or *P. novaehollandiae*. While most of the former species attain a manageable 2.75in (7cm), the latter generally grow larger and require spacious accommodation. Practically all the common names given to pygmy basslets are misnomers; these fish are not "grammas" at all, even though they are closely related to the gramma family. Proper grammas live in the Atlantic, and do not share any common waters with pygmy basslets.

Very little is known about the breeding habits of this family. Spawning in captivity is rare and success has been limited.

● *Will more than one species of pygmy basslet share an aquarium?*

... Basslets are extremely territorial and will fight with members of their own, or similar, species; therefore, it would be wiser to maintain one individual per tank.

● *Do pygmy basslets have to be housed in an invertebrate aquarium?*

No, but the tank should contain a great deal of rockwork, forming a myriad of passages and hiding places; which is normally the case in the invertebrate aquarium.

● *When choosing a healthy pygmy basslet, what should be looked for?*

Always try to pick a fish that is highly coloured and not "washed out" in appearance. Fins should be intact and there should be no tendency to scratch against rocks or other surfaces. Shyness and hiding is quite normal.

◀ *Its brilliant magenta colouring readily identifies the Strawberry Gramma (Pseudochromis porphyreus). Watch out for its pugnacious and territorial nature.*

◀ *The Neon-Back Gramma (Pseudochromis dutoiti) makes a wonderfully colourful addition to the mixed fish-invertebrate aquarium.*

Tank Conditions and Care

HABITAT: A mixed fish-invertebrate tank with plenty of rockwork would be ideal.

Tank size At least 48in (120cm) long with a volume of 45 gallons (205 l; 54 US gallons).

pH	8.1–8.3
Temperature	25–26°C (77–79°F)
Ammonia	Zero
Nitrite	Zero

Nitrate 5ppm or less total NO_3 in the fish-invertebrate aquarium; 20ppm maximum in a fish-only aquarium.

Specific Gravity	1.020–1.024
Dissolved Oxygen	6–7ppm

Water Changes 15–25% every two weeks with filtered tapwater.

Filtration Efficient protein skimming and activated carbon as standard, with ultraviolet sterilization and ozone filtration where possible.

Lighting Basslets prefer subdued lighting but will adapt to the intense lighting demanded by the invertebrate aquarium inhabitants.

FEEDING: Pygmy basslets particularly relish live brineshrimp but are happy to consume any meaty marine fare such as cockle, squid and mussel. It must be remembered, however, that they will only take food drifting in the current and not from the substrate.

HEALTH: There are no particular health problems in high quality water.

Lionfish FAMILY: SCORPAENIDAE

LIONFISH ARE ALSO KNOWN AS SCORPIONFISH, Turkeyfish, Zebrafish, Dragonfish and Fu Manchu. Their appearance is unmistakable. The rays of the pectoral and dorsal fins are grossly extended and, in many species, embellished with decorative tissue. The effect is like an exploding firework, indeed another common name is Fireworksfish!

Lionfish are extremely efficient predators with a battery of defenses to deter potential larger enemies. The extended fin rays, easily misinterpreted as beautiful embellishments, are filled with a potent venom capable of inflicting a painful wound in humans and fatal injury to other fish species.

Hunter's Camouflage

Lionfish can use their cryptic markings to blend into their surroundings, while they wait, quite still, for a passing fish. The cavernous mouth engulfs the subject with lightning speed and accuracy. Some species will use the width of their spines to herd small fishes or shrimps into a confined area before gulping down several of the victims.

In the wild, lionfish may be found as lone individuals, but quite often they congregate in

Popular Species of Lionfish

	maximum adult size
Lionfish *Pterois volitans*	14in (35cm)
White-fin Lionfish *Pterois radiata*	8in (20cm)
Spotfin Lionfish *Pterois antennata*	8in (20cm)
Turkeyfish* *Dendrochirus brachypterus*	4in (10cm)
Twinspot Lionfish* *Dendrochirus biocellatus*	5in (12.5cm)

*Dwarf species

● *Are lionfish dangerous fish to keep?*

... Lionfish need to be treated with the utmost respect, but they are neither aggressive nor likely to deliberately harm their owner. Always be aware of their presence and keep a reasonable distance between your arms and the fish. Never feed lionfish by hand.

● *What action should be taken if a person is stung by a lionfish?*

Immerse the sting in hot water to coagulate the venom, then pour vinegar or alcohol over the wound to ease the pain. If stung by only one or two rays, most adults should be able to withstand the pain. However, there is a slight danger that the person will be allergic to the poison (the likelihood is increased if they are already allergic to bee or wasp stings). If an allergic reaction is suspected, rush the patient to a casualty department.

● *What is the safest way to handle lionfish?*

As little as possible! If a specimen must be netted, use a large net to encompass the whole of the fish and transfer it keeping hands well clear. Turn the net over and allow the fish to disentangle itself (which it will do). Do not try to free the fish using your hands.

● *Can lionfish be kept with others of its own kind?*

Yes, they are quite compatible but larger specimens require a great deal of space.

● *Are lionfish safe with other fish?*

Yes, as long as they are non-aggressive and too large to be swallowed. Larger angels, moray eels, groupers, grunts and triggers make suitable tankmates.

● *Are there dwarf lionfish species?*

Yes. Although there are relatively few species of lionfish, they can range in full-grown adult size from 4in (10cm) to 14in (35cm). Obviously, it would be wise to be certain that a "dwarf" lionfish is not just a juvenile of a much larger species!

small groups during the day within caves or beneath shady overhangs before dispersing at dusk to feed. Several species are known to be fully nocturnal hunters and never venture into open water during the hours of daylight.

Although there are no reliable external differences between male and female, aquarium observations have revealed that female lionfish release a gelatinous ball of eggs while a mating pair rise together in the water column. The male fertilizes the ball which breaks up after reaching the surface. Breeding in commercial quantities has not been successful so far, but this behaviour indicates the possibility of success in the future.

▶ *Owing to their placid non-aggressive nature, fishkeepers often forget that the fin rays, clearly seen on this specimen* (Pterois volitans) *are tipped with venom and capable of inflicting a very painful wound.*

Tank Conditions and Care

HABITAT: For tank and water conditions see Angelfish page 114.

FEEDING: Most newly caught fish will only accept live foods such as goldfish, guppies, mollies, river shrimp and brineshrimp. Many aquarists will feel unhappy with this but with a little patience all lionfish can be weaned onto frozen marine foods. This may include lancefish, mussel and cockle. The following procedure has proved very successful: tie the chosen food loosely onto the end of a piece of cotton and let it fall slowly in front of the lionfish's nose. If the lionfish ignores it, wiggle the offering. When the fish eventually takes the food, the cotton should slide off and be removed. The "conversion" may take days or even weeks; persevere and do not offer live food in the meantime or after conversion.

HEALTH: Lionfish are very disease-resistant, especially where water quality is kept high. They can survive for over 12 years in an aquarium.

Sea Basses and Groupers

FAMILIES: SERRANIDAE / PLESIOPIDAE

REPRESENTED IN EVERY TEMPERATE AND tropical sea worldwide, the Serranidae is an extensive one, including over 370 species. The largest is probably *Epinephelus lanceolatus* reaching 9ft (2.7m), but several other species approach this size. At the other end of the spectrum *Plectranthias longimanus* is diminutive at only 1in (2.5cm). Many of the larger sea basses, or coral trout as they are sometimes known, are popular food fishes.

There are many instances of sex-change and simultaneous hermaphroditism in serranids. Hamlets are a good example – each fish has an ovotestis (an ovary and testes) and is capable of producing eggs and sperm at the same time. Such fish could produce several generations of self-fertilized offspring, but an influx of fresh genes would be required for long-term survival. The ability to change sex is common in reef fish. Among *Anthias* each fish begins life as a female, with the ability to become a male as a strategy for survival, enabling the species to continue even in the most difficult of circumstances. The change can be very swift, sometimes 2–3 days.

Popular Species of Sea Basses and Groupers

	maximum adult size

Comet Grouper/Marine Betta   6in (15cm)
Calloplesiops altivelis
Now classified in the family Plesiopidae.

▼ *The Comet Grouper* (Calloplesiops altivelis) *is a superbly marked, predatory fish best kept in a fish-only aquarium.*

Panther Grouper   12in (30cm)
Chromileptes altivelis
Often seen for sale as a 1in (2.5cm) specimen but ultimately this fish will need a very large aquarium!

Blue Hamlet   5in (12.5cm)
Hypoplectrus gemma
Available to the hobbyist on an erratic basis; easy to keep and very suitable for beginners. In common with other larger groupers, they will consume smaller fish.

Sixline Grouper   10in (25cm)
Grammistes sexlineatus
Has striking markings and is rather shy. It will eat smaller tankmates and there are reports that this species exudes a poison into the water when badly frightened, injured, or dying.

◆ *Wreckfish* (Anthias squamipinnis) *have clear sexual differences. Although they all begin life as yellow-orange females, dominant red males develop (see bottom fish) to command a small harem.*

● *Are groupers difficult to keep?*

The true groupers, which tend to exceed 10in (25cm), are very tolerant of poor water conditions and as such are easy to keep. The smaller serranids such as Swiss Guard and Wreckfish require optimum water conditions at all times.

● *What tankmates are suitable for groupers?*

Only those that are far too big to be swallowed! Many groupers can extend their jaws to some considerable size and will eat unsuspecting tankmates. The smaller and more peaceful members of the family will not usually harm other species.

Tank Conditions and Care

HABITAT: All species appreciate plenty of rockwork and hiding places.

Tank size Large groupers may require tanks in excess of 150 gallons (682 l; 180 US gallons) when fully grown. Smaller species need a minimum of 40 gallons (182 l; 48 US gallons).

pH	8.1–8.3
Ammonia	Zero
Nitrite	Zero

Nitrate Up to 50ppm total NO_3 for large species; less than 10ppm for smaller, sensitive species.

Specific Gravity	1.021–1.024

Dissolved Oxygen Larger species 5–7ppm; smaller species 6–7ppm.

Water Changes 15–20% every fortnight. Use only high quality filtered water for sensitive species.

Filtration Excellent biological, chemical and mechanical filtration is required. Efficient protein skimming and activated carbon filtration should be used as standard.

Lighting Most serranids prefer subdued lighting, although *Anthias* are used to very bright reef conditions.

FEEDING: Larger groupers will thrive on live river shrimp and frozen meaty marine fare such as cockle, mussel, squid and lancefish. Smaller serranids enjoy frozen brineshrimp, mysis and even marine flake food.

HEALTH: Most of the larger groupers are disease-resistant and rarely suffer if kept in a large enough tank. The smaller species are more delicate and require excellent water quality.

Shy Hamlet   5in (12.5cm)
Hypoplectrus guttavarius
As for Blue Hamlet

Wreckfish   5in (12.5cm)
Anthias squamipinnis
The most popular and attractive of the serranids. First-class water conditions are essential.

Swiss Guard   4in (10cm)
Lioproproma rubre
An attractive, shy species, very peaceful, and commanding a high price.

Coral Trout   18in (45cm)
Cephalopholis miniatus
A bright-red fish with neon blue dots. It usually outgrows the domestic aquarium and may eat its tankmates when mature!

Rabbitfish FAMILY: SIGANIDAE

RABBITFISH, NAMED BECAUSE OF THEIR herbivorous nature, are a relatively small family of fish with only about 25 species divided between two genera. *Lo* and *Siganus* are distributed throughout the Indo-Pacific, although at least two species, *Siganus luridus* and *S. rivulatus* have made their way into the eastern Mediterranean, probably by way of the Suez Canal.

They are usually to be found in the turtle grass beds and sandy areas of lagoons, often in large shoals of juvenile fish, sometimes mixed with surgeonfish. Mature specimens tend to leave the larger shoals and form strong pair bonds, wandering far wider over the reefs. Some siganids are regularly seen feeding in fresh water having travelled into river estuaries.

Grazing on Algae

Small mouths and rasping teeth are specially adapted for grazing on algae, and like all herbivores rabbitfish spend a great deal of time on feeding activities in order to supplement a diet that is relatively poor in nutrition by the sheer quantity of their intake.

Siganids are also known by the alternative common name "Spinefoot". Both the dorsal

and anal fin rays are venomous and if the fish is trodden on, or otherwise handled without proper respect, is capable of inflicting an extremely painful wound! Should the fish be attacked by another species, it will adopt a typical defence posture of head down with dorsal spines extended toward the opponent.

Breeding usually occurs in the early morning or late afternoon and more often in small groups. The eggs are sticky and demersal (sinking to the bottom) or attach themselves to algae. No parental care takes place. Some species are reported to have spawned in captivity, and the fry have been successfully reared to adulthood.

Popular Species of Rabbitfish

	maximum adult size
Foxface or Badgerfish	10in (25cm)
Lo vulpinus	

Extremely attractive species with a bright-yellow body and black and white stripes over the head for which the common title of Badgerfish is well-suited. Peaceful and lively is a good description of its behaviour.

Silver Badgerfish	10in (25cm)
Siganus virgatus	

Less commonly seen than *Lo vulpinus* and is not so brightly coloured. However, it recommends itself to the careful aquarist by

grazing on filamentous algae, often regarded as a nuisance by many hobbyists. This also is a peaceful species.

Other species that may be encountered from time to time include:

One-Spot Foxface	8in (20cm)
Siganus unimaculatus	
Brown-Yellow Foxface	8in (20cm)
Siganus uspae	
Red Foxface	8in (20cm)
Siganus magnificus	

Tank Conditions and Care

HABITAT: For tank and water conditions see Surgeonfish page 80.

FEEDING: Rabbitfish demand a constant supply of algae. If this is unavailable, blanched lettuce or spinach leaves must be placed in the aquarium every day. Other foods are also accepted such as brineshrimp, mysis and even flake food on occasions.

HEALTH: Many rabbitfish adopt a completely different coloration when stressed or at night. This usually takes the form of brown blotches and is thought to be a cryptic night-time camouflage technique. Once settled, a fish will regain its former bright coloration.

◀ *The Silver Badgerfish* (Siganus virgatus) *makes an ideal addition to the fish-only aquarium. It is a peaceful species that dislikes being bullied.*

◀ *The most attractive siganid for the hobbyist is probably the Foxface* (Lo vulpinus). *However, the spines of the dorsal and anal fins are venomous.*

● *Are rabbitfish suitable for the beginner?*

... Given the proper water conditions, and a constant supply of green food, they are not difficult fish to keep.

● *Do rabbitfish grow quickly?*

Yes. Given good conditions they will reach their full adult size within several years. Suitably large accommodation must be supplied or the fish will outgrow their surroundings.

● *What should be done if stung?*

Rabbitfish stings are very painful but are not dangerous unless there is an allergic reaction. Treat the pain in the same way as Lionfish (Scorpaenidae) stings by immersing the wound in very hot water. This will help alleviate the pain, which will eventually subside after several hours.

● *Are rabbitfish compatible with invertebrates?*

No, they can be very destructive, pecking at sessile invertebrates in particular.

Seahorses and Pipefish

FAMILY: SYNGNATHIDAE

THE SEAHORSE IS AN EXTRAORDINARY AND captivating creature. Its inherent charm and curious nature have lured hobbyists into marine fishkeeping with varying degrees of success; for seahorses are difficult to keep and not suitable for beginners. They have an ancient lineage, descended from pipefish-type animals millions of years ago. As their ancestors spent longer periods in still water they ceased to need a strong swimming capability and relied on camouflage to protect them from enemies. The seahorse of today is slow-swimming, relying on a rapidly beating dorsal fin and a pair of barely visible fins just behind the ear openings. It is able to adapt its body colour to its surroundings, and has a hard external skeleton capable of deterring potential predators. Its eyes move independently enabling it to identify food with one eye, while the other watches for any approaching threat. It also has a prehensile tail, by which it can attach itself tightly to any suitable piece of algae, rock or gorgonian coral. Hence the old name "Sea Monkey".

Reproduction is performed by one of the strangest acts in the whole animal kingdom. The female uses her ovipositor to deposit eggs within the male's abdominal pouch where they are fertilized and develop in complete safety. Other than that initial act, the female plays no further part in the development of the young.

Some two to eight weeks later, depending on the species, the "pregnant" male will be displaying a hugely distended abdomen and soon "gives birth" to tiny replicas of the adults. The babies have a fully functioning tail and grip any convenient object while they feed voraciously on plankton. Pipefish may not be as attractive as seahorses to the hobbyist, but they share many of the same characteristics and should be treated in much the same way within the aquarium.

● *Do seahorses have an internal skeleton as well as an external one?*

... Yes. The internal one is just like a normal fish, whereas the external one is made up of horny plates that expand and develop as the seahorse grows.

● *Which species are best for the experienced fishkeeper to start with?*

Seahorses are notoriously difficult to identify and it would be easier to consider them either as "giants" which may grow up to 10in (25cm) in length and live for 5 years plus, or as "dwarfs" which hardly ever achieve more than 4in (10cm) and live for 1–2 years. The giants are generally easier to feed.

➤ *The Yellow Seahorse* (Hippocampus kuda) *may alter its coloration to suit the surroundings. In the wild it generally inhabits the quieter lagoons and bays, hidden among the eel grass and algae.*

● *A male seahorse has given "birth" to babies; what should they be fed on?*

Baby seahorses can be fed brineshrimp and rotifers. However, their dietary requirements are still not properly understood and large-scale breeding has not been successful to date.

● *What tankmates would be suitable for seahorses?*

Pipefish, mandarinfish and Scooter Blennies are all ideal companions.

➤ *The Bluestripe Pipefish*
(Doryrhamphus excisus) *needs the same tank conditions as its close relative the seahorse.*

Tank Conditions and Care

HABITAT: Seahorses require a "quiet" aquarium where they will not be bothered by boisterous fish that may also deprive them of food. Plenty of anchorage points should be provided in the form of gorgonians, sea fan skeletons and algae. Seahorses may kill live gorgonians, sea whips or sea fans owing to their habit of remaining stationary for long periods, preventing the invertebrates from extending their polyps and feeding.

Tank Size A minimum of 36x15x12in (92x38 x30cm) is necessary to house four giant specimens, or eight dwarf seahorses.	
pH	8.1–8.3
Temperature	24–25°C (75–77°F)
Ammonia	Zero
Nitrite	Zero
Nitrate	Less than 10ppm total NO_3
Specific Gravity	1.021–1.024
Dissolved Oxygen	6ppm
Calcium	400–450ppm
Phosphates	Zero
Filtration Efficient biological filtration, protein skimming and activated carbon as standard.	
Lighting	Moderate, not too bright
Water Changes 15–20% each fortnight with high quality water of the same temperature and salinity.	

FEEDING: It is difficult to wean seahorses off live foods onto frozen marine fare, so copious quantities of live brineshrimp are usually offered. On its own, this diet can lack vital minerals and vitamins, and should be supplemented with live mysis shrimp, *Daphnia*, glassworm and bloodworm. In the wild, seahorses are constant planktonic feeders and this should be replicated in the aquarium by four or even five feedings each day.

HEALTH: Seahorses suffer many health problems. Whitespot, *Oodinium* and gill flukes may be treated using medication. Gaseous bubbles (possibly linked with tiny changes in osmotic pressure as a result of variations in salinity) may form in the pouch or body, and are potentially fatal. Body bubbles can be pricked with a sharp needle, and pouch bubbles eased out gently with a blunt cocktail stick.

Pufferfish FAMILY: TETRAODONTIDAE

PUFFERS ARE FOUND IN THE TROPICS; SOME species stray into brackish water and even fresh water. There are 118 species, but only a few are found in the aquarium trade.

Tetraodontids have smooth, soft bodies and the scales are missing altogether; this allows the puffers to inflate with water in excess of twice their normal size when danger threatens. Such inflation techniques, shared by the porcupinefish (page 94), increase the size of the fish until it is too large to be swallowed by a potential predator. Should that prove ineffectual, the mucus, skin and visceral organs are poisonous. Even so, there are predators that seem immune, and will consume puffers on a regular basis.

Species in the genus *Fugu* are particularly prized as a restaurant delicacy in Japan. Their organs contain some of the most toxic poisons known to man, and chefs have to be specially trained to prepare the fish safely. People die regularly from poisoning, but this dish continues to be highly regarded.

The dorsal and anal fins have soft rays and provide the main propulsive power; there are

Tank Conditions and Care

HABITAT: For tank and water conditions see Porcupinefish page 95.

FEEDING: Puffers enjoy crustaceans and molluscs with the exoskeleton (shell) left on. They are greedy feeders and will eat almost constantly, if allowed to.

HEALTH: In common with boxfish and porcupinefish, puffers are prone to eye infections should water quality deteriorate or the fish be in a constant state of stress. If the eyes seem cloudy, perform a 50% water change and treat with a bactericide. Other than that, puffers are remarkably disease-resistant.

no pelvic fins. Puffers are highly manoeuvrable and can easily swim backwards if the occasion demands. They breed by forming pairs or small harems scattering demersal (sinking) eggs within a territory defended by the pair or female, depending on the species. Eggs hatch after a month and the larvae migrate into the plankton layer to develop. Breeding in captivity is still very rare, but some species have been reared to adulthood.

Popular Species of Pufferfish

	maximum adult size		
White-Spotted Blowfish *Arothron hispidus* Very peaceful towards other fish.	10in (25cm)	White-Spotted Toby* *Canthigaster jactator* Requires a moderate amount of space.	3.5in (8.75cm)
Spotted Puffer *Arothron meleagris* Does well in a large aquarium. Often found in a bright yellow as well as a brown form.	12in (30cm)	Honeycomb Toby* *Canthigaster janthinoptera* An attractive small fish.	3.5in (8.75cm)
Dogface Puffer *Arothron nigropunctatus* Has an endearing face much like a dog. It is found in several colours, yellow, grey and even yellow and grey!	10in (25cm)	Sharpnosed Puffer* *Canthigaster solandri* Attractive and very peaceful to other fish dissimilar to itself.	3in (7.5cm)
Spotted Toby* *Canthigaster amboinensis* Extremely attractive, peaceful and easily housed.	6in (15cm)	Valentine Puffer* *Canthigaster valentini* Has a reputation for fin-nipping.	3in (7.5cm)

* These relatively smaller species are often referred to as Tobys or Sharpnosed Puffers. They are more sensitive to poor water conditions than their relatives.

● *Can puffers be kept with invertebrates?*

... No, even the smaller species can be very destructive.

● *How long do puffers live?*

On average about 5–7 years, although specimens in large public aquaria have survived much longer.

● *If the teeth grow so long that it can barely eat, what should be done?*

A vet that specializes in fish should be asked to file down the teeth while the fish is under an anaesthetic. This procedure is quite common and usually successful. Regular feedings of molluscs, crab or lobster (in their shells) will keep the teeth worn down.

● *Should puffers be encouraged to inflate?*

No. It is very stressful on the fish and may encourage them to shed poisonous mucus into the water, thereby putting at risk other tank inhabitants, and itself!

● *Do puffers shed their poisonous mucus into the tank water regularly?*

No. In high quality water and with peaceful tankmates there is no reason why it should ever shed mucus.

◆ *Sharpnosed Puffers* (Canthigaster solandri) *are peaceful and endearing fish that bring interest and colour to the fish-only aquarium. Tankmates should also be peaceful as puffers are easily stressed by bullying.*

◆ *This close-up of a White-Spotted Blowfish* (Arothron hispidus) *shows the typical mouthparts of a Tetraodontid. As the name suggests (tetra = four,* dontid *= teeth), they have four incisors, similar to beaks, two in each jaw. The teeth grow constantly and are worn down by crushing molluscs and exoskeletons of crustaceans.*

Unusual Fish

THE THREE FISH IN THIS SECTION ARE NOT related. Each may be the only representative of its family kept in a domestic aquarium. None of them is difficult to keep, but some specimens may take a while to locate, or require a special order through a dealer.

Pine-Cone Fish *(Monocentrus japonicus)*
Family: Monocentridae

This is a genuine living fossil; it has existed in its present form for millions of years. Rarely exceeding 6in (15cm) in the aquarium, its body is covered in very large, yellow coloured scales, fused together to create a texture similar to that of a pine cone. Its most remarkable feature is the light-generating organ on its lower jaw, which may help to locate other members of the species at night as well as assisting in the search for food. Pine-Cone Fish are generally peaceful and may be kept in a fish-only tank with other large and peaceful specimens or, alternatively, an invertebrate aquarium without crustaceans or small fish.

● *Could I keep all three of these species in the same tank?*

... Yes, provided that the tank was large enough, they would all share the same space peacefully.

● *Where can I see the light-emitting organ on the Pine-Cone Fish?*

It is just under the eye and may be seen in darkened conditions as the mood of the fish dictates.

● *Would a Remora attach itself to a fish sharing the same tank?*

It is possible, if the other fish were very large, but the Remora generally ignores its tankmates.

● *Will trumpetfish eat smaller species?*

Yes. They have an extendible jaw capable of accommodating fish that might otherwise appear to be too large to be eaten.

Tank Conditions and Care
Pine-Cone Fish

HABITAT: For water conditions see Large Angelfish on page 114.

Tank Size A minimum tank size of 48 x 15 x 18in (122 x 38 x 46cm) will be required for small specimens.

Lighting Subdued, with shady caves as a retreat.

FEEDING: Newly imported individuals may only accept live river shrimp and brineshrimp. With care and patience they can be weaned onto frozen, meaty marine fare.

HEALTH: Pine-Cone Fish are normally quite resistant to disease as long as water quality remains high.

▲ *Their large, distinctively shaped scales are a fascinating feature of the Pine-Cone Fish.*

Tank Conditions and Care
Trumpetfish

HABITAT: For water conditions see Large Angelfish page 114. They need good filtration, but are not fussy about lighting.

Tank Size A tank in excess of 6ft (2m) will be required for fully grown specimens as plenty of swimming space is essential.

FEEDING: Live food such as river shrimp are appreciated as a staple diet initially, although frozen shrimp and other meaty foods will be taken as they settle into aquarium life.

HEALTH: Optimum water conditions must be maintained if trumpetfish are to flourish.

◀ *The Atlantic Trumpetfish* (Aulostomus maculatus).

Trumpetfish (Aulostomus spp.)
Family: Aulostomidae
This elongated fish may reach 24in (60cm) in the aquarium. It is highly carnivorous and very intelligent, especially in finding food. In the wild, it is a solitary species that chooses a lofty vantage point from which to ambush small fish, shrimps and other crustacea. In captivity it can be trained to take shrimp from its owner's fingers. Trumpetfish lead a very sedentary life and must not be kept with other boisterous tankmates; a species tank would suit them much better.

Body colour varies with the species, but trumpetfish available to the hobbyist are generally either green or yellow. The sexes are easily distinguished as the male develops a long anterior fin ray on the first dorsal.

Tank Conditions and Care
Remora

HABITAT: For tank and water conditions see Large Angelfish page 114. Since this fish is mainly inactive, it does not need a very large tank, but well-aerated water is appreciated.

FEEDING: Remora relish live river shrimp and other meaty marine fare.

HEALTH: Not vulnerable to disease so long as water quality remains high.

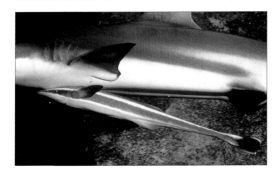

Remora (Echeneis naucrates)
Family: Echeneididae
Remora possess a very effective suction disc (a modified dorsal fin) above their heads which they use to attach themselves to marine mammals and larger fish. Once attached, they will feed on scraps of food discarded by their host. They are also capable of feeding independently and surviving without a host. Remora are very lethargic and may stay attached to the aquarium glass for very long periods. They are generally peaceful and will not bother similarly sized tankmates. Specimens offered for sale may be small, but this fish is capable of attaining 3ft (90cm) under ideal conditions.

◀ *Remoras generally have a lethargic nature within the aquarium, but in the wild their streamlined body enables them to keep pace with fast, large fish and aquatic mammals.*

137

Sharks and Stingrays

CLASS: CHONDRICHTHYES

UNLIKE THE PRECEDING SPECIES, ALL OF which have bony skeletons, the skeletons of sharks and rays are formed from cartilage. In addition, there is a marked difference in the physiology of bony and cartilaginous species. Cartilaginous fish are particularly sensitive to copper medications and heavy metals, and cannot always be treated for diseases in the same way as bony fish.

Sharks

There are about 357 species of shark worldwide, the smallest being the female *Squaliolus laticauda* which rarely exceeds 7in (17.5cm) fully grown. At the other end of the scale at 40ft (12m) is the gigantic Whale Shark *(Rhincodon typus)*. A totally harmless plankton feeder, the Whale Shark is the exception to the rule – practically every other species is strictly carnivorous and actively hunts for fish, crustacea and molluscs.

Sharks are supreme hunting machines. Every part of their body is tailored for killing. Their streamlined shape is capable of terrific bursts of speed. Forward pointing eyes focus mercilessly on the victim and a device in the nose, the "Ampullae of Lorenzeni", detects electrical impulses given off by the muscular movements of potential prey. It is so sensitive, that the breathing of a flat fish can be detected under several centimetres of sand. It can also pick up signals from distressed fish that may be well out of sight.

Pre-fertilized egg capsules, "Mermaids Purses" are imported from tropical regions and hatch into tiny replicas of their parents. In 3–5 years most of these sharks will reach a minimum of 3.3ft (1 metre) in length. Many public aquaria are now reluctant to accept any more sharks that have out-grown domestic tanks. The sheer size of the fish is not the only problem. In most species the caudal (tail) fin supplies most of the speed and direction, while the pectoral fins act as ailerons to go up or down, limiting manoeuverability in a confined space. Sharks do not have swimbladders, consequently they sink once forward motion has ceased. Couple this with the fact that they have no "brakes" and you have a fish that is very unhappy in an aquarium. Some specimens injure their noses against the sides of the tank, damaging the "Ampullae of Lorenzeni" and becoming stressed.

Stingrays

Very few species of stingray are suitable for the domestic aquarium as most grow too large or are relatively unattractive. Only the Blue-Spotted Stingray *(Taeniura lymna)* is seen with any regularity in the trade. It rarely exceeds 10in (25cm) and can be accommodated within a large tank. Like most stingrays, this attractive fish is a substrate dweller, sifting through the sand, mud and coral rubble in search of its favourite food, molluscs and crustaceans, which it crushes in its powerful jaws.

Popular Species of Sharks

	minimum adult size
Bamboo Shark *Chiloscyllium indicum*	2.5ft (75cm)
Brown Carpet Shark *Chiloscyllium griseum*	2.5ft (75cm)
Banded Catshark *Chiloscyllium plagiosum*	3.3ft (1m)
Brown Spotted Catshark *Chiloscyllium punctatum*	3.3 ft (1m)
Leopard Shark *Triakis semifasciata*	5.5ft (1.65m)
Epaulette Shark *Hemiscyllium ocellatum*	3.3ft (1m)
Nurse Shark *Ginglymostoma cirratum*	14ft (4.2m)

Nearly all will achieve these minimum sizes in 3–5 years, irrespective of the aquarium size.

● *Can sharks and rays be fed by hand?*

... No, they may inflict a serious injury. Feed using plastic aquarium tongs.

● *What are suitable tankmates?*

Large, hardy, fast-swimming fish will usually be suitable and these may include: Scats *(Scatophagus argus)* and Monos *(Monodactylus argenteus)*. Fish that are likely to irritate the shark are best avoided, e.g. triggerfish.

● *How can in-tank maintenance be carried out safely?*

Use a screen to isolate the shark or ray from the area of the tank that you are working in. Never assume that it will be safe for you to work in among the fish.

● *Are the stings associated with rays dangerous?*

Yes. They can cause serious illness in humans. Frequently, exporters clip off the sting to make the fish safer. It is unclear whether the sting regenerates and becomes venomous once more.

➤ *The Blue-Spotted Stingray* (Taeniura lymna) *is probably the most popular ray on offer to the hobbyist. Individuals often become very tame, coming close to the surface to take food offered in aquarium tongs.*

Tank Conditions and Care

HABITAT: Decoration or rockwork is unnecessary, as it takes up valuable swimming space.

Tank Size A hatchling will require an aquarium of at least 3ft (90cm) but will quickly outgrow the space available and a tank with an eventual size of 8ft (2.4m) will be essential.

pH	8.1–8.3
Temperature	24–25°C (75–77°F)
Ammonia	Zero
Nitrite	Zero
Nitrate	25ppm maximum total NO_3
Specific Gravity	1.021–1.024
Water changes	10% weekly

Filtration Highly efficient biological, mechanical and chemical filtration are all essential.

Lighting	Subdued
Heating	Undertank mats

FEEDING: Lancefish, squid, mussel, cockle, shellmeat, live river shrimp and even cubes of fresh fish are all constituents of a balanced diet. Feed once each day.

HEALTH: Sharks and rays are very resilient to disease and rarely need treating. If an ailment is positively diagnosed, then do not treat with medications that contain copper.

Invertebrates

Most marine hobbyists aspire to creating a "reef-type" aquarium at some point in their fishkeeping careers. This involves stocking the tank with invertebrates as well as fish. Setting up and maintaining an effective miniature reef requires the aquarist to master the more difficult aspects of the hobby, including being able to accommodate the needs of all the individual creatures that he or she intends to acquire.

Invertebrates are very sensitive to water quality, lighting, correct feeding and other tank conditions – considerably more so than most marine fish. Consequently, they demand a higher level of knowledge from the aquarist if he or she is to achieve the same level of success in maintaining an attractive display in the long term. The section that follows attempts to provide an essential insight into caring for these beautiful and fragile creatures.

INVERTEBRATE PROFILES

Cleaner Shrimp (Lysmata amboinensis) *see page 176*

What is a Marine Invertebrate?

INVERTEBRATES ARE ANIMALS WITHOUT A backbone or a vertebral column. Although a relatively loose term, "invertebrates" encompasses the overwhelming majority of animals on this planet. It is estimated that there are at least 2 million species sharing our world and of those a staggering 97% are invertebrates. A significant proportion of this figure is made up of terrestrial insects, worms and spiders, but experts believe that sea-dwelling invertebrates could account for nearly half of all known species. The vast majority are microscopic, but the giant squid (*Architeuthis harveyi*), which can reach a span of 66ft (20m), is also an invertebrate. Some animals are half invertebrate, half vertebrate. Sea squirts (see page 197) produce tadpole-like larvae that have a stiff backbone-like rod, although the sessile adult does not.

Saltwater invertebrates have developed into a multitude of fascinating shapes and sizes. For example, anemones are little more than a bag of skin, but when inflated with water, they become delightful flower-like creatures with deadly protective tentacles. Instead of an internal skeleton, crustaceans wear their skeleton on the outside, which they shed from time to time enabling growth to take place. Sea fans and sea whips possess a flexible support structure that is without a nervous system and acts only as a convenient attachment point for the multitude of polyps surrounding it. Cephalopods, such as octopuses and cuttlefish, are free-swimming invertebrates of great intelligence and formidable predatory skills. And so the list goes on, including such intriguing creatures as starfish, sea urchins, clams, sea slugs, jellyfish, tubeworms, sponges, soft corals, polyp colonies, and hard corals.

Marine aquarists are mostly concerned with those invertebrates that inhabit the shallow, tropical waters of the world, but similar species are represented in all oceans and seas from the tropical equatorial zones to the freezing waters of the polar regions. Indeed, polar waters possess an amazing diversity and quantity of anemones, sponges, tubeworms and shrimps.

The adaptability of invertebrates has been a never-ending source of wonder. In 1977, scientists discovered thriving colonies of crabs, shrimps, sponges, giant tubeworms, molluscs and other animals living at formerly impenetrable ocean depths 1.5mi (2.4km) beneath the surface! Far beyond the rays of the Sun, this ecosystem is nourished in a totally unexpected way, through a synthesis of chemicals converted by bacteria into food. The primary source of energy was identified as a chain of volcanic vents in the ocean floor, providing heat and chemicals vital for life.

● *Are invertebrates suitable for beginners?*

... No. These are far more sensitive creatures than fish, on the whole, and require a much better understanding of basic aquarium water chemistry, filtration and lighting. By having a fish-only tank for between 6–12 months, the novice will get a good grounding in these areas with animals that are generally far more forgiving.

● *Are there any substances that invertebrates find particularly noxious?*

Yes, copper-based medications are fatal to invertebrates, even in minute quantities. Copper treatments are commonly used to cure certain fish ailments, but all calcareous materials such as tufa rock, coral sand and gravel possess the ability to absorb and retain copper, only to reintroduce it back into the aquarium water at a later date. Therefore, it would be dangerous to house invertebrates in aquaria previously treated with copper without first replacing any affected materials.

➥ *What they lack in mobility, invertebrates often compensate for in variety of form and colour. Here orange polyps nestle among a colony of pink sponges.*

Historic Coral Reefs

The first corals appeared around 500 million years ago and can now be identified as fossilized examples inland, well away from today's coastlines. In fact, modern reef growth is estimated to have begun only very recently, around 5,000 years ago. This is because sea levels are dramatically higher now and have drowned previous structures. As recently – in geologic terms – as 7,000 years ago, sea levels were 66ft (20m) lower than they are today; 20,000 years ago they were 394ft (120m) lower!

Even these relatively slow-growing invertebrates are able to adapt to new environmental conditions. It is therefore not surprising that massive structures such as the Great Barrier Reef are only around 5,000 years old.

Considering the delicate eco-structures of the coral reefs, collecting for the aquarium hobby accounts for a tiny amount of sustainable harvesting. The marine aquarists' responsibility is, at all times, to maintain their tank systems properly and keep these animals alive, growing and, hopefully, multiplying.

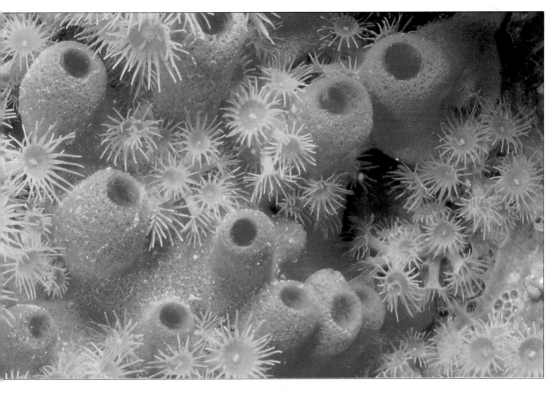

Sponges PHYLUM: PORIFERA

SPONGES ARE EXTREMELY PRIMITIVE ANIMALS and have changed little in the course of evolution. There are approximately 9,000 species, mostly in marine waters, with a further 150 adapted to freshwater. They are represented in all the oceans of the world, but are most common in sub-tropical and tropical waters. They range from a diminutive 0.4in (1cm) to 6.6ft (2m), with the largest species to be found in the Caribbean and the Antarctic seas. The deep-water species are commonly white, green or pale-yellow, but the more numerous shallow-water species encompass bright red, yellow, green, orange and purple. Colours are produced by pigments within the tissues, but the purpose of these pigments is poorly understood. They may either act as warnings (many sponges being toxic) or provide protection from harmful wavelengths of sunlight.

Sponges are sessile, filter feeders; they are also easy targets for predators. Angelfish and butterflyfish may feed on them exclusively for their whole lives. Large sea turtles find many sponges irresistible, as do a host of nudibranchs. To guard against their own destruction, sponges multiply speedily in an effort to compensate for such losses.

Homes for Other Species

Sponges are sometimes known as "living hotels" since their internal chambers make ideal "apartments" for a host of marine organisms, as diverse as shrimps, crabs, worms and small bottom-dwelling fish, such as gobies. The external surfaces of sponges may be colonized by algae, mushroom corals and other polyps. Some sponges do not tolerate such colonization; the larval stages of invertebrates in search of a home or the spores of algae are killed by sponge toxins should they attempt to establish permanently on or in the body of the sponge.

Shapes

As much of their development is governed by environmental factors such as space, water current and the substrate to which they are attached, sponges do not conform to any uniform shape. Species in turbulent waters are more likely to form rounded or flattened clumps, whereas species developing in slack

▼ *Sponges can be extremely colourful additions to the invertebrate aquarium. Pictured here are three attractive species available: Red Tree Sponge* (Haliclona compressa), *Yellow Tree Sponge* (Axinella vericosa) *and Red Ball Sponge* (Cliona lampa).

● *Are sponges easy to keep?*

... Most species require water of the highest quality and stability. They can present quite a challenge and are not for the beginner.

● *Which are the more reliable species?*

All the encrusting species seem to do well in the reef aquarium, especially the Blue Tubular Sponge (*Adocia* sp.), which, despite its common name, will encrust rocks and glass. The Orange Cup Sponge (*Axinellid* sp.) and Red Tree Sponge (*Haliclona compressa*) also do well.

● *How can a healthy sponge be recognized?*

It will have no pale or transparent edges and the colour will be deep and rich. Avoid specimens that are in any way disintegrating, unless it is a Blue Sponge (see below).

● *How do I "bag-up" a sponge to take it home?*

Sponges must never be removed from the water as air pockets can form leading to a premature demise. Leave enough water in the travelling bag to cover the sponge completely.

● *Is water circulation important?*

Yes. A moderate flow around the sponge at all times is preferable. Stale water, lacking in oxygen must be avoided.

● *Is it possible to see a sponge pumping water?*

Only with extremely good eyesight, although it has been estimated that a healthy sponge 4in (10cm) high and 0.4in (1cm) in diameter can pump 5 gallons (22.5 l; 6 US gallons) of water a day!

● *A Blue Sponge has disintegrated into smaller pieces, what should I do?*

This is not uncommon and each little piece may form into a new animal. If possible, distribute the pieces around the aquarium and monitor their growth.

● *Can a bath sponge be used as an ornament in the marine aquarium?*

No. While they would not be unsafe, such fibrous sponge skeletons are very light and porous, so almost always float!

water are taller and branching in form. The many encrusting species will simply take on the shape of the solid object that they grow over. These factors have made reliable identification of species very difficult; most species can only be identified by close observation of their structural features, which are often microscopic.

Internal Structure

Sponges have no organs or true tissues, but are just a simple aggregation of cells incapable of movement. The interior is a system of canals and chambers that open to the surface through a series of visible pores; indeed, the phylum name Porifera literally means "pore-bearer". Many of the internal surfaces are covered by whip-like hairs, known as flagella, which draw fresh oxygen-laden water and accompanying organic nutrients into the sponge. Once processed, the stale water is pumped out through exit pores by other flagella. Such is the efficiency of the filtering mechanism that even minute particles and bacteria can be absorbed, enabling sponges to thrive in nutritionally impoverished waters. Some sponges contain single-celled photosynthetic algae, blue-green algae and symbiotic bacteria, which may also provide nutrients for the sponge.

Sponges possess a "skeleton" that is made up of either spicules (elaborate rigid, supporting slivers of calcium carbonate or silica) or a fibrous material made of protein called spongin (the very same material we may use at bath time). These skeletons are not only beautiful, but are also the only dependable means of identification.

Tank Conditions and Care

HABITAT: For tank and water conditions see Hard Corals pages 151.

Temperature Within the range 21–25.5°C (70–78°F). Higher temperatures will cause stress.

Lighting Subdued conditions are preferred as they dislike being smothered by the algae normally encouraged by intense lighting. If bright conditions are required by other invertebrates sharing the same tank, then position the sponges in a shady position, perhaps within a cave or rock crevice.

FEEDING: Direct feeding is not strictly necessary; juices from frozen fish food will be enough to sustain most sponges. Extra feeding may cause pollution.

HEALTH: If aquarium conditions are poor, sponges can deteriorate, leaving only spicules or a spongin skeleton.

Sponges are capable of both sexual and asexual reproduction. Some may release eggs that are fertilized by sperm from another sponge of the same species; the fertilized eggs drift up into the plankton layer where they develop into larvae. At a pre-determined point of maturity, the larvae settle on the seabed and grow into a new sponge. Typically they reproduce asexually by budding off new individuals. More remarkably, complete sponges can reproduce from small pieces detached from a mature animal. This procedure is commonplace within the aquarium environment. Blue tubular sponges (*Adocia* spp.) are often introduced as a single animal only to "explode" into many fragments, each developing into a new sponge.

Purple sponges are highly desirable specimens owing to their beautiful coloration. Sporadic availability means that such specimens command high prices.

Hard Corals ORDER: SCLERACTINIA
(MADREPORARIA)

ASTRONAUTS HAVE REPORTED THAT THE Great Barrier Reef can clearly be seen from space, confirming it to be the largest animal-created structure in the world. At well over 1,200 miles (almost 2,000 km) in length, it is incredible to imagine that its construction is almost entirely due to the activity of hard (or stony) coral polyps! While thousands of invertebrates live on the reef, the hard corals quite literally are the reef. These unique polyp colonies abstract calcium carbonate from the sea water to form the calcareous skeletons in which they live. As they die, new polyps build their skeletons on top of the old ones, maintaining and expanding the reef.

Hard corals have only been studied closely for a relatively short period, but we know that they grow very slowly and are extremely long-lived compared with other sessile invertebrates. However, putting an accurate age on

The Bubble Coral (Plerogyra sinuosa) *has gained its common name from its unique bubble-like structure.*

● *Are hard corals to be recommended to the beginner?*

... Absolutely not! The aquarist will need at least 1–2 years of success with reef tanks, excluding hard corals, before attempting to keep these sensitive animals.

● *Can fish be a problem in the same tank?*

Their waste can pollute the water and put hard corals under stress. Never allow fish stocks to exceed 1in (2.5cm) of fish length for every 6 gallons nett (27 l; 7 US gallons) of water.

● *Is it safe to introduce hard corals into an aquarium with nuisance algae?*

No, nuisance algae indicates that water conditions are poor and not suitable for hard corals.

any particular animal or colony is very difficult and complicated by interruptions in growth owing to tropical storms and hurricanes. Study areas can be swept away in a few hours and formerly accurate information reduced to little more than guesswork.

We also know that they need special conditions for sustained healthy growth. The sea should be constantly warm, certainly never falling below 21°C (70°F); the water must be well oxygenated and unpolluted; and they need high-intensity sunlight, typically found in tropical and equatorial regions.

This need for intense sunlight is a key factor governing the survival of hard corals, for like their cousins, anemones, the tissues of hard corals are home to various species of algae, collectively known as zooxanthellae. This relationship is truly symbiotic as neither can live without the other; the algae provides the coral with oxygen and nutrients, while the coral gives the algae a safe home.

Reproduction

Reproduction is achieved in one of two ways. Either new colonies are established by fragments "budding-off", or totally new polyps begin to grow as a result of water-borne larvae finding a new home. In common with many other sessile invertebrates (those that are fixed in one place and unable to move)

● *Do hard corals "fight" with each other?*

... Hard corals need plenty of space and sense the proximity of competing species. The dominant species may attack the weaker one on two fronts. Stinging cells can be released into the water which will damage the "intruder" at a distance; and long tentacles, tipped with stinging cells, can be extended to damage another coral. The weaker coral will appear "burned" or retract from its attacker. Should "fighting" be suspected, move the corals as far apart as possible. An efficient filtration system will help remove stinging cells.

◀ *"Sweeper tentacles" have extended from this Anchor Coral* (Euphyllia fimriata) *to sting a nearby soft coral. Many hard corals use this effective method of attack to maintain sufficient space in which to grow.*

● *Where would it be best to site hard corals?*

Plenty of good quality, intense lighting is essential, so it makes sense to place the corals as close to the lighting source as possible, which in most cases means very high up on the rockwork. Secure placement is vitally important as corals injured in a fall are extremely difficult to restore to full health. A small area of damage will spread to affect the whole animal.

● *Is good water circulation necessary?*

Yes, it is essential. If possible variable pulsed pumps should be used to vary the direction of the water flow.

● *Are supplements necessary for good health?*

Supplements of molybdenum and strontium seem to help prevent some species from parting company with their skeletal bases. Iodine supplements have also proved beneficial. However, if good quality (ie reverse osmosis) water changes are performed as prescribed or a constant water change facility is in operation, there should be little or no need for supplements.

● *What precautions must be taken when buying hard corals?*

Always purchase healthy specimens that are fully expanded, with no signs of detachment or damage. Specimens should be fully coloured rather than pale.

● *How should hard corals be introduced?*

Acclimatize specimens to a new environment very slowly, preventing pH or osmotic shock. Over a period of 30 minutes slowly mix the tank water with the water in the travelling bag until the two are identical in make up. Always make sure there is enough space to accommodate a fully spread hard coral.

● *Are there any hard corals that do not require intense lighting?*

Yes, Sun Coral *(Tubastrea aurea)* is devoid of symbiotic zooxanthellae algae and lives in shady caves and crevices. Being a beautiful golden colour, it is very popular with hobbyists, but difficult to keep. Sun Coral needs a shady cave with good water circulation, and a diet of live rotifers and brineshrimp nauplii. Encourage the polyps to expand by squeezing the juices of a shrimp head over the colony. Excellent water quality is absolutely essential to the survival of this particular species.

◀ *It is easy to understand how this magnificent Sun Coral* (Tubastrea aurea) *gained its common name. Unfortunately, its characteristic golden polyps usually only become extended at night.*

The *Tooth Coral* (Euphyllia picteti) *exhibits its small multiple mouths amongst the tentacles.*

sexual reproduction enables a far wider dispersal of the species. It is a wonder of nature that on most reefs sexual reproduction takes place on only a few chosen nights each year! On those nights billions of eggs and sperm are released simultaneously from the same species, hundreds, sometimes thousands of miles apart. The resultant activity causes the water to become clouded for many miles! These mass spawnings work on a policy of overwhelming numbers, predators being allowed to satisfy their hunger while the massive majority of fertilized eggs escape to form a significant part of the plankton layers circling the tropical oceans. Lunar cycles seem

Popular Species of Hard Corals

Species for the experienced hobbyist

Tooth Coral	*Euphyllia picteti*
Frogspawn Corals	*Euphyllia* spp.
Anchor Coral	*Euphyllia fimriata*
Bubble Coral	*Plerogyra sinuosa*
Plate Coral	*Fungia actiniformis*

Species for the very experienced hobbyist

Organ Pipe Coral	*Tubipora musica*
Gonioporas	*Goniopora* spp.
Brain Corals	*Leptoria* spp.
Brain Corals	*Trachyphyllia* spp.
Moon Corals	*Favites* spp.
Sun Coral	*Tubastrea aurea*

Tank Conditions and Care

HABITAT: An almost exclusively invertebrate tank, established for at least 4–6 months in which the following exceptional conditions are maintained.

Tank Size   A minimum of 48 x 18 x 12in (122 x 46 x 30cm), or 40 gallons (182 l; 48 US gallons).

pH	8.2–8.3
Temperature	25–26°C (77–79°F)
Ammonia	Zero
Nitrite	Zero
Nitrate	Zero
Specific Gravity	1.021–1.026
Dissolved Oxygen	7–8ppm
Calcium	400–450ppm
Phosphates	Zero
KH	A natural seawater level of 7°dKH
Redox Potential	350–400mv

Lighting   Metal halide lighting is ideal with one 150 watt lamp at 6,500k per 2 sq ft (0.18 sq m). High-intensity fluorescent tubes in the right quantity would be acceptable – a 5ft (1.5m) tank would need 5 or 6 tubes plus reflectors. A continuous photoperiod of 12 hours each day.

Substrate   None, avoiding detritus build-up

Circulation   Good water turbulence is essential using several pulse-controlled pumps (see Water Circulation pages 46–47).

Filtration   External trickle filtration with excellent water circulation. Efficient protein skimming with additional ozone. Use the highest quality activated carbon filtration.

Water Changes   Either 15–20% per fortnight without fail or a constant water change system which would prove much more successful. Reverse osmosis or deionized water is strongly recommended (toxins in mains water usually prove fatal). Use only finest quality salt.

Extras   Ultraviolet sterilizer, oxygen reactor, redox controller, dosing pumps for calcium supplements etc, platinum chiller to keep temperature stable as lighting and possibly the weather will tend to increase it unacceptably.

FEEDING   Most hard coral will benefit from feeding with small pieces of squid and lancefish once a week. Live foods such as brineshrimp and rotifers supplement the coral's symbiotic algae. Much of this food will be wasted should the fish be too numerous, as they will devour it before the corals have a chance to benefit. Should the corals reject the food all traces need to be syphoned off promptly to prevent pollution.

HEALTH: Nearly all health problems are associated with poor water quality. The flesh becomes detached from the skeleton, never to become re-attached; polyps retract further back into the skeleton each day until they do not extend at all; the white skeleton becomes more exposed as the animal shrinks. It is usually impossible to stop deterioration, even by an improvement in water quality. Prevention is better than cure.

---

to trigger mass reproduction; spawning begins one or two nights after a full moon in late spring or early summer, though the greatest activity takes place on the fourth, fifth and sixth nights. Scientists still have a great deal to learn about these events.

As the larvae complete their growth, they descend to the reef in order to find a suitable place to settle. They must choose carefully, for this is where they will spend the rest of their lives. Recent research has shown that the larvae of some species can change their minds, at least in the initial stages. If the first site proves unsuitable, the larvae can detach themselves and may land on a better one.

Although still uncommon, both types of reproduction have been observed in the aquarium, which goes to show that given optimum conditions hard corals can not only thrive, but multiply. Breeding hard corals in the aquarium is likely to be very rewarding.

Degrees of Sensitivity

Hard corals represent a challenging prospect, but there are varying degrees of sensitivity from species to species. Excellent examples are to be found by comparing brain corals (*Trachyphyllia* spp) with the Tooth Coral (*Euphyllia picteti*). Brain corals are tremendously sensitive and require not only highly intensive lighting but also a superbly clean and stable environment that the average hobbyist just cannot provide. On the other hand, Tooth Coral will tolerate slightly less demanding conditions and the marinist can expect greater success with this species.

Gorgonians FAMILY: GORGONIDAE

SURVIVING THE TURBULENT CURRENTS OF THE coral reef is not an easy task. Most sessile invertebrates cling to their anchorage points to avoid being swept away. Sea whips and sea fans, on the other hand, actively seek out areas of strong water movement and grow, in some cases, to a height of 10ft (3m) in perfect security. The secret lies in their ability to bend with currents that would easily destroy other corals. But why choose to live in the most exposed and dangerous areas of the reef? The answer is simple – food. These turbulent locations are extremely rich in plankton, which is swept through the branches of fans and whips and captured in large quantities.

These animals are called gorgonians after the Gorgon, a monster from ancient mythology. Later the protein gorgonin, a flexible horny substance, was identified as common to the group, and named after the animals. Sea whips and sea fans qualify as gorgonians because their supporting skeletal stems are made of gorgonin. Others have a calcareous skeleton, but these species remain small and prefer sheltered, shady positions. The stem is covered by a crusty, often brilliantly colourful substance called coenenchyme, in which dense colonial polyps are embedded. The stem is attached to a hard surface, usually limestone, and the rest of the structure branches from that point.

Architectural Beauty
Although closely related, sea whips and sea fans are radically different in the way they grow. Sea fans have a central stem, devoid of polyps; a lacy structure on one flat plane branches out from it. Sea whips do not have a central stem but branch out from a point close to the base into vertical, whip-like extensions pointing in different directions.

Gorgonians are found in a myriad of colours, from subdued beige through to reds, oranges, purples and yellows. Polyps may not extend during the day and some species are exclusively night-time feeders. Of those that prefer daytime feeding, the polyps usually harbour symbiotic algae from which they supplement filter feeding. Being exposed to such nutrient-rich waters, gorgonians attract others ready to take advantage of a feeding platform. Sponges, sea squirts, hydroids and brittle stars abound in their intricate branches.

▼ Plexaurella *sp.* is a Caribbean sea whip that does well in the invertebrate aquarium.

Q&A...

● *Are gorgonians difficult to keep?*

They do not do well in the average invertebrate aquarium. Beige sea whips (mostly from the Caribbean) are the least sensitive and do noticeably better.

● *Are there any unsuitable tankmates?*

Yes, some shrimps and seahorses will rest on the branches preventing them from extending their polyps to feed – death may result. Sea urchins, starfish and cowries may cause the structures to topple over.

● *Do gorgonians have enemies?*

Ovulid snails are particularly destructive, as are certain species of nudibranchs that feed on the polyps.

● *Will gorgonians grow?*

Yes, under favourable conditions they may exceed 1in (2.5cm) of growth every month. However, a more usual rate is a few millimetres each month.

● *Where should sea whips and sea fans be placed within the aquarium?*

Always in a strong current and never in slack water. Some species like a well-lit position while others prefer shaded areas. Do not allow the branches to rub against rocks or corals, as this will cause "stripping".

● *What if the polyps on sea whips never extend?*

Gorgonians can refuse to extend their polyps for weeks, even months, and still remain healthy, but eventually they will "strip" and die. Make sure water parameters are correct and that the sea whip is in a fierce water flow. Decide on what lighting it requires and alter the position of the animal accordingly.

● *Which are the best specimens to choose?*

Never purchase specimens that have "stripped" exposing a black or white skeleton; they rarely recover and usually get worse. Always try to witness the polyps fully extended in daytime-feeding species. Thicker branching species do better than spindly species, which are mostly deepwater night-time feeders.

● *How are base-less gorgonians made secure?*

Quite often fine specimens will be found to have little or no anchorage point. Gouge out a hollow in a piece of tufa rock and wedge the base in it; the specimen will become firmly embedded within a few weeks. Underwater epoxy resins are now available that are safe to use in marine aquaria and can mount a base-less gorgonian in practically any location.

Tank Conditions and Care

HABITAT: For tank and water conditions see Hard Corals page 151.

FEEDING: Polyps are often large enough to capture brineshrimp nauplii, rotifers, sieved *daphnia* and cyclops. Dead foods and liquids are usually rejected. Feed sparingly once or twice a week when the polyps are fully extended. Some species are self-sustaining in the aquarium and under intense lighting will survive purely on their symbiotic algae.

HEALTH: Bacterial infections mean that the coenenchyme covering becomes discoloured, often blackening, and finally disintegrating, leaving the horny skeleton. The causes of this "stripping" include physical damage, poor water conditions, insufficient water circulation and even a build-up of filamentous algae among the branches. Under optimum conditions regeneration is possible.

Mushroom Corals FAMILY: ACTINODISCIDAE

MUSHROOM CORALS ARE OFTEN REFERRED TO as false corals because they occupy the middle ground between anemones and corals.

Marine aquarists will know these creatures by a variety of common names – coral anemones, disk anemones, plate anemones, mushroom polyps, mushroom anemones and so on. Whatever you choose to call them, they all belong to the family Actinodiscidae and most species are to be found in relatively shallow tropical reef locations that are spread throughout the world. As a general rule, they live in areas of slack water current in preference to more animated areas of the reef.

Feeding in the Wild

Despite being found at varying depths from just below the low water mark down to 12ft (40m), all species possess symbiotic zooxanthellae algae within their tissues as a reliable and constant source of nourishment. Even so, mushrooms can gain further sustenance from more direct methods. Many species cover themselves in a mucus layer that traps waterborne nutrients and transports them to a central mouth. Various other species have a

● *Why do mushroom corals detach themselves from rocks?*

... The detachment of one, several, or all of these animals from the rocks where they have been growing is a very common problem for the hobbyist. Among the many and varied possible reasons are: **1** incorrect lighting, **2** loss of zooxanthellae, **3** poor water quality, **4** overgrowth by algae, **5** a water current that is too powerful, **6** attack or threat from a neighbouring coral. Overcrowding of the colony may also cause polyps to detach and reproduce by dispersal to set up new colonies in the immediate vicinity. In many cases, providing that the tank environment is improved, individual polyps will re-attach themselves to the substrate (if it is coarse enough) or to other rocks nearby.

● *Have mushroom corals any enemies?*

Mushroom colonies have very few enemies. Other stinging corals can pose a threat if they are placed too close together, although mushrooms of different species will live in complete harmony no matter how closely they are situated. One of the greatest problems is that colonies may be overrun by nuisance algae (see pages 68–69). They respond badly to this threat and often individual polyps will detach themselves in the search for better conditions. Very hungry shrimps and crabs will sometimes cause a little damage, as will incompatible fish. Some nudibranchs, usually accidental additions, will eat mushroom polyps. Since they are night-time feeders, these nudibranchs are best located during the hours of darkness by torchlight. Once found, it is an easy task to dispose of them.

Actinodiscus striatus, *sometimes called the Striped Disk Anemone, is very common on the reef, especially in shallow areas where the sunlight is of a high intensity. The larger "mother" polyp has probably produced the smaller surrounding mushrooms.*

more dramatic approach. Giant elephant ears (*Rhodactis* spp.) can transform their flat disks into a hollow ball in which they trap small fish and crustaceans; 12–18 hours later, the hapless victim has been consumed and the disc shape is assumed once more. It is true that not all *Rhodactis* species are able to perform this feat, but the aquarist should be aware that those specimens capable of extending to 12–15in (30–38cm) in diameter should be investigated before they are housed with small fish, shrimps and crabs.

Reproduction

In common with many other sessile invertebrates, colonies of mushroom corals are capable of reproducing by several methods. Division is an asexual procedure whereby an individual polyp will develop two or more separate mouths, finally dividing into several animals. Sometimes, however, these animals will remain fused together giving the appearance of one animal with several mouths. Budding-off is another asexual practice commonly found in anemones. The term describes a method by which a mother polyp will bud-off one, or several, small and identical young polyps. These young animals stay under the shade of the mother polyp until they are big enough to move away to become a mature animal in their own right. Sexual reproduction is essential to all species wanting to spread their own kind to distant locations. On certain evenings throughout the year, identical species will release eggs and sperm into the water simultaneously (see Hard Corals page 150). The fertilized eggs form part of the plankton layers of the sea to develop into larvae before descending to their chosen location to build their own colony.

Why a particular colony should reproduce by one method rather than another at any given time is not absolutely clear. All these reproductive practices have been witnessed in the aquarium, with asexual methods being

Its deep turquoise coloration indicates that this Actinodiscus sp. *has been collected from deeper waters. Maintain the rich hues by placing it in medium lighting.*

quite common under optimum water conditions. Crowded colonies are much more likely to reproduce than sparse individuals.

Sunburned Mushrooms

Under the intense tropical sun, mushroom polyps inhabiting shallow water can suffer sunburn! The damage is caused by ultraviolet light that has not yet been absorbed by the seawater. Under these conditions, the symbiotic zooxanthellae will produce a yellow, green or turquoise pigmentation in order to reflect and counteract the effects of the potentially damaging light wavelengths.

Conversely, deeper water species are often blue or red, enabling them to gather as much light as possible. These richly coloured species are much sought after by the hobbyist and consequently command a high price. You can maintain their health and deep colours by placing them in subdued lighting.

Self Protection

Mushroom polyps are quite capable of defending themselves, not only do they produce a toxin to keep other invading corals at a distance but they are also very resistant to

● *How will I know what kind of lighting to adopt?*

... If the polyps shrink or retract, then they require less light. Alternatively, if colonies extend or "reach" then they will require more intense lighting. You will be able to choose from a range of lighting — specialized fluorescent tubes, metal halides and mercury vapour (see pages 12–15). If possible, use them without tank cover glasses which filter out valuable wavelengths.

● *Is there any useful advice to be followed when keeping mushroom colonies?*

1 Disturb the colonies as little as possible, they resent too much movement and may shed polyps as a result.
2 Position the rock so the polyps can expand properly.
3 Make sure that they cannot come into contact with stinging corals.
4 Keep colonies free of nuisance algae.
5 If the polyps were fully extended and healthy in the dealer's tank, try to replicate the same tank conditions.
6 If you need to re-position colonies, allow at least a week to assess whether the move was successful.
7 Newly purchased colonies need at least 7–14 days in which to settle down properly. Do not feed or re-position before then.
8 Detached polyps can be grouped together to produce an attractive "colony" in an area of the substrate with slack water flow.

Tank Conditions and Care

HABITAT: Rocky walls, outcrops, shallow reefs with very clear water. Best kept in reef aquaria.

Tank Size	Over 20 gallons (91 l; 24 US gallons)
pH	8.1–8.3
Temperature	24–26°C (75–79°F)
Ammonia	Zero
Nitrite	Zero
Nitrate	Less than 10ppm (preferably zero)
Specific Gravity	1.022–1.025
Phosphates	Less than 0.5ppm (preferably zero)
Redox Potential	350–450 mv

Filtration Trickle filtration is preferable. Efficient protein skimming and activated carbon filtration as standard.

Water Changes 15–25% change every two weeks using high quality, filtered water.

Fish Stocking Level Absolute maximum of 1in per 6 gallons (2.5cm per 27 l; 1in per 7.2 US gallons).

Water Circulation Moderate flow over the colonies

Lighting As described in main text, in conjunction with correct placement of colonies.

FEEDING: *Rhodactis* spp. should be offered pieces of mussel, squid or lancefish. Other smaller species may be fed on live or frozen rotifers, frozen fine zooplankton and the juices from other frozen fish foods. Liquid fry food and artificial substitutes are not recommended as they may cause pollution. Many colonies will survive quite successfully without additional feeding supplements, but if feeding is necessary, do so very sparingly and no more than twice each week.

HEALTH: The two main health risks faced by mushroom polyps are detachment and shrinking. Large polyps can shrink from healthy disks down to tiny buttons less than 10% of their normal size. The main causes are poor water quality or unsuitable lighting. Once these conditions have been improved, mushrooms should recover slowly.

toxins produced by encroaching species. In the confines of the invertebrate aquarium, such poisons will need to be removed on a continuous basis by the use of activated carbon filtration.

Although all mushrooms are disk shaped, the sheer variety of colours, spots, stripes, dimples, fringing tentacles and textures, is astounding. The vast majority of these fascinating creatures have yet to be classified properly which is quite understandable as there

▲ Mushroom corals (Actinodiscus sp.) of varying colours and forms can often be seen growing within close proximity in perfect harmony.

could be the work of several lifetimes here! Therefore, do not be surprised if you try to identify a prized specimen, only to find that it is simply referred to as *Actinodiscus* sp. As with many invertebrates, the exact taxonomy is generally a lower priority to marinists than correct husbandry of the animal.

157

Anemones
(including Sea Pens) ORDER: ACTINARIA

THESE ANCIENT ANIMALS OCCUPY ALL THE oceans and seas of the world and species are to be found throughout the very coldest to the very warmest regions, such is their ability to diversify and adapt. Anemones are very closely related to corals, but whereas corals are made up of polyp colonies, anemones are one large polyp. Their structure is extremely simple and has changed remarkably little over millions of years. They are basically a "bag of skin" that is inflated with water to give it a shape. Some species have a sucker-like foot used to cling onto rocks, while in others the foot is more adapted to burrowing. Above the slender body is a disc with a mouth in the centre and tentacles radiating out from the middle. Every tentacle is tipped with a battery of stinging cells called nemato-cysts and these are used to deter predators and capture prey. Each nematocyst is spring-loaded with a hollow, barbed thread, through which a paralyzing poison can pass. The firing of each cell is governed by it coming into contact with anything edible – a structure lacking in protein is usually ignored. Once

Sand anemones (Heteractis sp.) *locate their feet deep in the substrate; if disturbed, they can withdraw from sight very swiftly.*

Condylactis gigantea *is a Caribbean species that is colourful and less sensitive than many other anemones. Coming from the tropical Atlantic, it does not provide a natural home for clownfish.*

Tank Conditions and Care

HABITAT: For tank and water conditions see Mushroom Corals page 156.

FEEDING: A healthy anemone can be fed small pieces of lancefish, squid, cockle and mussel once each week to keep it in good condition. Small pieces should be pressed lightly into the tentacles and never forced into the mouth as this will cause serious damage. If food is rejected, remove it and do not try again for another week. Many anemones will remain perfectly healthy without such gross feeding, taking adequate nutrition from their zooxanthellae exclusively. Where fish are kept in the same tank, the juices from frozen fish food is often enough to keep anemones healthy. Nuisance anemones such as *Aiptasia* spp. must not be fed if they are to be kept under control.

HEALTH: The most common ailment is when anemones turn white, shrink and eventually die. This can be due to several factors including lack of light, poor water quality, or lighting in the wrong colour spectrum. Anemones possess a symbiotic algae within their tissues and as this dies the anemone loses its colour and shrinks in response to a lack of nutrients and oxygen. Once the process of degeneration has begun, the anemone may lose its power to attach and death usually follows soon after. This scenario is much more likely with the clownfish-types (e.g. *Heteractis* spp.), rather than the hardier Caribbean species. Once an anemone starts to break up and disintegrate, it should be removed from the aquarium immediately, to avoid massive pollution.

● *Are there any anemones that are not desirable in the aquarium?*

... Yes, triffid, glass or rock anemones (*Aiptasia* spp.). (See Invertebrate Pests page 201) These small 1–2in (2.5–5cm), brownish anemones can multiply into plague proportions and will ensnare any small fish that gets too close. They can be very difficult to eradicate from the aquarium once established.

● *What is the best way to treat an anemone sting?*

Rinse the wound with vinegar or alcohol and then apply a paste of equal parts sodium bicarbonate and water. Once the pain begins to subside, or the paste dries out, apply a dusting of talcum powder or papain, which is a meat tenderizer used in barbeque cooking and contains an ingredient that can neutralize venom. This treatment can also be used to relieve the pain from the stings of venomous fish.

● *Why do anemones periodically deflate and then expand again?*

Anemones are simply bags of water. When fully inflated they absorb oxygen and nutrients from this "captured" water. After a while, the water becomes stale, devoid of oxygen and has to be exchanged for a fresh supply. The anemone deflates for a short period of time, expelling the unwanted liquid and accompanying waste products. A healthy anemone in high quality water will generally complete the whole process of deflation to reflation within 5–10 hours.

● *Is there any useful advice when buying anemones?*

Yes. If an anemone is attached to a rock, rather than remove it and risk damage, purchase the rock as well if practicable. Never buy anemones that are very pale or white and have obviously lost their symbiotic algae. Refuse anemones that are unattached and rolling about in the tank.

▶ *A pair of clownfish* (Amphiprion percula) *bask in the protection of a* Heteractis gelam *anemone. This anemone is readily identified by the bulbous ends of its tentacles.*

ensnared by the barbed hooks, the prey is then passed through the tentacles and continually stung until it ceases to struggle, finally being engulfed by the central mouth.

Symbiotic Relationships

Anemones are to be found in many attractive hues; green, yellow, red, pink and purple. However, in nearly all cases the underlying colour is brown, caused by the presence of single-celled algae called zooxanthellae that live within the tissues of most species. The relationship is truly symbiotic with the anemone deriving oxygen and nutrients from the algae, while the algae have a secure home in bright sunlight and can utilize the anemone's waste products, such as carbon dioxide, to photosynthesize. Without the benefits of zooxanthellae, most species of anemone would find survival almost impossible.

Reproduction may be either by division ("budding-off" tiny versions of the mother animal), or sexually, by producing eggs and sperm. Many species have multiplied successfully under favourable aquarium conditions.

Clownfish are most often pictured in association with anemones, but this is not a fully symbiotic relationship as many species of anemone are unsuitable hosts, and in the Caribbean there are no clownfish to take advantage of their protection. Some species of shrimp and crab do have a similar relationship with the Caribbean anemones. Anemones of the genera *Heteractis* (formerly *Radianthus*), *Anthopsis* and *Stoichactis* are suitable partners for clownfish. However, *Condylactis* and *Pachycerianthus* spp. should be avoided, being exclusive to the Caribbean; they are best kept in an invertebrate-only tank because of their highly predatory natures.

Sea Pens

These fascinating animals are closely related to anemones, although distinct in appearance. They are only seen in the aquarium trade occasionally, and hobbyists may be unaware of what they are and how to maintain them. Sea pens have a tubular body; the upper portion is supported by an internal calcium spine, resembling an old-fashioned quill. Like anemones, they possess a foot that enables the animal to burrow and anchor itself safely in turbulent water. Being mostly nocturnal feeders, sea pens are quiet during the day, showing only a white, buff, yellow or orange column protruding from the substrate. As darkness descends, the animal begins to expand, covering its body in a mass of feathery polyps ready to feed on waterborne food particles. The most commonly available species is *Cavernularia obesa*.

● *Are clownfish always immune to the stings of anemones?*

... No. Clownfish often require a "settling-in" period whereby they adapt to a new anemone. In the process they may get stung, or even consumed by the anemone.

● *Are anemones suitable for newcomers?*

They require excellent water conditions and intense lighting of the correct quality. It is best for beginners to gain experience with less sensitive marines, preferably fish-alone, before advancing to more delicate invertebrates such as anemones.

● *Can I move an anemone if I don't like its position?*

No, moving the anemone will damage its foot no matter how careful you are, and it may simply move back again. Sometimes anemones settle on the front viewing glass, in which case a move can be excused. However, the foot must be eased off very gently.

● *What causes an anemone to "wander" about the aquarium?*

Poor water conditions, insufficient lighting, or both, are the primary reasons. The anemone is searching for a more favourable spot, where all its requirements will be met. In the absence of correct conditions, the anemone will continue to "wander".

● *Is it safe to keep small fish with anemones?*

Most fish possess an instinctive caution when it comes to anemones, but very small fish may fall prey to their stinging tentacles, especially in the dark.

● *Can the sting of an anemone be dangerous to humans?*

Yes. Carpet anemones (*Stoichactis* spp.), *Condylactis* spp. and tube anemones (*Pachycerianthus* spp.) all possess ferocious stings and should not be touched with bare skin, particularly on sensitive areas, such as the forearms or backs of hands. *Heteractis* species may also produce a stinging reaction. In addition, some people may be allergic to the poison reacting with a rapidly spreading rash or, in rare cases, anaphylactic shock (complete collapse of the respiratory system). Both require immediate hospital attention.

▶ OVERLEAF *Carpet anemones* (Stoichactis gigas) *possess very short tentacles, giving them the appearance of a round carpet. In the wild, this species is favoured by many clownfish because of the protection afforded by a prodigious sting!*

▲ *Sea pens, such as* Cavernularia obesa *seen here, must have a deep substrate into which their foot can burrow for firm anchorage.*

Star Polyps FAMILY: CLAVULARIIDAE

CLAVULARIA IS NOT A DIFFICULT CORAL TO maintain and can perform a vital function for the well-being of an aquarium. Members of the family Clavulariidae have long been confused with genera such as *Xenia* (see pages 166–167) which they resemble superficially; so much so, that star polyps have been commonly named *Xenia*, quite erroneously.

Star polyps come in an enormous range of colour, but they do have certain unifying qualities that make them easy to identify. First, while retaining an eight-point star-like symmetry to their tentacles, the stem is short – never more than 0.5in (12mm) and holds the polyps close to its base. The base is often a fused, rubbery encrusting mass; usually purple, but it can be shades of brown in some species. The polyps can withdraw into their base leaving nothing for predators to attack, and giving full protection from all but the most determined of attackers. When the polyps do emerge, they mask the base entirely. Polyp coloration varies from species to species, but includes varying degrees of green, brown and silvery-grey. The "eye" of the polyp is often white, giving rise to the common name star polyp.

The most common method of reproduction in the marine aquarium is by division. This

▲ *The purple basal mass can be seen clearly as part of this species,* Clavularia viridis. *Given excellent aquarium conditions it will spread quickly over rock or glass.*

occurs as the basal mass increases in size and develops new polyps. Most hobbyists keeping *Clavularia* under optimum conditions have found that it spreads rapidly; as much as one centimetre every month, according to species. This rate of growth gives a new aquarium an established appearance remarkably quickly as the polyps cover previously bare rockwork or glass. In the wild, gorgonians and sea whips close to a colony may find the polyps spreading up their branches, gradually killing the "host". Star polyp "trees" are the result and are readily available in the aquarium trade. It would be wise to keep gorgonians and sea whips at a comfortable distance if they are to be preserved in their original state!

In the wild, *Clavularia* reproduces by shedding eggs and sperm into the ocean to found colonies in faraway locations but this rarely occurs within the aquarium and cannot be relied upon to spread a species to the other end of a large aquarium.

Tank Conditions and Care

HABITAT: For tank and water conditions see Mushroom Corals page 156.

FEEDING: It seems that star polyps do not feed on microscopic plankton but gain nutrition from the symbiotic algae within their tissues.

HEALTH: Clavulariid colonies are highly resistant to disease but they may be attacked by nudibranchs such as *Pleuroleura striata*. If the colonies are observed during the hours of darkness, predatory nudibranchs can be identified and removed.

● *Do star polyps have any special requirements?*

... Yes, good water circulation is essential; sluggish, stale water gathering around the polyps will result in a very poor showing, whereas heavy turbulence promotes good aeration and increased vitality.

● *How can star polyps be encouraged to spread in the aquarium?*

Portions of a well-established colony can be eased off a rock carefully and placed elsewhere. Species that form a mound-like structure can be cut with a very sharp scalpel and the pieces distributed accordingly. This may appear brutal, but the colonies recover very quickly and are soon ready to start spreading again.

● *If a colony refuses to extend its polyps for some weeks, what can be done?*

Although reasonably hardy, *Clavularia* will not tolerate deteriorating water conditions brought about by lack of water changes, overfeeding or overstocking with fish. Several large water changes will often help the star polyps into recovery. Dormant basal structures can sometimes be brought back to life if the environment is drastically improved.

◄ Clavularia *sp. Attractive colonies of star polyps are commonly available in the aquarium trade and make an ideal choice for the newcomer to invertebrates.*

● *Do* Clavularia *colonies need special attention?*

Yes. It is essential that they do not become smothered by nuisance algae or overgrown by decorative algae (see pages 52–55). Once established in a colony, it is almost impossible to eradicate the deeply rooted holdfasts.

● *Can* Clavularia *perform any useful function?*

Yes. Where an invertebrate aquarium is without a substrate, *Clavularia* can be encouraged to form a living mat of polyps over the base, disguising the bare glass.

● *Can* Clavularia *colonies be positioned close to each other?*

Yes, they present no threat to each other.

● *Are star polyps recommended for the newcomer to invertebrates?*

Yes, they are without doubt one of the most reliable invertebrates and ideal for the less experienced aquarist.

Pulse Corals FAMILY: XENIIDAE

THE FAMILY XENIIDAE IS MADE UP OF SEVEN genera, and even the most ardent hobbyist is unlikely to come across more than a few of the many species kept by the aquarist. The most common of these are usually the so-called pulse corals such as *Xenia umbellata, X. puertogalarea, X. elongata, Heteroxenia fuscescens* and *Anthelia glauca*. All of which hold eight pulsing pinnate tentacles on elongated stems. They are incapable of retracting fully but shrink in size considerably. This is the main physical difference between Xeniidae and Clavulariidae (pages 164–165).

Pulse coral polyps vary in colour, ranging from dark brown to light grey. Most species pulsate in a rhythmic opening and closing motion (30–40/min), believed to help the flow of freshly aerated water over the surface,

● *Are pulse corals easy to maintain?*

... No, only the most experienced hobbyists with advanced aquarium technology should attempt to keep them.

● *How can I recognize a healthy pulse coral?*

By the mere fact that the tentacles are pulsing! If the coral refuses to pulse, or the pulses are infrequent, do not buy it.

● *Why do Xeniids fail to pulse?*

The majority of aquarium specimens tend not to pulse normally, and the reasons are not fully clear. However, given optimum conditions, non-pulsating specimens can revive this behaviour.

▼ *Xenia sp. All Xeniids are difficult to keep in the marine aquarium.*

Xeniids are easily identified by the thick, branching trunk from which the pulsating tentacles originate. They are common in the wild, but difficult aquarium subjects.

assisting in respiration. Although assistance with feeding cannot be ruled out, nutrition is supplied in most cases by symbiotic algae within the tissues.

The various genera within the family Xeniidae differ in the methods of attachment to the substrate. *Xenia* spp. for example, possess a thick trunk from which the tentacles arise; whereas *Anthelia* spp. polyps branch at the point of attachment. Stem lengths vary from species to species. Some are just a few centimeters long, others such as *Heteroxenia fuscescens* may exceed 3in (7.5cm).

Tank Conditions and Care

HABITAT: For tank and water conditions see Hard Corals page 151.

FEEDING: No direct feeding is necessary.

HEALTH: If the best conditions are not supplied, pulse corals frequently stop pulsing, shrink and die. Other Xeniids, such as *Anthelia glauca* are far more reliable and will even multiply under optimum conditions.

Xeniids are not uncommon in the wild and are to be found encrusting rocks where there is a good flow of clean, unpolluted water and access to intense illumination. They suffer badly when transported and need the very best conditions in a captive environment.

Soft Corals

IDENTIFYING SPECIES OF SOFT CORAL IS NOT an easy task. They do not conform to an exact shape, form or coloration and many of the species are almost indistinguishable. However, this need make little difference to the enjoyment of the hobbyist as the vast majority of species respond in much the same way within the aquarium environment.

Sinularia

Sinularia species have an altogether different growth pattern to that of their leathery cousins. Although both emanate from a single basal attachment point, the vast majority of *Sinularia* spp. branch into many finger-like vertical lobes, covered in masses of much shorter polyps. A common exception to the usual form is *Sinularia brassica* – Cauliflower Coral – named because it produces tight communities of dark-brown rosettes, generated by masses of polyps, that closely resemble cauliflower florets; as the polyp tentacles retract, the whole coral can turn white. *Sinularia* are easy to keep in the well-tended invertebrate aquarium.

Sarcophyton

Sarcophyton species are often referred to as leather corals. This may seem an unusual common name, but both the texture and

Sarcophyton *species reproduce readily in the aquarium given favourable conditions. Here a "mother" leather coral has budded-off smaller specimens from the base. Long polyps are emerging from the top surface.*

◀ *Species of* Sinularia *can take on attractive shapes and are spongy to the touch. Polyps are generally diminutive compared to their* Sarcophyton *cousins.*

colour of the animals, when they have polyps withdrawn, are remarkably similar to tanned hide. Widespread throughout the tropical areas of the Indo-Pacific, some species of *Sarcophyton* can be seen forming undulating plates exceeding 3ft (1m) in diameter. From the upper surface springs a carpet of polyps sometimes exceeding 0.4in (1cm) in length. Using an eyeglass you can see that the delicate polyps are topped with a ring of eight tentacles, used for catching tiny planktonic particles that have been transported in the current. Inexperienced hobbyists might investigate *Sinularia* and *Sarcophyton* species as ideal first-time invertebrates to keep.

● *How do soft corals reproduce in the aquarium?*

... Most leather corals either "bud-off" smaller animals from around the base, or literally "fall apart"! In the latter case, pieces of the main plate quickly re-establish themselves at a different location and grow into replicas of the "mother" coral. It is also possible to propagate soft corals by cutting them into smaller sections using a very sharp razor blade or scalpel. This works particularly well with *Sinularia* species where natural division points occur. Place the "new" coral in a suitable hole in a rock, or gouge one into a piece of tufa rock. There they will quickly fix themselves and grow normally. The "mother" coral will heal over after several weeks.

● *Do soft corals have any enemies?*

Relatively few, but two to watch out for are the Rapa Rapa Snail (family Coralliophilidae) and a nudibranch, *Dendronotus* sp. The latter is pure white and less than 2in (5cm) long; the gills are attractive plumes grouped all over the body. Both are active only at night and have the ability to bore into the soft coral body and devour it from within. Large bristleworms have also been known to prey on soft corals, though the danger from these pests is far less of a threat. Nevertheless, it is worthwhile to check on these nocturnal predators with a torch. Any small snails or white nudibranchs found on, or around these corals, should be removed.

● *Is good water circulation essential?*

Yes, soft corals thrive in a brisk water flow which stimulates them and helps prevent bacterial infections.

● *Why do soft corals extend polyps at night?*

Although light-loving and possessing symbiotic algae within their tissues, most soft corals extend their polyps at night to capture small particles of planktonic food.

● *Should soft corals be kept away from other species?*

Yes. All hard corals, anemones and any other stinging invertebrates must be positioned at a reasonable distance. Soft corals have no protection and can be intimidated into "closing-down" permanently, until they eventually die, or are moved.

● *Is it best to leave soft corals where they are?*

Yes, soft corals do best with as little disturbance as possible. Resist the temptation to keep moving them around the aquarium. Let them establish themselves on the rockwork and leave them to prosper.

Tank Conditions and Care

HABITAT: For tank and water conditions see Mushroom Corals page 156.

Lighting Soft corals are very forgiving when it comes to lighting. They will do quite well under only a few fluorescents. However, the stronger the lighting, the better the animal will look, and grow. Watch them blossom under intense metal halide lighting!

FEEDING: A few drops of juice from some meaty marine fare can be introduced at night when the corals are feeding, but this is not essential, especially in a mixed aquarium where the fish are also being fed.

HEALTH: Soft corals suffer from bacterial infections due to poor water conditions. Rotting of the basal attachment point is fairly common, as is blackening of the tissues. Both these undesirable situations can be improved by restoring good water quality and an increased water circulation over the affected areas. Once this is achieved, many species will heal themselves, given time.

Highly Compatible

One of the most attractive qualities of soft corals is that, unlike their cousins the hard corals, they are non-aggressive and quite happy to live in close proximity with each other. Indeed, in the wild, soft corals will recolonize vacant portions of reef so quickly and so densely that hardly any other species are allowed access. As a consequence, mainly invertebrate or reef aquaria can be fully stocked with little fear of the kind of "burning" or coral warfare so often the case with hard corals.

Soft corals are highly variable in growth rates. Major governing factors include water quality, lighting and (not least) the particular species. Given optimum conditions, growth can be unexpectedly swift. Even under less than optimum conditions, soft corals will grow at a steady rate and require some extra space in which to expand to their full potential – and that can be quite considerable!

In common with other invertebrates, they use the surrounding water to inflate their tissues giving themselves a "living" appearance.

From time to time, however, the aged water is expelled and the coral takes on a shrivelled form with all polyps retracted. Any hobbyist who already keeps soft corals will know that these actions are part of a regular cycle of events that may occur as often as daily. Accompanying the "close-down" stage the coral may shed a mucus skin enabling it to rid itself of parasites or other encrustations that might be trying to establish a home on its skin. If necessary, any excessive mucus can be carefully syphoned off to prevent other invertebrates becoming fouled.

Dendronephthya

Although it is closely related to the genus *Sinularia*, *Dendronephthya* differs noticeably in that its body is supported by sharp calcium spicules and may be brightly coloured red, orange or white. It is found in relatively deep water and has no symbiotic algae within its tissues. During the day it is a small, uninteresting ball; at night, however, it expands into a cauliflower shape. Like *Sinularia brassica*, *Dendronephthya* species are also commonly

▲ *A Dendronephthya soft coral seen in close up reveals the calcium spicules that help support the water-filled structure. Like so many other beautiful corals, these can be difficult to maintain.*

known as Cauliflower Corals. They feed by drawing in tiny food particles as they expand, making them very difficult to feed properly in the aquarium. *Dendronephthya* prefers a shady position and dislikes being fouled by nuisance hair algae, which can get caught up in the "twiggy branches".

Tubeworms

MOST WORMS FAVOURED BY THE HOBBYIST are sedentary tubeworms belonging to two families: Sabellidae, commonly known as feather dusters or fanworms; and Serpulidae, often called Christmas Tree worms. All these species live permanently within tubes and exhibit one or more feathery plumes of tentacles with which they feed and breathe. Frequently, the plume is most attractive and brightly coloured in blue, red, yellow, white, black, orange, green, purple, mauve, beige and brown.

Fanworms and Christmas Tree worms trap tiny particles of food in their feathery crowns. From there it is passed to a central rib and into a mucus stream that flows down to a central mouth. The crowns are extremely sensitive to movement in the immediate vicinity, and often withdraw rapidly. Reactions are controlled by giant nerve fibres that run the whole length of the body within a central main nerve cord.

Feather Dusters (Fanworms)

These worms are usually found in the sand or mud of shallow intertidal zones. They mix tiny particles of mud with mucus to form a parchment-like tube in which to live. Sizes vary from an inch (2.5cm) in length, to well over 4in (10cm) depending on the species. Feather dusters are gregarious and live in extremely large colonies, especially where the food supply is abundant and rich. As a general rule, colours are rather muted and limited to beige, brown, black, dark red, mauve and white. The species most commonly available to the marine aquarist are *Sabellastarte magnifica* and *S. sanctijosephi*.

Christmas Tree and Coco Worms

Serpulid worms differ from the sabellid worms in that they produce a hard calcareous tube. Species such as *Protula magnifica* are solitary animals, with a tube that may reach 12in (30cm) in length with an aperture of up to 1in (2.5cm). The incumbent worm may display one, or several, colourful plumes and is consequently much in demand by the invertebrate keeper. They are referred to as Coco Worms by exporters, wholesalers and hobbyists alike, but the derivation is unclear.

The much smaller Christmas Tree worms embed their tubes within living hard corals such as *Porites*, often establishing large communities. The spiralling double crowns are normally 0.4in (1cm) in diameter and up to 50 worms may occupy a single rock of 11sq ft (1sq m). Resembling tiny twin Christmas trees, even a small portion of rock can display radioles (crowns) in a stunning variety of colours. *Spirobranchus giganteus* is possibly the most commonly available species, but in the aquarium it rarely achieves its potential size of 6in (15cm) across the radioles.

Tank Conditions and Care

HABITAT: For tank and water conditions see Mushroom Corals page 156. Christmas Tree worms should be given optimum water conditions as for Hard Corals page 151.

FEEDING: Tubeworms benefit from occasional feedings with live rotifers and brineshrimp nauplii. Squeezing the juices of a thawed mussel around the crowns can also be helpful.

HEALTH: Occasionally the worm will leave its tube; it can survive for many weeks in this state, or may die almost immediately. Owing to the lack of suitable materials, the worm cannot re-build a new tube and is ultimately doomed. Individual Christmas Tree worms may fail to appear one by one, until the whole colony is no longer showing. The cause is usually deteriorating water quality and lack of nutrition.

Q&A...

● *Are tubeworms suitable for any marine aquarium?*

... No, invertebrate aquaria are by far the best. Tanks containing fish produce too much waste, and fish may peck at the crowns, damaging them.

● *Why do tubeworms periodically shed their crowns?*

Poor water quality, unwanted attention from predators, the shock of being moved or, surprisingly, as a prelude to breeding. Or it may be that the crown has become old and not as efficient as a new one. There is every likelihood that the animal will produce a new crown within two to three weeks, providing that any adverse conditions have been improved.

● *If the* Porites *coral dies, will the Christmas Tree worms die also?*

Yes, it is very likely. Although there is no physical connection between the two, once the host coral has died, serpulid worms seem to do very poorly.

● *Do tubeworms require a sandy substrate?*

Feather dusters and Coco Worms can be embedded in sand or placed in a rock crevice; they do equally well in both locations.

● *How do tubeworms breed in the aquarium?*

If you have several specimens of the same species they may begin to emit a smoky plume early in the morning; it will contain either eggs or sperm. Adults generally shed their crowns to prevent them from eating the larvae, which form very quickly and settle on rockwork, glass, and substrate. By the time the adults have started to re-grow a new crown, tiny tubeworms will be appearing and should be fed with live rotifers at least three times each day if growth is to be assisted to adulthood. Feather dusters breed most successfully.

● *Can the tube be re-used if a Coco Worm dies?*

Yes. If you are certain that the serpulid worm has died, clean the tube with a brush and replace into the aquarium. A suitably sized feather duster can be inserted into the opening to give the redundant tube a new lease of life. Do not try to force the new occupant into the tube as the worm will pull itself down to the desired depth.

▶ *Feather duster worms, such as these colourful* Sabellastarte *species, are commonly available to the hobbyist, but do require careful feeding for long-term success.*

Shrimps, Crabs, Lobsters & Barnacles

PHYLUM: CRUSTACEA

CRUSTACEANS ARE GAINING VERY RAPIDLY IN popularity within the marine aquarium trade. Not only are many crustaceans colourful and mobile but they often provide a useful scavenging service, clearing up tiny morsels of food that would otherwise be a potential source of pollution.

The phylum Crustacea is a large one with over 40,000 species, many of which are of little interest to the marine aquarist. It also includes species that are commonly but wrongly attributed to other groups; barnacles (despite a mollusc-like appearance) are a good example. By far the largest group within the phylum is the class Malacostraca, which contains almost three-quarters of all known crustaceans. The vast majority, and the most popular crustaceans within the marine hobby, are decapods. As the name suggests, they have ten legs, which are arranged in five pairs, although some of the forward pairs may have developed into pincers or claws. Suitable decapods for the marine aquarium include crabs, lobsters and shrimps.

Shedding the Exoskeleton

These creatures share one fascinating feature – they wear their skeletons (properly called the exoskeleton or cuticle) on the exterior of the body. They possess the remarkable ability to shed it at regular intervals, allowing further growth and the regeneration of damaged or missing limbs. The exoskeleton is made of chitin and strengthened with carbonate and other calcium salts, which can make them very hard indeed. Mineral salts and other useful substances are absorbed from the old exoskeleton before it is discarded, making the whole process all the more remarkable. When moulting, the animal inflates itself with water so that the cuticle splits at the thorax. The "new" animal squeezes backward through

● *Are crustaceans best kept in a mainly invertebrate aquarium?*

... Yes. They are sensitive to high quantities of fish waste and generally do better in an environment with very few compatible fish.

● *Can a variety of crustaceans be kept in the same aquarium?*

Within reason, yes. Shrimps and crabs are relatively safe to mix, but lobsters may be unsuitable.

● *Need a discarded exoskeleton be removed?*

No. It is inert, causing no pollution. Indeed, the exoskeletons of lobsters and some crabs are extremely attractive and may be removed, dried and preserved intact with a coat of varnish.

● *What lifespans can be expected from crustaceans?*

This is very difficult to answer as so much depends on the species, the age when bought, and water conditions. Generally, shrimps should live 2–3 years, crabs 4–5 years and lobsters 5 years plus.

● *What is the difference between a shrimp and a prawn?*

Scientifically speaking, nothing at all.

● *Why do many cleaner shrimps lose their cleaning behaviour in the aquarium?*

When the aquarist feeds them with copious food on a regular basis, they learn to wait for food to come to them, rather than go in search of it.

● *Can shrimps be persuaded to appear in the day?*

Individuals or very small groups are most reticent to make an appearance, but in larger numbers (as in the wild) they gain complete confidence. Larger groups also tend to look more impressive.

● *Can shrimps be raised in the aquarium?*

Newly-hatched shrimps are extremely difficult to rear. Some commercial breeders and universities have had success, but even experienced aquarists usually fail owing to the inability to provide the correct initial diet.

the split, leaving a hollow replica of itself behind. After it deflates back to normal size, the new exoskeleton will still be soft and the crustacean will be vulnerable to predators for a few days. The unwanted cuticle is often left in an exposed place (perhaps as a diversion) while the vulnerable animal goes into hiding nearby. The amount of energy required to complete the process is considerable; not all individuals manage it successfully, and some die in the process.

Shrimps

Many of the shrimps kept by the marine aquarist would normally be found performing an invaluable service within the coral reef community – cleaning fish of parasites. So much in demand are they that fish actually queue at certain "cleaning stations" for the

▲ *If a fish such as this Banded Goby* (Cryptocentrus *sp.) approaches a Cleaner Shrimp* (Lysmata amboinensis) *it will be inspected for parasites and irritants. Many fish find this attention pleasurable and return for more.*

privilege. The distinctive red and white livery of many such shrimps is a clear signal for the waiting fish to remain perfectly still and let the crustacean wander at will over its body, fins, eyes and even into the mouth and gills, consuming offending parasites as they go. This fascinating behaviour is often repeated in the aquarium, especially on larger fish or anything perceived as a large fish, such as a human hand. However, shrimps often constitute the greater part of the diet of many fish, for example hawkfish, pufferfish and triggerfish. Therefore, despite their relative immunity, care must be taken to ensure that a newly introduced shrimp, cleaner or otherwise, does not become an expensive snack! It must also be remembered that natural behaviour on the open reef and within the confines of the aquarium are not always compatible. The persistent attentions of a cleaner shrimp can often lead to an irritable fish eating the shrimp in an effort to rid itself of the problem.

Mostly-fish tanks are less than perfect accommodation for shrimps, which usually fare best in a mixed fish-invertebrate or in an invertebrate-only aquarium. If a scavenger is sought for a mostly-fish tank, then a suitable alternative would be a hermit crab (*Dardanus* spp.). Not only is it well protected, but it is also able to withstand varying water conditions and a certain amount of copper-based medication.

The following shrimps are worthy additions to the marine aquarium:

Cleaner Shrimps (*Lysmata amboinensis* and *L. grabhami*) are stunningly beautiful in their red and white livery with arrays of long, white antennae. They can be kept singly or in groups and many individuals become hand-tame quite quickly. Cleaner shrimps are usually on view much of the time. These species can frequently be seen holding eggs in their swimmerettes.

Boxing Shrimps (*Stenopus* spp.) are popular and colourful, but have a menacing appearance owing to their large, outstretched claws. They are best kept singly, as two are likely to fight if they are not a matched pair. Although active at feeding times, boxing shrimps are reasonably shy and tend to hide for long periods among rocks.

Dancing or **Candy Shrimps** (*Rhynchocinetes* spp.) are the type most frequently seen on sale. They are good scavengers, peaceful, attractive, hardy and relatively cheap. They are particularly recommended for any newcomer to invertebrate keeping. *Rhynchocinetes*

▲ Rhynchocinetes regulosus *is one of several species commonly known as dancing or candy shrimps. They are happier when kept in groups rather than singly.*

uritai is the best known species, but others of the same genus become available from time to time from dealers. Individuals tend to hide from view in rocks, but in large groups they become bolder.

Blood or **Scarlet Shrimp** (*Lysmata debelius*) is exceedingly beautiful and usually commands a high price. They are not difficult to keep and are totally peaceful, but they are quite wary of well illuminated areas and may not be seen very often. Specimens can vary in colour from bright red to dusky crimson and tend to remain inactive until feeding times. They do best in groups of three or more.

Anemone Shrimps (*Periclimenes* spp.) are exquisitely delicate creatures resembling painted glass ornaments. As the name suggests, they require the protection of the kind of anemone usually suited to clownfish (see Anemones page 160). There is a risk, however, that if the anemone is already host to clownfish, the shrimp will be constantly harassed and driven from the tentacles.

Saron or **Monkey Shrimp** (*Saron rectitostris*) is an attractive nocturnal scavenger rarely seen during the day.

The following shrimps are far less desirable for the general marine aquarium:

Mantis Shrimps (*Odontodactylus* spp. and *Squilla* spp.) are predatory ambushers, feeding on fish and other suitable livestock to satisfy their large appetites. They usually arrive in the aquarium within the crevices of living rock (see pages 50–51). If kept in a species tank, they can become interesting subjects for study. (See Invertebrate Pests page 202).

Pistol Shrimps (*Synalpheus* spp.) are hardly ever seen, but often heard, hence the common name. They can produce a loud crack with their claws, not unlike the sound of glass breaking! Most aquarists find the sound too alarming to tolerate and have to remove the specimen.

Harlequin Shrimps (*Hymenocera* spp.) are gorgeous creatures that devour live starfish! The majority of marinists would find the demands of these shrimps hard to accommodate both ethically and financially.

Crabs

Many species of unidentified crabs arrive in the marine aquarium within pieces of living rock. Some will remain small and innocuous, while others will increase in size and become very destructive. Being mostly nocturnal, the only clue to their presence is the discarded exoskeleton, left in a prominent position. The following species are among the most common:

Arrowhead Crab (*Stenorhynchus seticornis*). This unusual crab resembles an underwater spider and is not at all popular with arachnophobes! However, they make a worthwhile addition to any invertebrate aquarium. Keep singly if fighting is to be avoided. Some develop a taste for bristleworms and can help to keep this difficult pest under control.

Porcelain or **Anemone Crabs** (*Neopetrolisthes* spp). These crabs are easy to keep; much of what has been said about anemone shrimps applies equally here.

Hermit Crabs (*Dardanus* spp.) have a reputation for hardiness, making them ideal scavengers for the fish-only tank where they will

◆ Dardanus megistos *is a larger species of hermit crab and is mostly unsuited to the invertebrate tank.*

◆ *This crab* (Neopetrolisthes maculatus) *often occurs in association with carpet anemones* (Stoichactis *spp*).

tolerate less than perfect water conditions and even a certain amount of copper-based medication. Hermit crabs come in a variety of colours and sizes. Their legs may be red, yellow, blue or grey; they range from tiny 0.4in (1cm) specimens, to fist-sized specimens that can do incredible damage in the invertebrate aquarium. As hermit crabs have no shell of their own, they occupy the empty shells of univalve molluscs (gastropods) taken by chance or force. Growth is only possible if larger shells are available.

Anemone Hermit Crab (*Dardanus pedunculatus*). Like its close relatives, the Anemone Hermit Crab occupies the shell of a univalve mollusc, but this species deliberately places small anemones on its shell for protection. When it changes shell, it takes its anemones with it. Owing to the sensitivity of the anemones, very good water conditions are required as in a mainly invertebrate aquarium.

The Shame-Faced Crab (*Calappa flammea*). This species takes its common name from the

● *Are there any species of crab that should not be considered under any circumstances?*

Yes, swimming crabs (*Macropipus* spp.), which are easily recognized as their rear legs are flattened into "paddles", enabling them to swim after and catch fish. They also grow very large and will consume just about anything edible.

● *Are crustaceans susceptible to any medications?*

Yes. Copper-based medications are lethal to all crustaceans with the exception of hermit crabs, which will endure mild doses. Other medications are generally tolerated very poorly and are best not used in the same tank.

● *Is it safe to house univalve molluscs (gastropods) and hermit crabs in the same aquarium?*

No. Hermit crabs will eat the molluscs and take their shells. Turbo Snails (*Turbo fluctuosus*) in particular, are often introduced to graze on the algae within an invertebrate tank. Hermit crabs will commonly prey on these molluscs, even though the empty shell may prove useless to them.

way it appears to be hiding its face behind large, but weak claws. It spends most of the day hidden beneath the sand or under rocks and it should not be kept with molluscs, which it will eat.

The **Boxing Crab** (*Lybia tessellata*). These fascinating creatures carry an anemone on each claw for protection. Although very small, approximately 1in (2.5cm) in length, they make an excellent addition to most invertebrate aquaria.

The **Decorator Crab** (*Camposcia retusa*) is a master of camouflage, attaching suitable pieces of algae and detritus to its legs and body in order to break up its outline. It is peaceful and easy to keep.

Lobsters

Lobsters have large appetites and will eat other crustaceans and fish. They also like to burrow in order to make a suitable retreat. This behaviour will cause chaos within the aquarium and is a convincing argument to house all lobsters in a species tank. Lobsters are highly territorial and must be kept singly if serious fighting is to be avoided.

The **Purple Spiny Lobster** (*Panulirus versicolor*) is a very attractive but large-growing species, reaching up to 8in (20cm) in length and requiring plenty of space. It has a good appetite and is easy to keep.

Red Dwarf Lobsters (*Enoplometopus occidentalis*) are extremely attractive nocturnal creatures capable of growing to a modest length of 5in (12.5cm).

Reef Lobsters (*Enoplometopus* spp.) are extremely colourful lobsters rarely growing larger than 6in (15cm). Once a suitable "home", in the form of a cave or burrow, has been found, they settle down well.

Barnacles

These interesting crustaceans can occasionally be acquired in small colonies or as individuals sharing the same rock as other sessile invertebrates. Aquarists are often fascinated to see the feathery feet constantly wafting small particles of food into their mouths. Unfortunately, barnacles require constant supplies of tiny food particles to remain in good health. Not only is this impractical in many cases, but the uneaten food puts a great strain on water filtration systems. As a consequence, most species usually have a limited lifespan within the marine aquarium.

▲ *Goose barnacles may be too demanding in their food requirements for most hobbyists to keep them successfully. This particular species is* Lepas anserifera.

◀ *Red Dwarf Lobsters* (Enoplometopus occidentalis) *are enthusiastic excavators and will often short-circuit an undergravel filter through their digging activities.*

Tank Conditions and Care

HABITAT: For tank and water conditions see Mushroom Corals page 156.

FEEDING: It is preferable to feed shrimps, crabs and lobsters regularly on suitably sized meaty foods rather than to let them scavenge. Shy feeders may be tempted out of hiding by offering a small piece of squid in a pair of aquarium tongs close to their regular retreat. Barnacles can be fed four or five times each day by squirting live rotifers and brineshrimp nauplii gently at their feathery appendages.

HEALTH: Shrimps, crabs and lobsters will normally remain healthy so long as water conditions are good. Barnacles often die owing to lack of sufficient nutrition.

Clams and other Bivalves
CLASS: BIVALVIA

BIVALVES ENCOMPASS SOME 15,000–20,000 species. They have earned their name because, being filter feeders, each species has an inhalant and exhalant syphon within a pair of symmetrical hinged shells, held together by a pair of powerful muscles. Oysters, mussels, scallops and cockles all belong to this group.

Clams

Slightly more unusually, clams also have a pair of large gills which not only enable the animal to breathe but also act as a food filter. Water is drawn in through the inhalant syphon, passed over the gills and any plankton or food particles are trapped on a sticky mucus layer; thereafter, tiny beating cillia carry the food to the mouth and the waste water is disposed of through the exhalant syphon. In common with many invertebrates, filter feeding is not the only method of obtaining nutrition; the fleshy mantle of most clams is home to various species of symbiotic algae, enabling the clam to feed and grow in the absence of food available for filtering.

Each species of symbiotic algae (zooxanthellae) gives the clam its distinctive colour and patterning which may be in shades of blue, green, brown, grey, white, orange, gold, yellow, purple or red. Many of the colours have an iridescent quality which, when

● *Are the various species of clams easy to identify?*

... Most clams are identified by their shells and not the coloration of the mantle. It is unwise to rely on a particular colour or pattern as a guide to species recognition.

● *Which is the inhalant syphon and the exhalant syphon and where are they?*

Both syphons are to be found in the mantle. The inhalant syphon is the large, elongated slit, within which the gills can be seen; the exhalant syphon is the smaller circular mound.

● *If one clam is put in a tank, will baby clams appear?*

No, for two reasons. Marine clams are either male or female, so a minimum of one male and one female of the same species is needed for successful reproduction. Secondly, clams are very difficult to raise under aquarium conditions owing to a larval stage requiring a specialized rearing technique. Having said that, semi-wild "clam farms" do exist in several, mainly tropical, countries, and these successfully supply much of the aquarium and food trades.

● *Can a clam be positioned anywhere in the tank?*

Only in brightly lit areas that have good water turbulence. If possible, move the clam higher up the rockwork to enable it to take full advantage of the intense illumination.

Tank Conditions and Care – Clams

HABITAT: For tank and water conditions see Mushroom Corals page 156.

Lighting Moderate to intense lighting is essential. This can be fluorescent, mercury vapour or metal halide but it is important that 10–12 hours of light falls directly onto the mantle every day.

FEEDING: In the brightly-lit aquarium, the symbiotic algae within the mantle provide all the food a clam requires. Liquid foods tend to pollute the tank as they are difficult to regulate; for most tanks liquid foods are not necessary.

HEALTH: Clams suffer from very few diseases so long as water quality is high and water circulation is good. However, if mistreated, the muscle holding the two shells together sometimes detaches and the clam separates into a "gaping" position. Some specimens recover, others deteriorate quickly and should be removed. Predatory bristleworms can be a problem as they can crawl into the syphons and devour the clam from the inside. Therefore, all tanks containing clams should be cleared of these worms at regular intervals. For advice on dealing with bristleworms see pages 198–199.

arranged in attractive patterns make clams some of the most stunningly beautiful animals anywhere in the sea. As a result, many marine aquarists find them difficult to resist.

Many bivalves attach themselves to a firm substrate by means of strong fibres called byssus threads. These are exuded from the byssus gland located at the base of the animal. The byssus (as the whole "root-like" structure is called) anchors the bivalve to the substrate, minimizing the threat of being swept away by a strong current. Should it prove necessary to move an established clam, these threads may be cut with a sharp blade close to the area of attachment, not near the base of the clam. Pulling at the animal may damage delicate tissues and must be avoided.

Clam flesh is very desirable to many predators, so at the first sign of any perceived threat the clam closes its shell rapidly as its only defence. Each clam has a row of tiny dark dots around the edges of the mantle; these are light receptors and are capable of detecting the shadows cast by potential predators.

Some of the most popular and commonly available species fall into the genus *Tridacna* and include *T. crocea*, *T. maxima* and *T. gigas* (cultured). Aquarium specimens tend to be quite slow growing but given intense lighting and regular calcium supplements to aid shell growth, clams can be long-lived and exhibit a steady, if slow, growth rate.

◄ *This Giant Clam* (Tridacna gigas) *is a cultured specimen exhibiting an impressive colourful mantle. As the animal is fully open, the exhalant syphon is visible.*

▶ *The full impact of this* Tridacna maxima *is lost as the specimen is semi-closed. As it settles in the aquarium, the mantle will usually become fully visible.*

Other Bivalves

The Caribbean Spiny Oyster (*Spondylus americanus*) is most frequently available to the marine aquarist, although other similar *Spondylus* species are to be found in the Indo-Pacific. In common with Flame Scallops *(Lima scabra)* and Green Mussels, lack of suitable food is a common cause of a rapid demise, as well as predation from other aquarium inhabitants.

Green Mussels may be on sale as individuals, or more often in clusters. The green iridescent shell makes them an attractive proposition. Unfortunately, they are generally not long-lived in the marine aquarium for two reasons. Firstly, they have large appetites and must be fed frequently on plankton or live rotifers as a substitute; to most aquarists this can become an impractical chore and as a result the mussels slowly starve. Secondly, clusters have a habit of parting, as individuals throw out their byssus threads and pull themselves into inaccessible locations within the rockwork. This makes feeding almost impossible and the mussels gradually starve in the nutrition-free water. In common with scallops, the flesh is very appealing to many fish and other invertebrates, and losses can be

Tank Conditions and Care
other Bivalves

HABITAT: Invertebrate aquaria only. For tank and water conditions see Mushroom Corals page 156.

Lighting Unimportant as none of these species have symbiotic algae that rely on intense light.

FEEDING: Once or twice daily with rotifers or brineshrimp nauplii as these bivalves are heavy feeders and will starve in "clean" reef aquaria.

HEALTH: Nearly all fatalities are due to lack of proper feeding.

high if they are housed with shrimps, crabs, lobsters, bristleworms and the like.

Flame Scallops have become very popular with marine aquarists owing to the intense red coloration of their flesh. They come from the Caribbean and rarely exceed 2.5in (6.25cm). By clapping the two halves of their shells together a jet of water can be exhaled, which provides the propulsion for swimming, albeit jerkily. However, scallops much prefer to stay in one position, firmly attached by their byssus threads, and should be encouraged to establish a position at the front of the aquarium display. All too often, these bivalves make their way to the very back of the rockwork where they remain unseen and eventually die. Scallops do not possess a symbiotic relationship with any algae, therefore all their food must be obtained by filtering the water. They are heavy feeders and it is recommended that live rotifers or brineshrimp nauplii are squirted in their vicinity at least twice each day. Without a reasonable amount of food, these attractive bivalves gradually starve to death. Many fish find scallop flesh very inviting and those specimens showing signs of predation are likely to have received the unwanted attentions of incompatible fish.

◀ *Flame Scallops* (Lima scabra) *may starve in the absence of suitable food.*

Nautiluses SUBCLASS: NAUTILOIDEA

NAUTILUSES ARE SOME OF NATURE'S GENUINE living fossils, having remained in their present form for millions of years. Until recently it was thought to be very rare. However, large numbers have been caught off the reefs in the Indo-Pacific on night-time feeding forays. During the day they retreat back to the ocean depths, sometimes as much as 650ft (200m) and beyond the reach of collectors.

This amazing daily migration can only be achieved because of its unique body design. The mother-of-pearl shell contains chambers that may be filled alternatively with liquid or gas, depending on whether the creature wants to rise or fall in the water column. It moves by forcing jets of water through the exhalant syphon, in the same manner as its relatives octopuses and cuttlefish. Unlike its cousins, it produces no sepia ink and cannot avoid danger by a swift swimming action.

The sexes are distinct, the female becoming much larger than the male. Toward the end of their lives, the shells of the females fill with eggs and with this precious cargo they drift into the shallows to die. Thousands of tiny nautiluses are then released from the shell at varying intervals.

 Nautilus macromphalus *is popular with hobbyists.*

Fully grown, the female nautilus measures some 20in (50cm) across, and is a formidable predator, capable of extending its tentacles to catch fish and shrimp. Owing to its highly developed predatory nature, nautilus are best kept singly in a species tank or with sessile invertebrates only. A well known species is *Nautilus pompilius*, the Pearly Nautilus.

● Will a nautilus reach its full potential size in the aquarium?

... Most young male specimens rarely exceed 8in (20cm) in captivity, although females are likely to grow larger depending on the species.

● Are nautiluses suitable for the beginner?

Absolutely not. These creatures can only be recommended to the advanced, committed and well-prepared hobbyist.

● Are nautiluses commonly available?

No. A special order will almost certainly have to be placed, and the specimen will be very expensive.

Tank Conditions and Care

HABITAT: For water conditions see Cuttlefish page 187.

Tank Size Juveniles can be housed in tanks as small as 48x15x18in (122x38x46cm) but will require an aquarium in excess of 72x18x24in (183x46x61cm) as a fully grown adult.

FEEDING: Live river shrimp is eagerly accepted in the initial stages. Frozen shrimp, lancefish, cockle and mussel will also be accepted, especially as it falls through the water. Any food on the substrate may be ignored and have to be removed or re-presented.

HEALTH: Little information available.

Octopuses FAMILY: OCTOPODIDAE

OCTOPUSES ARE MOLLUSCS BELONGING TO THE class Cephalopoda of which there are about 650 species. The largest is the Giant Pacific Octopus measuring 20ft (6m) across, but most are quite small, spanning no more than 12in (30cm) arm tip to arm tip. They live in all the temperate and tropical oceans, usually in shallow areas and tide pools.

Millions of years ago octopuses had a shell like most other molluscs. Today this is little more than two small slivers embedded in the mantle (the fleshy body). However, there are a number of similarities between octopuses and their near relatives – clams, oysters, scallops, limpets and cowries. They all breathe through an inlet-outlet syphon which, in the case of octopuses, combines with the mantle to form a pump to jet-propel through the water away from danger. The discharge of a dark-brown ink known as sepia is a further escape strategy. Pursuers are disorientated, giving an octopus a better chance to escape.

Octopuses have voracious appetites. Their favourite foods are crabs, shrimps and other crustaceans but fish will be taken readily. Night-time feeding forays are normal, but hunger may force daytime hunting especially if a convenient opportunity presents itself. Prey stands little chance once engulfed by eight strong arms, each lined with rows of unyielding suckers. However, octopuses do have their own enemies and often make a favourite meal for moray eels.

A Formidable Intelligence

Of all the invertebrates, cephalopods have the largest brain and the best eyesight, enabling them to be trained in captivity to perform "tricks" that require high intelligence and a good memory. These tasks may include pressing certain buttons or touching a series of colours in a particular order before being rewarded with a morsel of food. Possibly the

---

Tank Conditions and Care

HABITAT: For water conditions see Cuttlefish page 187. Avoid open uplifts, trickle filter overflows, etc., as these are excellent escape routes!

Tank Size A single octopus can be kept in a tank 36x15x12in (91x38x30cm).

Lighting Subdued at all times

FEEDING: Newly imported octopuses will relish live river shrimps but as time progresses should be introduced to a varied diet of frozen shrimps, cockle, mussel, squid and lancefish.

HEALTH: Diseases are very rare – escape from the aquarium is the biggest risk to health. Never use copper-based medications.

---

most famous trick is to put a shrimp in a screw-top bottle, and watch an octopus unscrew the cap, and eat the shrimp!

Pigment cells called chromatophores allow the octopus to alter its skin colour. This is particularly useful for camouflage but can also confuse predators, demonstrate mood swings or convey colour-coded messages to a potential mate.

Reproduction

On meeting, a male and female will go through an elaborate courtship ritual with colour-change messages being exchanged and the male stroking the female with his arms. After a time, the female will be aroused enough to allow the male to transfer a sperm packet, located on the tip of one of his arms, into her mantle cavity where the eggs are fertilized. Following this encounter the female will find a crevice in which to lay her eggs, and will stand guard over them. She rarely feeds during this period and dies soon after the eggs hatch. Commercial hatcheries have reared the young for educational purposes as well as the aquarium trade.

● *Are octopuses easy to keep in the marine aquarium?*

... Reasonably easy, providing good water quality is sustained and the tank has plenty of rockwork forming caves and crevices in which they can hide.

● *Are there any species to avoid?*

Yes, Blue Ring Octopus *(Hapalochlaena maculosa)* though very attractive, has a lethal bite. Reports confirm that humans, if bitten, die within minutes!

● *Does the tank need to be covered?*

Yes, it is absolutely essential! Octopuses are consummate escape artists and can squeeze through the tiniest gaps. Keep heavy cover glasses tightly fitted!

● *Is an octopus likely to "ink" in the tank?*

No, not unless seriously upset. If it does ink in the tank this does not usually prove fatal if fresh carbon is fitted immediately to filter it out.

▲ *The Common Tropical Octopus* (Octopus cyaneus) *is the most popularly available species in the aquarium trade. It measures about 12in (30cm) across its full span and can become very tame. Other very similar species are available from time to time.*

● *Is an octopus likely to bite humans?*

If it thinks fingers are food, yes! Octopuses very soon learn where their food comes from and will extend their arms out of the water in expectation. This tempts the owner to feed by hand and encourages a possible bite. Be on the safe side and offer food with the use of plastic aquarium tongs.

● *Are octopuses compatible with any other fish or invertebrates?*

They will eat most fish and all invertebrates that are not sessile. A species tank is almost essential.

● *Can two octopuses be kept in one tank?*

Unless it is extremely large, no, as they will fight until one or both are dead.

Cuttlefish FAMILY: SEPIDAE

CUTTLEFISH ARE MORE ACTIVE PREDATORS than their close relatives, octopuses. They are fast swimming, have excellent eyesight and will fearlessly catch crabs, shrimps and fish. Like octopuses, cuttlefish have eight arms but, in addition, they also possess two long rapidly extendible tentacles with which to capture prey at a reasonable distance. After capture, a strong parrot-like beak inflicts the fatal wound whilst the radula (similar to a tongue) rasps it into digestible pieces.

These creatures are highly intelligent and communicate feelings and messages by their appearance. Large pigment cells just below the surface of the skin can alter the patterning and colour of the body in a split second. Some species can send waves of colour washing from front to back in hues of red and black. Individuals will perform spectacular kaleidoscopic "shows" during courtship or when potential prey has been discovered. Crabs and shrimps are almost mesmerized, and become an easier target. Cuttlefish may also change colour to blend in with the background, or to exhibit fear or aggression.

Most species establish a pair bond between males and females for a brief period during the summer mating season and the resultant eggs, which resemble bunches of grapes, are attached to algae or protected areas where a good flow of water is to be found. The female

◄ *The Common Cuttlefish* (Sepia officinalis) *is an impressive beast. Special cells called chromatophores are just below the surface of the skin and produce rapid changes in pattern and colour. The unusual eye (seen here in close-up) is that of a hunter. Once located, prey rarely escapes from this most determined predator.*

may guard the eggs for a short while after laying but rarely remains to see them hatch. Sometimes eggs are washed up on the beach and interested aquarists can hatch them in a suitable marine aquarium.

Coldwater aquarium enthusiasts would certainly be interested in the Common Cuttlefish (*Sepia officinalis*), which grows to around 12in (30cm) long, or the Atlantic Cuttlefish (*Sepia atlantica*) at a more manageable 2in (5cm), an interesting contrast to the giant Indo-Pacific cuttlefish, *S. apama*, which may grow to a massive 3ft (1 metre).

"Inking" in the Tank

Many people are concerned about the cuttlefish's ability to "ink" as a defensive measure in such a confined space as an aquarium. Experienced keepers of this invertebrate have found that the ink does no harm to the cuttlefish, or any other tank inhabitants and the discoloration tends to clear in about an hour. Imported specimens tend to ink far more often than tank-reared cuttles, but inking is not an uncommon event and the hobbyist will just have to accept the situation. Certainly any maintenance activity such as rearrangement of rockwork can cause inking; so can tapping on the glass or sudden, unexpected movements in front of the aquarium. Life expectancy in captivity is estimated at between two and six years.

● *Can a coldwater species be kept in the tropical marine aquarium?*

... Provided that they are raised from eggs, yes; experienced cuttlefish keepers have found no problem with the higher temperatures, but adults respond very poorly.

● *Where can cuttlefish eggs be obtained?*

They have to be collected from the seashore as the vast majority of retailers are unable to supply them.

● *Are the fry easy to rear?*

They are about the size of a freshwater cyclops upon hatching and require copious and regular amounts of live food such as brineshrimp nauplii. Success can be very variable from batch to batch.

● *Are the fry quick growing?*

Yes, very quick. They can reach 3in (7.5cm) in length in only 6 weeks! Within 10 months the specimens can reach 9in (22.5cm). However, excellent water quality is essential at all times, as is very regular feeding if this growth rate is to be sustained.

● *Can cuttles be housed with any other creatures?*

Only sessile invertebrates. Fish, crustacea and all other livestock will all be seen as food and eaten.

● *Is the background rockwork important?*

Yes, if you want to witness the enormous variety of colour changes that the cuttlefish can produce. Avoid bland rock such as tufa but introduce various shades of darker lava rock and slate. Various corals will also help to bring out the best in them.

Tank Conditions and Care

HABITAT: Cuttlefish occupy open water and require plenty of clear swimming space. It is not necessary to have a lot of rockwork.

Tank Size Juveniles can be housed in tanks as small as 48x15x18in (122x38x46cm) but will require an aquarium in excess of 72x18x24in (183x46x61cm) as a fully grown adult.

pH	8.1–8.3
Temperature	21–24°C (70–75°F)
Ammonia	Zero
Nitrite	Zero
Nitrate	10ppm total NO$_3$ or less
Specific Gravity	1.021–1.024
Dissolved Oxygen	6–8 ppm

Filtration Efficient protein skimming and activated carbon filtration as standard. Biological filtration must be efficient and capable of coping with the large amounts of waste produced.

Lighting Preferably subdued but will adapt to moderate or bright conditions.

Water Circulation	Moderate

Water Changes 15–25% every two weeks with high quality water.

FEEDING: Cuttlefish will greedily accept live river shrimp, frozen prawns, cockle, mussel and all meaty marine foods.

HEALTH: Given good water conditions, cuttlefish suffer no particular health problems.

Sea Slugs ORDER: NUDIBRANCHIA

● *How do sea hares protect themselves?*

... If attacked, they release a poisonous dye from a gland in the mantle. It is best to house them with peaceful fish.

● *Will sea hares consume nuisance slimy algae (Cyanophyceae)?*

Unfortunately not. They are not attracted to this particular type of algae.

◀ *While the Striped Nudibranch* (Chromodoris quadicolor) *is a highly desirable sea slug, lack of suitable food generally causes it to shrink and die.*

Tank Conditions and Care

HABITAT: For tank and water conditions see Mushroom Corals page 156.

FEEDING: Sea hares require a constant supply of green algae, both micro and macro. They consume vast quantities of nuisance algae but will not discriminate against decorative algae and can decimate carefully cultured growths. Most highly coloured sea slugs starve to death in the aquarium. Should they happen on a suitable food source, it will usually be a prized coral which they will feed upon until it is dead.

HEALTH: Given good water quality sea slugs do not suffer from any particular diseases. However, insufficient food will cause shrinking and inactivity; death usually follows.

SEA SLUGS ARE OFTEN KNOWN AS NUDIBRANCHS – a word meaning naked gill – and belong to a group of gastropods called opistobranchs. These univalve molluscs possess either a very reduced shell, or no shell at all. Some species, such as the Spanish Dancer (*Hexabranchus imperialis*) are graceful and agile swimmers; however, the vast majority creep over the seabed and have little or no ability to swim.

Many sea slugs are beautiful creatures with remarkable coloration and markings, making them particularly desirable additions to the marine aquarium. Their flamboyant vividly coloured appearance acts as a warning to potential predators that they are poisonous. The feathery tufts adorning their backs are external gills, and some species have the unusual ability to withdraw them into the body should danger threaten. Other species lack these decorative plumes altogether, and respire directly through their skin.

Beautiful But Deadly

Contrary to popular belief, only a few sea slugs are herbivores. The vast majority are grazing carnivores feeding on specific hard corals, soft corals, gorgonians, anemones, sponges, and other invertebrates. The most beautiful sea slugs are usually the most carnivorous and can prove highly destructive to sedentary invertebrates. The vast majority of these species, though they are commonly available for sale, cannot be recommended for the marine aquarium.

One group of species that performs a useful service is the sea hares (*Aplysia* spp.), which grazes on algae at a prodigious rate. The Caribbean Sea Hare can grow to 12in (30cm) in length, but the Indo-Pacific species supplied to the aquarium trade are generally only 3.2in (8cm). Sea hares are good swimmers and are able to move quickly to fresh feeding sites, or remove themselves from danger.

Cowries FAMILY: OVULIDAE

COWRIES ARE PROBABLY OF MORE VALUE TO shell collectors than to marine fishkeepers; for although their shells are often beautiful, in the aquarium cowries are capable of causing considerable inconvenience.

Cowries are nocturnal univalves that generally remain hidden during the day. When darkness falls they emerge to forage, dislodging carefully positioned corals with their powerful foot. Although a few species are herbivores, the vast majority are carnivores and will feed on gorgonians, soft corals and other sessile invertebrates. Even those species that enjoy a diet of macro-algae regularly turn their attention to living corals, often to the great dismay of the hobbyist.

The attractive shell is a hard, highly polished dome and is usually fully, or partially, covered by a relatively uninteresting fleshy mantle to provide camouflage.

▼ *The strong foot of the Tiger Cowrie* (Cypraea tigris) *will dislodge precious corals with ease.*

● *Can cowries be introduced accidentally into the aquarium?*

... Yes, they can arrive clinging to sea fans and sea whips on which they feed. The Flamingo Tongue *(Cyphoma gibbosum)* from the Caribbean is often introduced in this way.

● *Are cowries suitable for the fish-only aquarium?*

No, cowries demand the higher water quality of an invertebrate aquarium or species tank.

● *Which species are suitable for the aquarium?*

Tiger Cowrie *(Cypraea tigris), C. arabica, C. pantherina* and *C. nucleus.*

Tank Conditions and Care

HABITAT: For tank and water conditions see Mushroom Corals page 156.

FEEDING: Most aquarium cowries will graze on macro-algae such as *Caulerpa* spp. supplemented with lancefish and shellmeat.

HEALTH: Given a balanced diet and good water quality, cowries tend to be healthy.

Basket Stars, Brittle Stars & Sea Lilies

PHYLUM: ECHINODERMATA
CLASSES: OPHIUROIDEA, CRINOIDEA

BOTH BASKET STARS AND BRITTLE STARS ARE ophiuroids. In common with sea lilies (crinoids) they have a central disk, five legs, but no suckers on the end of their tubed feet.

Basket Stars

The five arms of a basket star are sub-divided many times to form a delicate tracery trap in which to capture tiny food particles drifting in the current. During the day, they close their arms and rest as a loose ball, frequently in prominent places. Such behaviour means that they are already positioned for the hours of darkness when the arms are fully extended and feeding begins.

These creatures are very large when feeding, with some species exceeding 20in (50cm) across the tips of the arms. They are not suitable for small aquaria, and are to be recommended to the experienced hobbyist only.

Brittle Stars

Being efficient scavengers by nature, these starfish are suited to the reef aquarium where they will co-exist peacefully with other invertebrates. They differ from other starfish in that the central disk of the body is somewhat flattened and the five arms may be spiny or have other forms of extensions. As the common name implies, brittle stars are very fragile and frequently lose arms, which are quickly regenerated. Brittle stars are not completely ideal aquarium inhabitants as they are nocturnal and spend much of daylight hours hidden from view. When active, these unusual creatures have extremely mobile legs and can move remarkably quickly to capture food or avoid danger. Sometimes they will entwine themselves among the long spines of *Diadema* urchins for protection; a common trait in the wild. In nature, brittle stars can often be seen in massive congregations some several animals deep!

This basket star, Astrophyton muricatum, *is just beginning to extend its deceptively long arms into the current to feed on tiny food particles.*

Brittle stars such as this Ophiomastix venosa *have a keen sense of smell which leads them to food.*

Sea Lilies

Also termed feather stars, these creatures are crinoids. They have a long ancestry which can be dated as far back as 500 million years. In common with brittle stars and basket stars, sea lilies are extremely fragile and their arms are easily broken by rough handling, strong water currents or the unwanted attentions of fish. Regeneration is reasonably quick, providing that the source of aggravation has been eliminated.

Sea lilies are filter feeders and are largely nocturnal. However, they may make an appearance during the day, especially if food is available. Optimum water quality must be provided at all times since they will not thrive if conditions are constantly changing. The Red Crinoid, *Himerometra robustipinna*, is one of the most commonly imported species from East Asia, popular because of its attractive deep red coloration. Other species are available from time to time but they tend to be much less colourful.

This Red Crinoid (Himerometra robustipinna) *has a typically feathery structure, accounting for the sea lilies' alternative common name, the feather star.*

● *Are any of these creatures to be recommended to the beginner?*

... Brittle stars can be kept successfully by the newcomer, but the others require experience and a wider understanding of invertebrate needs.

● *Will they damage sessile invertebrates?*

No, in this respect they are very compatible with other invertebrate species.

● *Are any special procedures required when moving these creatures from tank to tank?*

Yes, they react very poorly to changes in water quality, especially salinity and pH. Move them in plastic bags with some of the aquarium water from the first tank and float the open bags (with the tops turned down) in the new tank. Gradually add the new aquarium water into the open bag a little at a time, allowing 20-40 minutes before you free the stars completely. Handle carefully as their arms are easily broken.

● *What would cause basket and feather stars not to feed properly?*

Lack of sufficient water current, a low oxygen content or poor water quality will all result in a lack of feeding stimulus, and to a more general inactivity.

Tank Conditions and Care

HABITAT: For tank and water conditions see Mushroom Corals page 156.

Lighting Unimportant but feeding behaviour may best be observed by the use of a low wattage tungsten bulb or blue fluorescent tube (see Lighting pages 12–15).

FEEDING   Offer basket and feather stars live brineshrimp nauplii and/or live rotifers every evening when they are in feeding mode. Freshly thawed molluscs can also be squeezed in the water nearby as a good food supplement. Brittle stars can be offered small pieces of fish and shellmeat. Circulatory pumps are best switched off during feeding to allow the animals maximum time in which to absorb the food without it being drawn into the filters and lost.

HEALTH: Long life cannot be expected if correct nutrition and optimum water conditions are not supplied.

Sea Urchins

PHYLUM: ECHINODERMATA
CLASS: ECHINOIDEA

THERE ARE AN ESTIMATED 750 SPECIES OF SEA urchin all belonging to the class Echinoidea. They live in tropical, temperate, or icy oceans; in shallow or very deep water; in fact anywhere that suitable food is to be found. The species are so varied that the smallest has a body or "test" no larger than 1.2in (3cm) in diameter, while the largest is 10in (25cm). Depending upon the species, spines may exceed 12in (30cm) or be barely noticeable. The word urchin derives from the old French *heriçon* meaning hedgehog. Dickens enthusiasts will also be interested to note that the phrase "street urchin" arose because their unkempt spiky hair resembled a hedgehog.

Most species graze on algae using five powerful jaws on their underside; waste material is excreted through the anus on top of the test. However, a few species have only three jaws and still fewer look more like a sea cucumber with an elongated body, jaws at the front and anus at the rear. Not all species are herbivores, so aquarists must be careful that they do not introduce uncommon species that make a meal of soft-bodied invertebrates such as anemones and leather corals.

Sea urchins are true "jugglers of the sea". Not only do they possess moveable spines but they have a group of smaller secondary spines and rows of feet with which they can perform many useful tasks such as clearing the body of debris, ridding it of harmful larvae looking for a home, manoeuvring pieces of food into the mouth, as well as helping in the general locomotion of the animal. Always use aquarium tongs if you must move an urchin but never pull on the spines; try to dislodge it from beneath.

Apart from one or two isolated cases, all urchins are either male or female. Since they live in large groups, reproduction involves mass spawnings at certain times of the year. Eggs and sperm mix together locally before

Tank Conditions and Care

HABITAT: For tank and water conditions see Mushroom Corals page 156.

FEEDING: Most species need large quantities of algae to graze on. This may be macro- or micro-algae. They do not favour nuisance algae.

HEALTH: The most common health problem is casting off spines. Little is known about why some urchins shed their spines, all at once, or a few at a time. The shock of being moved can trigger it, as can poor water conditions such as low pH and water poor in calcium. Some "bald" urchins survive and re-grow their spines very slowly if conditions improve, but most die.

◀ *The Banded Sea Urchin* (Echinothrix calamaris) *is long-lived and an excellent choice for the aquarium.*

fertilized eggs are dispersed far and wide in the plankton layers to develop into larvae. Sea urchin larvae is so distinct that species are easily identified by the larvae alone. When fully formed, the young adults migrate back to the sea floor where they mature. Sea urchins have not yet been bred in captivity.

● *An urchin has not moved for days, is it dead?*

... Urchins are nocturnal, and some species wander round at night, returning to the same spot by morning, giving the impression of never having moved. Give the animal a light tap with a pair of plastic aquarium tongs; if it falls off easily and shows no sign of righting itself, then it is probably dead. If it cannot be dislodged then it is likely to be a healthy specimen.

● *Are urchin stings dangerous?*

The ferocity of a sting varies markedly from species to species. The Pencil Urchin (*Heterocentrotus mammillatus*) and the Mine Urchin (*Eucidaris tribuloides*) have very blunt spines and are incapable of stinging at all. The Long-Spined Urchin (*Diadema savignyi*) has very sharp venomous spines that can give a painful wound. Some species such as *Toxopneustes pileolus* – the Poison Urchin – can be fatal to humans, but these species are hardly ever found in the aquarium trade.

● *Can urchins be destructive?*

They are capable of dislodging rocks and corals and, in confined spaces, sharp-spined species can pierce soft corals and anemones.

● *What is a good beginner's urchin?*

The Pencil and Mine Urchin are good for beginners as is the Common Urchin. Long-Spined Urchins, while readily available, are slightly more sensitive.

● *How should a sting be treated?*

Dip the wound in alcohol or vinegar and do not try to extract the tip of the spine if it is completely embedded in the skin. Although painful for a couple of hours) the tip usually dissolves under the skin quite quickly. If an allergic reaction sets in (generally in people already allergic to bee and wasp stings) then get to the nearest hospital casualty department as soon as possible!

➤ *The Pencil Urchin* (Heterocentrotus mammillatus) *derived its name because its spines can be used to write on a stone slab or slate.*

Starfish

PHYLUM: ECHINODERMATA
CLASS: ASTEROIDEA

STARFISH ARE FOUND ON SHORELINES AND IN shallow seas through every part of the world. Species can live in the coldest arctic waters, in temperate and sub-tropical zones, or in the very warmest tropical regions. They belong to a large invertebrate group of approximately 6,000 species called echinoderms. The group also encompasses feather stars, sea urchins, sea cucumbers and sea lilies, all of which have found some place in the marine aquarium.

Starfish, like other echinoderms, have no head, brain or complex sense organs. A simple nervous system extends down the arms and across the skin which responds, rather ponderously, to touch and surrounding water quality. Food is detected by the same process. Locomotion is fascinating to observe as

◀ *The Blue Starfish* (Linckia laevigata) *is an attractive species and one of the more successful on offer to the hobbyist. Always choose the most brightly coloured individuals.*

Popular Species of Starfish

The following are commonly available and generally do well in the marine aquarium:

Blue Starfish *(Linckia laevigata)*
Bun Starfish *(Culcita novaeguinea* and *Culcita schmideliana)*
Red Starfish *(Fromia elegans)*
Orange Starfish *(Fromia monilis)*
Red-knobbed Starfish *(Protoreaster lincki)*
Common knobbed Starfish *(Pentaceraster mammillatus)*

This orange starfish will contentedly graze on algae; most starfish will not.

● *Can a starfish be housed in a mainly fish tank?*

... No, this is not advisable. Starfish are very sensitive to fish waste.

● *Are starfish safe introductions to an invertebrate aquarium?*

Yes, most species do very well in such an aquarium, but some specimens feed on clams and other molluscs as well as sponges.

● *Is it true that nearly all starfish will feed on algae?*

Most definitely not! Most species require a diet of meaty shellfish or sponge; a few species will feed solely on algae, while some, like the infamous Crown-of-Thorns Starfish *(Acanthaster planci)* scavenge on almost anything.

● *Will a starfish topple corals or rockwork?*

If the corals or rocks are not properly seated then a starfish might very well cause some to fall. On the whole, starfish do very little damage.

● *Why do starfish hide during the day?*

Most species are nocturnal and remain stationary during the day. However, many specimens will make daytime hunting forays if they are hungry or if they learn that food is available at a certain time each day.

starfish seem to glide over even the roughest terrain. They have hundreds of pairs of tubed feet connected to a water vascular system, unique to echinoderms. Each leg incorporates a canal filled with sea water which can, by a system of valves and muscles, control each pair of feet.

The mouth of the starfish is at the centre of the underside and many species are capable of pushing their stomachs out through the mouth to engulf and digest food outside of the body. This is common in species that feed on bivalve molluscs, using their strong feet and arms to pull the two shells apart just enough to insert the stomach and digest the shellfish within its own shell.

Starfish are also capable of extraordinary regeneration and reproduction. Lost limbs are quickly re-grown, but more extraordinary than this, many species, when cut in half, develop into two separate animals! Commercial oyster and mussel fishermen discovered this to their cost when plagues of starfish fed on their valuable shellfish cultures. They tried to destroy the starfish by cutting them in half and throwing them back into the sea, only to find that they had doubled their numbers! Normally starfish reproduce by ejecting eggs and sperm into the water, where the larvae develop until adulthood, when they settle on the sea bed.

Tank Conditions and Care

HABITAT: For tank and water conditions see Mushroom Corals page 156.

FEEDING: Initially offer meaty foods such as shellmeat, cockle, mussel, lancefish, prawn, squid or mysis to establish a preferred diet. Blanched spinach may also be offered. Feed every 1–3 days. If there are fish or crustaceans that would steal the food first, place a small piece of food on the floor of the aquarium and place the starfish directly over the top. Otherwise, position the food right next to the starfish and let it move over it.

HEALTH: If water quality deteriorates and the correct diet is not provided, starfish often suffer bacterial infections leading to open wounds. Being quite sedentary, they may also attract the unwanted attentions of crustaceans and inquisitive fish which may do some damage; therefore, tankmates must be chosen with care.

Sea Cucumbers CLASS: HOLOTHUROIDEA

THESE FASCINATING CREATURES ARE EASY TO identify as they have a group of feathery tentacles at one end of the body, which sweep food particles into the mouth constantly. Sea cucumbers move slowly on several rows of tubed feet ranged along the length of their bodies and would be at the mercy of any passing predator if it were not for two effective means of diversion. They are capable of passing the whole stomach, intestines and the contents thereof, through the anus and into the water for the attacker to feed upon while the cucumber makes good its escape. Amazingly, these vital organs are soon regenerated and the animal can return to a normal life once more. Secondly, some species possess the ability to squirt out sticky threads, confusing and entangling enemies.

Sea Apples

The most popular species for the domestic aquarium is *Pseudocolochirus axiologus*, also known as the Sea Apple, probably because of the reddish blush on parts of its body, vaguely reminiscent of some types of apple.

All too often, both traders and hobbyists inexplicably regard these fascinating animals quite wrongly as algae eaters and neglect to feed them properly. If the required nutrition is not made available in large enough quantities, sea cucumbers shrink dramatically in size and finally die of starvation.

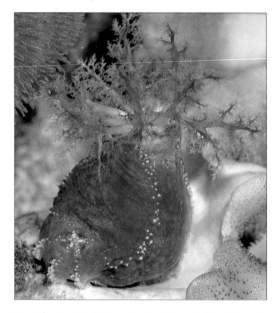

← *The Sea Apple* (Pseudocolochirus axiologus) *is not an easy invertebrate to keep in the aquarium.*

Tank Conditions and Care

HABITAT: For tank and water conditions see Mushroom Corals page 156.

FEEDING: When the tentacles are active, copious quantities of brineshrimp nauplii and/or live rotifers should be introduced into the vicinity. Large specimens will require feeding at least twice a day. Feeding is best undertaken with all circulatory pumps switched off to prevent food being swept into the filters.

HEALTH: Sea cucumbers will remain healthy if the correct food and water conditions are provided. Shrinking bodies and inactive tentacles are sure signs that these vital requirements have been neglected.

● *Are sea cucumbers suitable for the inexperienced hobbyist?*

... No. Although widely available, these animals need the special care and understanding that comes with experience.

● *Why do fish die after sea cucumbers have tried to breed in the aquarium?*

Sea cucumbers occasionally shed eggs and sperm into the water. The eggs are poisonous to the many fish that enjoy feeding on them.

● *Are they likely to expel sticky threads or internal organs into the aquarium?*

Only if seriously threatened by aggressive fish or crustaceans.

Sea Squirts CLASS: ASCIDIACEA

THERE ARE OVER 1,000 SPECIES OF SEA SQUIRT but hardly any are deliberately made available to the hobbyist. They usually arrive by accident on pieces of living rock or accompanying other sessile invertebrates. Some species live in colonies forming a living "mat", others are large individuals 20in (50cm) long. Depending on their appearance, some species are confused with certain species of sponge.

Sea squirts feed by drawing water in through one syphon, filtering it for particles, and then expelling the "cleaned" water through another. The aquarist can make good use of these interesting creatures as an aid to better water quality. They do very well in the invertebrate aquarium and may spread quite freely if conditions are favourable.

According to the species, the colour may be red, blue, green, white, yellow, beige or transparent. Occasionally, some species also act as hosts to symbiotic algae.

▼ *Sea Squirts are an interesting and attractive addition to the aquarium and are easy to keep.*

● *Are sea squirts invertebrates?*

They form the link between invertebrates and vertebrates as the larval stage possesses a stiff rod, or notochord, which acts like a backbone.

● *How did they get the common name sea squirts?*

If they are held out of the water and squeezed, a jet of water is squirted from the syphons. This is more noticeable in larger specimens, but is not a practice recommended to the hobbyist.

Tank Conditions and Care

HABITAT: For tank and water conditions see Mushroom Corals page 156.

FEEDING: Sea squirts are efficient filter feeders and can often survive without any special attention. However, live brineshrimp nauplii, live rotifers and the juices from a freshly thawed mollusc are all readily accepted to assist with growth and the preservation of good health.

HEALTH: Ascidians normally remain healthy even if water conditions are less than perfect.

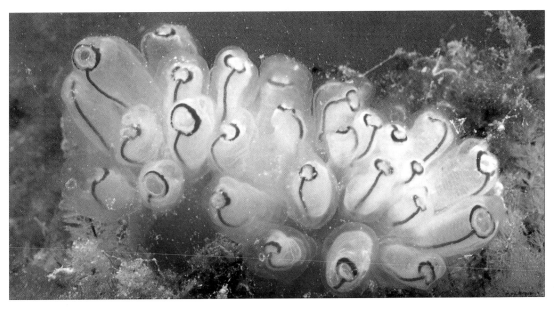

Invertebrate Pests

ANY HORTICULTURIST WILL TELL YOU THAT there is no such thing as a garden without weeds and diseases, and such is the case with the marine aquarium. Like the gardener, the marinist must be vigilant to prevent troublesome pests from ruining an otherwise impressive display. Unfortunately, some pests initially appear to be attractive additions to the aquarium and only later manifest themselves as harmful plagues or vicious hunters that are extremely difficult to eradicate.

The following examples are well known to the experienced hobbyist, but most aquarists will only become aware of their presence when the situation is already out of hand. Therefore, newcomers to the hobby are advised to familiarize themselves with the more common pests and avoid their introduction in the first place.

Bristleworms (Class: Polychaeta)

There are several species of bristleworm that find their way into the home aquarium, each able to multiply rapidly either sexually or asexually. They are segmented marine worms with fully functioning destructive mouthparts and rows of barbed, stinging hairs flanking the body. The smaller species may only be about 2in (5cm) long and the width of a small rubber band, but the larger species grow well in excess of 12in (30cm) long, and reach the width of an adult's little finger.

Bristleworms are scavengers and predators. They sift through detritus searching for algae and morsels of food, but they can also attack living prey such as clams, tubeworms, sessile invertebrates and fish that "lock" themselves into crevices at night.

Large specimens are capable of biting humans, and even the smallest produce a painful rash. Beware of sliding a hand beneath rockwork in an effort to move it as this is a likely way to get bitten or stung.

Feeding forays are nearly always at night and the day is spent hiding among rocks, or buried in the substrate. The best way to gauge how many occupy the hidden depths of a tank is to examine the tank with a dull torch beam after it has been in total darkness for several hours. If it is badly infested, dozens will be moving over rocks, sand and corals. Practically every tank will possess one or two specimens, which may be acceptable; but infested tanks must be cleared for the safety of other livestock and the hobbyist.

The Solution: Bristleworms can be removed with a pair of plastic aquarium tongs during the hours of darkness. A dim light will locate the smaller species, but you will probably need to set a trap for the larger, more destructive worms. Commercial traps are available and work very well but you can make a homemade trap using a 1in (2.5cm) diameter pvc tube about 4in (10cm) long, capped at both ends. Each cap has a small drilled hole through which the worms squeeze to get to a bait of squid, mussel or cockle. Unable to find the exit, the worms are trapped, to be disposed of at leisure. The trap is best baited and positioned between a rock and the substrate as the lights go out. It can be emptied

BRISTLEWORM TRAP

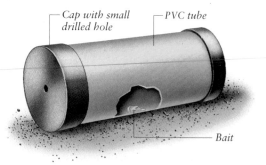

Cap with small drilled hole — PVC tube — Bait

▲ A bristleworm trap will catch specimens in the immediate vicinity, but it will need to be moved around to clear them from the whole tank.

● *What is the best course of action if badly stung by a bristleworm?*

... Remove as many of the barbed hairs as possible with a pair of tweezers and then rinse the area in vinegar or alcohol to ease the pain. Reddening and swelling may take several days to clear.

● *Nuisance flatworms are difficult to see. Is there an easy way to identify them in a domestic or retail aquarium?*

Yes. Many of them gather on the front glass just below the water line. This makes them very easy to locate with the naked eye or a small magnifying glass.

➤ *Flatworms and bristleworms are two of the most insidious marine pests. (Below) flatworms* (Convolutriloba retrogemma) *infest a disk anemone; (below right) bristleworms attack* Lythrypnus dalli.

in the morning and re-set that night; repeat every night until no more are captured. It would be wise to set the traps about every two months.

Some fish will eat bristleworms but can get badly stung in the process. There are reports of worms wrapping themselves around the face of the fish, blinding it permanently and leading to a premature death.

Brown or Planaria Flatworms
(*Convolutriloba retrogemma*)

Although this flatworm species is only a few millimetres in length, it can reproduce both sexually and asexually, so it takes only one specimen to infect a whole tank. Given the right conditions, flatworms will spread over everything that does not move, including rocks, glass, equipment, algae, corals and sand. Within months the sheer weight of numbers will smother sessile invertebrates to the point of destruction! If left unchecked, the end result could be a brown, lifeless mass.

Brown Flatworms arrive on living rock and corals, generally from tanks that are already infected. They can be difficult to locate, and have the ability to move out of sight into the safety of tiny cracks in the rocks relatively quickly. Not only do they feed on micro-organisms, but they also have a symbiotic algae within their tissues providing sustenance, so they thrive in brightly lit aquaria, often occupying the most brilliant locations.

The Solution: Fish-only aquaria can easily be treated with a copper-based medication, but alternatives must be found for the reef aquarium. If small colonies are spotted at an early stage, then syphoning the area several times each day should clear the problem fairly quickly. Some species of fish have been known to eat flatworms; these include mandarins, wrasses, damsels, butterflyfish and tangs. However, experience has shown that it is generally only particular individuals within these groups and not the groups as a whole that will devour this pest.

Consistently reliable and specific chemical controls are unknown for the invertebrate aquarium. Once it has become badly infected, the unlucky aquarist can only limit the damage by frequent syphoning. Smaller aquaria may eventually recover, but larger tanks may house controlled populations for the rest of their existence.

Giant Elephant Ear Polyps
(*Rhodactis* spp.)

Most mushroom colonies feature polyps between 0.5in and 2.5in (1.25–6.25cm) in diameter. However, a few species grow much larger – in excess of 12in (30cm) is not uncommon – and they devour live fish! In their normal state, giant elephant ears look like a dinner plate; this is the "open" stage of a subtle trap. When a fish settles on the polyp, it slowly closes around the victim, trapping it in a giant ball. The fish dies quite quickly and is consumed through the central mouth. Substrate dwellers such as mandarins, hawkfish, blennies and gobies are particularly at risk, but clownfish have also been known to take shelter in these traps. Even basslets and grammas are not safe; they

see the entrance to the polyp in its "ball state" as a cave in which to shelter, and become the polyp's next victim.

The Solution: Giant polyps of this kind have no place in an aquarium with small fish and shrimps. The only solution is to remove them, possibly taking them back to the retailer.

Triffid, Glass or Rock Anemones
(*Aiptasia* spp.)

Triffid anemones are the proverbial wolves in sheep's clothing. They are beautiful creatures, so impressive and attractive to look at that they are often given priority treatment, only to multiply into a dangerous and unsightly plague! They have a prodigious sting capable of killing (as a prelude to eating) small fish; even larger fish can sustain a nasty injury. Reef tanks suffer particularly badly, for as the anemones spread amongst the polyps, corals, clams and other anemones they tend to sting everything they touch. As a result, if their neighbours are not killed, they will show the "burn" marks from having brushed against these fearsome predators.

→ *Despite the delicate appearance of this triffid anemone* (Aiptasia *spp.*), *it is a hardy and invasive pest.*

◀ *Giant elephant ear polyps* (Rhodactis *sp.*) *are highly predatory and will close around an unsuspecting victim. Once trapped, there is little chance of escape.*

One anemone can produce copious offspring in a few weeks owing to an extremely rapid reproductive ability, especially if the tank is consistently overfed. Several months after that, a whole aquarium may be covered in a mass of these anemones if nothing is done to bring matters under control.

Triffid anemones have an elongated body stem lodged far down in a rock crevice or among a polyp colony, making it virtually impossible to remove. At the slightest disturbance it will disappear into the safety of its inaccessible home. To make matters worse, if the whole animal is not destroyed, it can regenerate itself from a small piece of remaining tissue. They can also live in total darkness quite successfully, so check all water routes, especially pipes and other areas of limited access, when trying to eradicate them from the system.

The Solution: Fish-only aquarists are relatively fortunate, and have a range of options. The easiest is to remove any pieces of rock where colonies are established and scrub them under hot running water. Alternatives are to introduce fish species that regard these anemones as food (larger angelfish and most butterflyfish, for example) or to kill the anemones with copper-based medication.

The reef hobbyist is not quite so lucky. Anemone-consuming fish or invertebrates tend to be indiscriminate where other livestock is concerned and may consume the very corals the aquarist is trying to save. Perhaps

● *What is the best way to avoid problems with* Aiptasia *anemones?*

... Make sure that new corals and living rock are free from these pests before purchase. If the dealer has them in the sale system avoid buying from that source.

● *Is there any way of telling if a giant elephant ear polyp has eaten a fish?*

About 24 hours after feeding, a pellet of waste material is slowly ejected from the mouth. If you see that the polyp has formed a ball, check to make sure that all your livestock are accounted for. Trapped fish can be rescued if you get to them early enough.

the most effective option is to use a syringe to inject the offending anemone with a lethal dose of calcium additive. This has the added advantage of being safe should any of the solution escape into the surrounding water. In fact, almost any additive could be used if the first proves ineffective. Another alternative is to fill a syringe with very hot water and squirt it at the base of the anemone. One drawback is that it could prove harmful to invertebrates in the immediate vicinity and therefore can only be used on isolated individuals. A strategy guaranteed to make many people wince, but effective, nonetheless, is to push a sharpened or red-hot screwdriver into the anemone's hiding hole and grind the animal out of existence.

Amphipods (Order: Amphipoda)

Amphipods are small crustaceans generally found feeding in the detritus at the bottom of an aquarium, within the filters, or even on the front glass. They are easily identified as laterally compressed grey shrimp-like creatures, half-moon in shape.

Amphipods rarely do any direct damage; however, some species may carry disease which they can pass on to other livestock. They are quite hardy and capable of multiplying into plague proportions when there is enough food, usually provided by an over-enthusiastic hobbyist.

The Solution: An immediate cure is to remove the creatures by syphoning them out of the tank. They will be found under rocks during the daytime and quick action will be necessary to allow for their surprising turn of speed. In the long term, a drastic reduction in the food supply will see a steady decline in numbers until they are barely

noticeable. Many fish would enjoy copepods as a food if they had access to their hiding places. Regular disturbance of the rockwork may reduce numbers as the fish learn to associate such activity with a potential meal.

Pistol Shrimps (*Synalpheus* spp.)

These are other pests introduced accidentally along with pieces of living rock. They are confirmed recluses and of little interest to most marinists. However, you are left in no doubt as to their presence owing to the noise they make, not unlike the sound of a pistol shot (or an aquarium cracking!) as they snap shut their huge claws. The shock waves are intended to stun passing prey.

The Solution: If you can tolerate the noise they make, then it is unlikely that much livestock will actually be lost to pistol shrimps and they are probably best left alone. If, on the other hand, the noise proves unacceptably irritating, then follow the advice for mantis shrimps.

Mantis Shrimps (*Odontodactylus* spp.)

Mantis shrimps are highly developed predators. They can emerge from a cave at lightning speed to beat to death a likely meal with their club-like claws. Fish, other shrimps, crabs, lobsters and aquarists' fingers are all potential targets. Their alternative common name of "thumb-splitter" is particularly apt.

A pistol shrimp (Synalpheus *sp.*) *is an extremely attractive creature, but rarely seen in open water. Its claw, the source of the characteristic erksome noise, can be seen bottom left.*

A *mantis shrimp* (Odontodactylus southwelli) *will occupy any suitable cavity from which to strike.*

● *How do amphipods arrive in the aquarium?*

... Within the crevices of living rock, or even as eggs or larvae in aquarium water. Unfortunately there is no guaranteed method by which to avoid their accidental introduction.

● *Should any precautions be taken when trying to capture mantis shrimps?*

Yes. Wear thick leather or rubber gloves to avoid injury.

● *Can mantis and pistol shrimps be kept as pets?*

Yes, quite easily. On their own, they make very good pets, being easy to feed and fun to observe.

Mantis shrimps normally arrive in pieces of living rock. They travel very well and rarely die in transportation. Depending on the particular species, size may range from 2in–12in (5–30cm) in length.

The Solution: Ridding a tank of mantis shrimps is not an easy matter. They are intelligent and can avoid traps set for them. If a shrimp settles in a favourite cave, you will have to remove the whole rock taking care that any back entrance is covered and that the creature does not slip out as the rock is lifted from the water. If no other solution can be found then, as a last resort, you may have to push scissors, skewers or a sharp stick into the cave to kill the shrimp by impaling or decapitating it.

Glossary

Absorption The process of taking in and retaining, the way a dry sponge takes in water. Liquid vitamins added to marine flake act in this manner.
Activated carbon Material used to remove pollutants from aquarium water (see page 36).
Adsorption The process by which organic molecules are bonded to a medium, such as ACTIVATED CARBON.
Aerobic Requiring oxygen.
Algae Primitive plants, which may be microscopic or large (e.g. kelp). They have plant characteristics, are almost exclusively aquatic, and do not flower.
Ammonia (NH_3) A gas that dissolves in water and is the first by-product of decaying organic material; also excreted from the gills of fish. Highly toxic to fish and invertebrates.
Anaerobic Not requiring oxygen.
Anal fin A single fin positioned vertically below the fish.
Asexual reproduction Reproduction without the fertilization of eggs with sperm, as in corals "budding off".

Barbel A whisker-like growth around the mouth, which detects food by taste.
Berlin System A filtration technique using living rock and a powerful protein skimmer only.
Biological filtration A means of filtration using bacteria, *NITROSOMONAS* and *NITROBACTER*, to change otherwise toxic AMMONIA-based compounds into safer substances such as NITRATES.
Bivalve A mollusc or shell-dwelling animal with two respiratory valves. (See page 180).
Bleaching The process by which corals or anemones lose or expel their ZOOXANTHELLAE owing to shock or pollution. They turn pale pale or white.
Brackish water Water containing approximately 10% sea water; found where freshwater rivers enter the sea.
Brineshrimp A saltwater crustacean, *Artemia salina*, whose dry-stored eggs can be hatched to provide live food for fish or invertebrates.
Buffering action The ability of a liquid to maintain its desired pH value. (See also CALCAREOUS).
Byssus gland A gland found in BIVALVE molluscs that produces sticky attachment threads.

Calcareous Formed of, or containing, calcium carbonate, a substance that can help aquarium water to maintain a high pH value.
Calcium An important element found in sea water, the metallic basis of lime.
Caudal fin A single vertical fin at the rear of the fish, also called the tail.

Caudal peduncle The part of a fish joining the CAUDAL FIN to the body.
Copper A metal used in copper sulphate form as the basis for marine aquarium remedies. It is poisonous to fish in excess, and to invertebrates at trace levels.
Counter-current skimmer An efficient PROTEIN SKIMMER in which the water flows against a current of air, thereby giving a longer exposure time for collection of waste, or sterilization if OZONE is used. (See page 28.)
Cyanobacteria A primitive form of life, having some characteristics of ALGAE and bacteria but regarded as different from both. Often called slime algae.

Deionizer A mains water filter using several purifying ion-exchange resins.
Demersal "Close to the sea floor." Demersal eggs are heavier than water and are laid in prepared spawning sites on the sea bed. The fertilized eggs are then guarded by one or both adults until hatching occurs.
Denitrification The process by which NITRATE is changed by ANAEROBIC bacteria into nitrous oxide and then into free nitrogen gas.
Diffuser Another name for an airstone.
Dorsal fin A single vertical fin on top of a fish; some species have two dorsal fins, one behind the other. Many marine species have venomous rays in the dorsal fin, so handle with care.

Filter feeder An animal (fish or invertebrate) that sifts water for microscopic food, e.g. pipefish, tubeworms.
Filter medium Used in filtration systems to remove dissolved or suspended organic substances from water.
Fluidized bed A biological filtration method. Unclean water is pumped through a cylinder containing millions of tiny 'beads' on which nitrifying bacteria have become established.
Foam fractionation A method of separating proteinous substances from water by a foaming action. Also called protein skimming. (See page 28).
Fry Very young fish (see LARVAE).

Gill flukes Trematode parasites, such as *Dactylogyrus*.
Gills Membranes through which fish absorb dissolved oxygen from the water during respiration.
Gravel tidy Plastic mesh fitted between layers of gravel to protect biological filtration systems from being exposed (and thus rendered ineffective) by burrowing fish. (See page 23)

Hydrometer A device for measuring the SPECIFIC GRAVITY (S.G.) of water,

especially useful when making up synthetic mixes. May be either a free-floating or swing-needle type.
Hydrophilic Attracted to water.
Hydrophobic Water-hating.

Impeller An electrically driven propeller that produces water flow through filters.

Larvae (1) The first stage of fish development after hatching; underdeveloped fish fry (2) The first reproductive stage of many invertebrates.
Lateral line A line of perforated scales along the flanks of fish, connected to a pressure-sensitive nervous system, used to detect vibrations in the water.

Marine Fungus A parasitic organism, causing cotton-wool-like growths on the body. (See page 73).
Mouthbrooder A fish that incubates fertilized eggs in its mouth.
Mulm A very fine particulate muddy deposit.
Mysis Commercially available marine shrimp used as live and frozen food.

Nauplii Newly hatched BRINESHRIMP.
Nitrate (NO_3) A compound derived from (and less toxic than) NITRITE by NITROBACTER.
Nitrate-Nitrogen (NO_3-N) A measurement of NITRATE levels in the water.
Nitrification The process by which toxic nitrogenous compounds are converted by AEROBIC bacteria into less harmful substances, e.g. AMMONIA to NITRITE to NITRATE.
Nitrite (NO_2) A toxic compound derived from AMMONIA by *NITROSOMONAS*.
Nitrobacter AEROBIC bacteria used in the biological filter to convert NITRITE into less harmful NITRATE.
Nitrosomonas AEROBIC bacteria used in the biological filter to convert AMMONIA into NITRITE.
Nuisance algae Hair (filamentous) or slime algae that can overrun a tank. (See CYANOBACTERIA).

Osmolator Equipment for replacing evaporated water so as to maintain the desired SPECIFIC GRAVITY.
Osmosis The passage of a liquid through a semi-permeable membrane to dilute a more concentrated solution. (See page 78).
Osmotic stress An adverse reaction caused in livestock when the SALINITY of its environment changes significantly. Also called osmotic shock.
Oxygen Reduction Potential (ORP or Redox Potential). A measurement of the water's ability to cleanse itself.
Ozone (O_3) A three-atom, unstable

form of oxygen used as a disinfectant. (See page 30).

Ozonizer A device that uses high-voltage electricity to produce OZONE.

Pectoral fins Paired fins, one on each side of the body, immediately behind the gill cover.

Pelagic "Of the open sea". Pelagic eggs are lighter than water and are scattered after an ascending spawning action between a pair of fish in open water.

Pelvic fins Paired fins, one on each side of the body, immediately below the gill cover. (Not all marine fish have them).

pH A measure of acidity or alkalinity; the scale ranges from 1 (very acid) through 7 (neutral) to 14 (very alkaline). Aquarium water should be kept in the range pH 7.9–8.3.

Phosphates (PO₄) Compounds that are waste products generated by livestock, also present in unfiltered mains water. (See page 37).

Photoperiod The length of time that aquarium lights remain on.

Phytoplankton Very small plants (e.g. unicellular algae) that drift in water.

Plankton The encompassing term for PHYTOPLANKTON and ZOOPLANKTON.

Power filters Also called canister filters. (See page 26).

Power head An electric IMPELLER system fitted to biological filter return tubes to create water flow.

Protein skimmer A device that removes proteinous substances from aquarium water. Also used in conjunction with ozonized air for sterilizing water. (See page 28).

Rays Bony supports in the fins of fish.

Reactor An isolated container, usually in or near a sump, for performing a particular task, e.g. increasing calcium or oxygen in the water, before it is reintroduced to the main system.

Reverse-flow filtration A biological filtration system in which water flows up into the tank through the base covering instead of the more usual downward flow. (See page 22).

Salinity The measure of saltiness of aquarium water. The hobbyist can measure salinity and SPECIFIC GRAVITY as one and the same.

Sexual reproduction Reproduction in which the eggs of the female are fertilized by the sperm of the male.

Silicone sealant An adhesive used to bond glass or stop leaks, or to create rock and coral formations.

Spawning The part of the reproductive process involving fertilization of eggs.

Specific gravity (S.G.) The ratio of the density of a measured liquid to the density of pure water. Natural sea water has an S.G. of around 1.025, but marine aquarium fish are normally kept at (1.020–1.023). (See SALINITY).

Stripping The process by which the crust of a gorgonian (the part housing the polyps) falls away.

Substrate Aquarium base covering.

Sump An undertank reservoir that usually holds a TRICKLE FILTER, mechanical and chemical filters as well as probes and REACTORS.

Sweeper tentacles Long stinging tentacles used by aggressive hard corals to

sting other nearby corals in order to establish a territory.

Swimbladder The hydrostatic organ enabling fish to maintain their chosen depth and position in water.

Syphon (1) A length of tube used to move water from one vessel to another (2) The inhalant and exhalant organs of a mollusc.

Total system An aquarium with built-in sophisticated filtration and other management systems providing full water treatment.

Trace elements Elements found in sea water in very small quantities, often much less than 1ppm.

Trickle filter A biological filter, filled with inert media (See page 24).

Turnover The water flow rate through a filter. For marine aquaria a high turnover is recommended.

Ultraviolet sterilizer An ultraviolet light tube, enclosed in a water jacket, through which aquarium water is passed to sterilize it. (See page 33).

Undergravel filter The substrate of an aquarium used as a biological filter.

Ventral fins see PELVIC FINS.

Water change The replacement of a proportion (usually 20–25%) of aquarium water with fresh sea water mix.

Zooxanthellae Symbiotic ALGAE found within the tissue of many corals, anemones and clams.

Zooplankton Extremely small animals (and their larval stages) that drift in the water.

Acknowledgments

ABBREVIATIONS

AQ   Aquapress
AOL   Andromeda Oxford Ltd, Chris Honeywell
ND   Nick Dakin
OSF   Oxford Scientific Films
PhM   Photomax, Max Gibbs
SAL   Salamander Books Ltd.

Title page PhM; 5 PhM; 7 ND; 8 David B. Fleetham/OSF; 9tr Aztec Europe Ltd; 9br 1 and 2, AOL; 9br 3, Interpet Ltd; 9br 4, 9bl AOL; 10 AOL; 11t ND; 13 P. Stiles; 14tr Les Holliday; 14b Interpet Ltd; 15 ND; 16 M.P. and C. Piednoir/AQ; 21 M.P. and C. Piednoir/AQ; 27r Eheim; 27l Interpet Ltd; 30 Courtesy of Energy Savers Unlimited Inc., Coralife; 33 Rainbow Plastics; 36, 37 AOL; 38 Wetpets Ltd; 41tl Biophoto Associates; 41tr Dr. W. J. Ingledew/Science Photo Library; 42–3 PhM; 46 M. Sandford; 47c Tunze; 47br Rolf C. Hagen (UK) Ltd; 48l, 48c Max Gibbs/SAL; 48r AOL; 49t, 49b Max Gibbs/SAL; 51 Les Holliday; 52 PhM; 53 W. Tomey; 54 D. Allison; 55tl PhM; 55br W. Tomey; 58–9, 59r, 60tr PhM; 60bl AOL; 66, 67 M.P. and C. Piednoir/AQ; 68, 69 Les Holliday; 71 PhM; 72tr Dr Chris Andrews/National Aquarium in Baltimore; 72br ND; 73tl Tetra; 73cl PhM; 75 ND; 77, 79, 80, 81, 82, 83, 85, 86–7, 88, 89, 90–1, 91tr PhM; 93 M. Dune/AQ; 95t, 95r

PhM; 96 ND; 97, 98–9, 99tr, 100, 101, 102, 104, 105 PhM; 106 ND; 107 D. Allison; 108, 109 PhM; 110 W. Tomey; 111, 112tr, 112b, 113, 115, 116, 117, 119, 120, 121, 123, 124–5, 125t, 127, 128bl, 128–9, 130, 131, 132–3, 133br, 135t PhM; 135br M.P. and C. Piednoir/AQ; 136, 137tl PhM; 137bl M.P. and C. Piednoir/AQ; 139 PhM; 141 P. Stiles; 142–3 N. Genetiaux/AQ; 144–5 PhM; 146 ND; 147 PhM; 148t ND; 148–9, 150 PhM; 152–3, 154–5, 155b ND; 157 M.P. and C. Piednoir/AQ; 158, 159 PhM; 160–1 ND; 161b W. Tomey; 162–3 PhM; 164 M.P. and C. Piednoir/AQ; 165, 166 ND; 167, 168 PhM; 169 ND; 170–1 Trevor McDonald; 173 PhM; 175 ND; 176 PhM; 177t M.P. and C. Piednoir/AQ; 177b M. Sandford; 178 PhM; 179 D.M. Shale/OSF; 181c ND; 181br Trevor McDonald; 182, 183, 185 PhM; 186b Rodger Jackman/OSF; 186t M. Sandford; 188, 189, 190t, 190b, 191, 192, 193, 194 PhM; 195 ND; 196 PhM; 197 OSF; 199t PhM; 199b D. Allison; 200 ND; 201 Svein A. Fosså; 202 PhM; 203 W. Tomey;

Artwork by Julian Baker

The author and publishers would like to thank Max Gibbs and Barry Allday of The Goldfish Bowl, Oxford, (U.K.) and Lynchford Aquatics, Farnborough, Hants., (U.K.) for their help in this project.